The Limits
of the Papacy

The Limits
of the Papacy

AUTHORITY
AND AUTONOMY
IN THE CHURCH

PATRICK GRANFIELD

CROSSROAD · NEW YORK

1987

The Crossroad Publishing Company
370 Lexington Avenue, New York, N.Y. 10017

Printed in the United States of America

Library of Congress Cataloging in Publication Data

Granfield, Patrick.
  The limits of the papacy.

  Includes index.
  1. Papacy.   2. Catholic Church—Government.   I. Title.
BX1805.G65   1987   262'.13   87–658
ISBN 0–8245–0839–4

In memory of
Johannes Quasten (1900–1987)
teacher, colleague, friend

Contents

Preface

Twenty-two years have passed since the end of Vatican II and nearly ten years since John Paul II became Pope. In those two decades, conflicts between centralized power and personal liberty have become a major concern for Roman Catholics. This issue, as old as Christianity itself, is a critical aspect of a larger concern: the effort of the Church to determine more precisely its identity in the post–Vatican II world.

The office of the papacy plays a crucial and controversial role in this updating process. It enjoys vast power and international prestige; it suffers manifold criticisms and virulent attacks. A recurring question emerges: does papal authority have any constraints? Can there be any limits if the Pope possesses "the supreme plenitude of power," and if "the First See is judged by no one"?

Catholics, in trying to answer these questions, usually start with three dogmatic truths. First, the papacy, as the continuation of the primatial ministry established by Christ in Peter, is of divine origin; it can be reformed but not abolished. Second, the episcopate, in succession to the apostolic college, received from Christ the authority to govern the local Churches and, under the leadership of the Pope, this College of Bishops has supreme authority. Third, all believers, through the *sensus fidelium*, manifest, when in harmony with Scripture and tradition, the infallibility of the Church.

Speaking less concretely, authority and autonomy form a dialectical relationship from which, ideally, there results a healthy tension, if neither opposed position exerts undue dominance. Thus, neither an absolutist nor individualist bias is acceptable: the former ignores the variety of gifts in the local Churches; the second makes ecclesial unity impossible. As a matter of fact, the idea of unity looms larger in the New Testament than does the role of supreme leadership. And rightly so, for leadership is a means of preserving and fostering the unity of the Church, the Body of Christ established by God for his people.

1

Dialectical tension, however, is not a purely political one, a question of superior power; rather it is a balancing of rights: the divine positive right of the hierarchy to teach and rule authoritatively and the God-given human right of the faithful to freedom of conscience. These are the components of the interaction, the poles of tension. Neither can be ignored without creating a serious imbalance.

This book examines, from the perspective of limits, the papacy as a term in the dialectics of Church unity—the unity within the Catholic Church as well as the broader unity of all Christian Churches. Ecclesiologists, past and present, have addressed the issue of the limitation of papal authority but only as a minor part of larger treatises on the papacy and the Church. To my knowledge, no one has given a complete and integrated analysis of the limits of the papacy, indicating its historical development, theological principles, and necessary implications.

The Pope needs a large measure of authority to discharge effectively the demands of his universal ministry. But the Pope, empowered though he is, remains a finite creature bound by a divine mandate. Any envisioned limitation, whether essential or voluntary, must be compatible with his office and the independence needed to fulfill its sacred mission.

To appreciate the delicate balance between the rights of the papacy and the limits of the papacy, intrinsic or voluntary, we look first at concrete examples of recent controversies in Chapter One. Then we discuss separately the claims of the papacy in Chapter Two and the possibility of limitation in Chapter Three. The rest of the book concerns the interaction of claims and limits in four major areas: collegiality (the cooperation of Pope and bishops) in Chapter Four; the status of the local Church (the authority of the Pope and the authority of the local bishop) in Chapter Five; the role of the faithful (the *sensus fidelium* and the reception and nonreception of magisterial teaching) in Chapter Six; and ecumenism (the quest for the unity of all Christian Churches) in Chapter Seven.

The sequence of chapters is dictated by the need to focus on one specific issue: the papal office and its limitations. The decision to order the book in this way should not overshadow the central affirmation that the Pope is always in union with the entire Church and the College of Bishops. Indeed, the Pope's universal ministry to the Church is rooted in his membership and leadership in the College of Bishops.

An ecclesiology of communion provides the fundamental framework for understanding the Church. The universal Church—comprised of believers who confess the Lordship of Jesus and who are united in faith and unity through the Spirit—comes to be in the communion of the local Churches. The universal Church is not an abstraction or a legal fiction; it is not simply an administrative federation of local Churches. Rather, the universal Church is the spiritual *communio* of local Churches in which the Bishop of Rome enjoys a unique leadership role.

Our analysis, seen in the light of recent history, reveals the complex functioning of the papacy as well as the self-correcting mechanisms of the entire Church. The purpose of this book is not at all to undermine the traditional prerogatives of the Pope, but rather to contextualize them and harmonize them with the needs and activities of the rest of the Church. The Petrine office is thus enhanced when it is appreciated not as narrowly adversarial, but as truly and cooperatively ministerial. Only thus can the dialectics of unity flower and bear fruit.

To resolve once and for all the tension between authority and autonomy, even in the Roman Catholic Church, would be unwise even if it were not impossible. The realistic goal, however, is not static resolution but vital balance. An enduring tension is intrinsic to every living community; it persists as an ongoing challenge. What enables one to face this challenge with hope is the revealed promise that the Spirit of Christ with unlimited power guides the incarnational Church, fraught though it be with human limitations, so that the communion of believers—bishops, priests, religious, and laity—properly using the rights given them by God, can approximate the lofty goal of full unity in love.

Before concluding, I wish to thank the many persons who have assisted me. Words cannot fully express my appreciation for the unstinting help and support given to me throughout the writing of this book by my brother, David Granfield. I am also indebted to several of my colleagues at the Catholic University of America who kindly agreed to read the manuscript and who made many helpful suggestions: the Reverend Avery Dulles, S.J., the Reverend Joseph A. Komonchak, Dr. William E. May, and the Reverend James H. Provost. I appreciate their comments, but I have not always followed their advice. Finally, I am grateful for the generous assistance provided by the staff at the Catholic University library and by my research assistants, Mark O'Keefe, O.S.B., Margaret Shawn Scanlan, S.N.D., and Rosemarie Gorman.

· I ·

The Primatial Authority in Action

Roma locuta est; causa finita est.
—*St. Augustine**

Roma locuta, ecclesia finita est.
—*George Tyrrell†*

P apal authority, its exercise and limitations, has emerged since Vatican II (1962-65) as a fundamental issue in the Roman Catholic Church. With the Council, a new era in Church history began. In what was both a theological and a cultural event, this Council of reform and reunion responded vigorously to John XXIII's call for *aggiornamento*. Its sixteen documents dealt with such major questions as the description of the Church, Scripture and tradition, liturgical reform and the use of the vernacular, the Church in the world, religious freedom, ecumenism, laity, religious and priestly life, and the relationship between the Pope and the College of Bishops.

John XXIII had repudiated the "prophets of gloom" and enabled the Church to confront positively the challenge of modernity. As a result, hopes and dreams filled Catholics throughout the world and expectations ran high. Many felt that they were seeing the beginning of an exciting transformation of Catholic Christianity. The ideals of Vatican II transformed Catholicism internationally and locally, altering the course that official Catholicism had followed for nearly two centuries.

From the start, it was immediately evident that the process of

---

* Derived from text of Augustine: Sermon 131, cap. 10. *Patrologia latina* 38: 734.

† Letter to Henri Bremond, January 27, 1907. Quoted in Thomas M. Loome, *Liberal Catholicism, Reform Catholicism, Modernism: A Contribution to a New Orientation in Modernist Research* (Mainz: Matthias-Grünewald, 1979), p. 53.

implementing Vatican II would be a long and arduous task. Deep divisions in the Church soon emerged sparked by differing interpretations of the Council documents due in no small part to a certain ambiguity within the texts themselves. Disputes developed between those who favored a literal and at times a selective reading of the texts and those who attempted to capture the more elusive "spirit of the Council."[1] Joseph A. Komonchak has noted that the "progressives" at the Council may have been correct in arguing that the reforms purified but did not destroy the essential nature of the Church. But the "conservatives" were more perceptive in recognizing the deeper implications of the Council and the unsettling fact that "what theologically is only 'reform' sociologically can be quite 'revolutionary.'"[2]

The Popes of the postconciliar years came to the same realization. Committed to Vatican II and desirous of making the Church responsive to present exigencies, they were also sensitive to tradition and fearful lest the passion for instant renewal dilute the unique meaning of Catholicism. Paul VI (1963–78) was a major force in implementing the ideals of Vatican II. He cautiously encouraged the development of collegiality, liturgical reform, lay participation, ecumenism, and the revitalization of priestly and religious life.

The most controversial event in Paul VI's pontificate was the encyclical *Humanae vitae* (1968) which unequivocally rejected the use of artificial birth control: the Pope declared that the unitive and procreative aspects of the conjugal act are inseparably joined, and therefore "each and every marriage act must remain open to the transmission of life" (no. 11). Outspoken critics and advocates of the encyclical launched a debate that was unprecedented in the Catholic Church. The reaction of the Holy See to those who openly dissented was remarkably restrained; a few bishops in Europe and the United States suspended some priests, but the Vatican itself issued no censures or excommunications. *Humanae vitae*, however, seriously weakened the credibility of the teaching authority of the Church. It marked the beginning of widespread dissent from other doctrinal and disciplinary norms.

---

1. Hermann J. Pottmeyer examines conciliar hermeneutics in "Ist die Nachkonzilszeit zu Ende?," *Stimmen der Zeit* 203 (1985):219–230.

2. "The Ecclesial and Cultural Roles of Theology," *Proceedings of the Catholic Theological Society of America* 40 (1985):23.

John Paul II, the first non-Italian Pope in 456 years, was elected in 1978. From the very start of his pontificate, he seemed to move toward a restoration of Roman Catholicism and the reaffirmation of an unambiguous Catholic identity.[3] Astutely, he linked this restoration with the full implementation of Vatican II. In his first address as Pope, the day after his election, he said that the primary duty of his pontificate would be "prompting with prudent but encouraging action the most exact norms and directives of the Council."[4] The Pope was convinced that if the Church was to maintain its uniqueness and fulfill its God-given mission, then it had to present its doctrine lucidly and to enforce its rules strictly. For him, the Catholic acceptance of Christ and the teachings of the Church inevitably contribute to a more visible unity within the whole human race.

John Paul II has made it clear that he is not pleased with many things that have happened since the end of Vatican II; he has taken steps to correct what he views as distortions. In this first address as Pope, he indicated the major governing principles of his program of restoration. Referring to the virtue of fidelity, he argued that it means obedience to the teaching of the magisterium, respect for liturgical norms issued by Church authority, and the rejection of "arbitrary and uncontrolled innovation."[5] In other speeches he has condemned false pluralism and misinterpretations of the Council, repudiated moral laxity, and insisted that priests and religious unselfishly accept celibacy. Above all, he has demanded a recommitment to the ideals of the Gospel and the teaching of the Church in order to foster doctrinal and disciplinary unity. He has not considered dissent a kind of "loyal opposition" but rather as something that harms the Church and renders it ineffective.

John Paul II's self-avowed mission is to bring the Church under control, to heal its divisions, and to make it a powerful and credible sign of God's grace in the world. He also wishes to strengthen the role of the papal office. Paul Johnson described this goal: "With all the strength of his faith, and all the power of his intellect, and all

---

3. This is a major theme in Paul Johnson, *Pope John Paul II and the Catholic Restoration* (New York: St. Martin's Press, 1981). See also Giancarlo Zizola, *La restaurazione di Papa Wojtyla* (Rome and Bari: Laterza, 1985).

4. *Origins*, October 26, 1978, vol. 8, no. 19:291.

5. Ibid., 293.

the magic of his personality, he is striving to rebuild the authority of the papacy."[6]

The program of John Paul II dramatically raises to public consciousness the topic of this book: the possible limits to papal primacy. This issue goes beyond theory to the reality of power and deals with areas of competence, specific conflicts, and the principles operative in decision making.

The last ten years have seen an increasing exercise of papal authority by the Pope personally and by Roman congregations with papal approval. Vatican interventions on a variety of controversial theological issues have increased. These actions are hardly marginal; they tell us much about how Rome understands and exercises its own authority; and they raise the obvious question about the limits of papal power. Critical assessment is necessary.

What papal and curial actions have caused so much notice and controversy? The following list does not pretend to be exhaustive; I have selected only the major and well-publicized examples of Roman interventions that graphically illustrate the direction of papal authority over the last decade. At this stage, I shall give only the facts, but in later chapters I shall interpret some of the central theological issues implied in these events. I have divided the principal targets of current Roman concern into three categories: theologians, priests and religious, and bishops.

Theologians

Recent Popes have been lavish in their praise of theology and even of theologians—in general. John Paul II, for example, has viewed theology as one of the most important tasks of the Church, because its function is to continue Christ's prophetic mission by interpreting God's self-communication in human history. He calls theologians "servants of divine truth" (*Redemptor hominis*, art. 19) and encourages them to engage in scientific research with responsible freedom and competence. In addressing German theologians at Altötting, the Pope said that theology is a science and "is free in the application of methods and analyses."[7] Yet theology must always

---

6. Johnson, *Pope John Paul II*. On dust jacket.
7. *Osservatore Romano*, English edition, December 15, 1980, p. 9.

operate in an ecclesial context and collaborate with the magisterium—the authentic interpreter of the Word of God. The indispensable respect for the magisterium, according to the Pope, does not deprive theology of its "unrenounceable autonomy": "The magisterium and theology have two different tasks to perform. That is why neither can be reduced to the other."[8]

At the same time, the Pope has been instinctively wary of abrasive theological dissent and impatient with those who question dogmas or engage in endless debates over their meaning. Although he spoke of a "certain pluralism in methodology" (*Redemptor hominis*, art. 19), which suggests a variety of theological approaches, he has held strongly that theological opinions should not confuse the faithful. The believer "has a right to know what he can rely on in practicing his faith."[9] "It is the right of the faithful not to be troubled by theories and hypotheses."[10] The Pope has rejected the liberal agenda, warned of violating the boundaries of revealed truth, and demanded obedience to the authority of the magisterium.

The desire of the Pope to ensure clarity in Catholic teaching and to correct those theologians who deny the Church's doctrine has been no idle wish. The Pope, especially through the Sacred Congregation for the Doctrine of the Faith (SCDF), has continued to judge the orthodoxy of theologians. An indication of the seriousness of Rome is evident in the following nine instances that are listed chronologically.

Anthony Kosnik, et al.

In 1972, the board of directors of the Catholic Theological Society of America established a committee to study human sexuality. Members of the committee were Anthony Kosnik (chairman), William Carroll, Agnes Cunningham, Ronald Modras, and James Schulte. In 1976, the board "received" the final report, noting that its action implied neither the approval nor disapproval by the Society or its board of directors. The report was published as a book the

---

8. Ibid.

9. Ibid.

10. At the Catholic University of America, *Origins*, October 25, 1979, vol. 9, no. 19:308.

following year: *Human Sexuality: New Directions in American Catholic Thought* (New York: Paulist, 1977).

The doctrinal committee of the National Conference of Catholic Bishops[11] and the Sacred Congregation for the Doctrine of the Faith[12] evaluated this book and both criticized it. The SCDF, for example, said that many of the conclusions made by the authors "either dissociate themselves from or directly contradict Catholic teaching as consistently proposed by moral theologians and as taught by the Church's magisterium."[13] The episcopal committee made a similar judgment, saying that the study "contradicts theological tradition and the Church's clear magisterial teaching refined over the centuries."[14] Although neither group ordered any punitive action against the authors, there was a difference in tone between the two statements. The U.S. evaluation was more circumspect in its criticism and made no direct reference to any specific course of action the authors must take. The SCDF report, however, pointed out that the authors "have an enormous responsibility for the erroneous conclusions and potentially harmful impact these ideas can have on the correct formation of the Christian consciences of so many people."[15] It invited the authors "to correct their errors."[16]

John J. McNeill, S.J.

In August 1977, John J. McNeill, a Jesuit moral theologian and psychotherapist, was informed by his provincial superior that the Congregation for the Doctrine of the Faith had serious objections to his book, *The Church and the Homosexual* (Kansas City, Mo.: Sheed, Andrews and McMeel, 1976). The Congregation ordered the withdrawal of the *imprimi potest* from all future editions and translations of the book and prohibited McNeill from promoting the book and from lecturing on the question of homosexuality or sexual ethics. The Congregation gave several reasons for its action. It said that his moral position on homosexuality and his advocacy of ethically responsible homosexual

---

11. *Origins*, December 1, 1977, vol. 7, no. 24:376–378.
12. *Origins*, August 30, 1979, vol. 9, no. 11:167–169.
13. Ibid., 169.
14. *Origins*, December 1, 1977, vol. 7, no. 24:376.
15. *Origins*, August 30, 1979, vol. 9, no. 11:167.
16. Idem.

relationships are contrary to the traditional teaching and pastoral practices of the Church. Moreover, the Congregation said the public appearances of McNeill had been a source of scandal: by giving false hopes that the Church will change its teaching on homosexuality, he had created confusion in the community.[17]

In September 1985, McNeill addressed the national convention of Dignity, a Catholic homosexual organization, on human rights, civil liberties, and the moral position of the Church. On October 19, 1986, the superior general of the Jesuits, supposedly at the urging of the Vatican, notified McNeill that he must avoid public comment on the subject of homosexuality and give up all public ministry to homosexuals or face dismissal from the Society of Jesus. "I have come to the conclusion that I cannot obey that order in conscience," McNeill declared.[18] He also issued statements to several newspapers critical of the October 1986 document on homosexuality issued by the Congregation for the Doctrine of the Faith.[19] In January 1987, he was dismissed from the Jesuits.

Jacques Pohier, O.P.

A French theologian, formerly professor at Le Saulchoir, Pohier specializes in the relation between moral theology and psychology. He received severe criticism from the SCDF in April 1979 for his book, *Quand Je dis Dieu* (Paris: Seuil, 1977). In particular, the Congregation said that he denied the following truths: the intention of Christ to give his passion a redemptive or sacrificial value; the corporeal resurrection of Christ; the survival, resurrection, and eternal life with God as a vocation of humankind; and the presence in Scripture of a teaching with objective meaning that the magisterium can determine authentically. These affirmations are "manifestly not in conformity with revelation and the magisterium of the Church."[20] In September 1979, the Congregation informed him that he could no longer preside at the eucharist, teach theology, preach, or organize public conferences.

---

17. The Vatican statement is in *Origins*, March 16, 1978, vol. 7, no. 39:612–615. Also see *Origins*, September 22, 1977, vol. 7, no. 14:218–219.

18. *New York Times*, November 8, 1986, p. 36.

19. Text of the Vatican document in *Origins*, November 15, 1986, vol. 16, no. 22:377–382.

20. *Origins*, April 19, 1979, vol. 8, no. 44:705.

Hans Küng

In 1967, the SCDF began its investigation of certain theological positions of Hans Küng, professor at Tübingen University in Germany. On February 15, 1975, it issued a document pointing out certain opinions of Küng that differed from the doctrine of the Church: his teaching on infallibility and the magisterium and his position on the possibility of valid consecration of the eucharist by a nonordained baptized person.[21] Although Küng repeatedly refused to go to Rome to discuss his case with the Congregation, communication between the two parties continued.

On December 15, 1979, the congregation issued a declaration that noted that some of his theological views continued to be "a cause of disturbance in the minds of the faithful."[22] It mentioned infallibility, "contempt for the magisterium of the Church," the consubstantiality of Christ with the Father, and the Blessed Virgin Mary. The Congregation declared that Küng "in his writings has departed from the integral truth of Catholic faith, and therefore can no longer be considered a Catholic theologian nor function as such in a teaching role." Stating that "he can no longer teach with the authority which he received from the Church," it referred to the section on canonical mission found in *Sapientia christiana*, art. 27, 1.[23] Subsequently, Küng was removed from the Catholic faculty of theology at Tübingen, but he remains as director of the Institute of Ecumenical Research. It should be noted that he was not excommunicated, declared a heretic, nor forbidden to exercise his priestly ministry.

Edward Schillebeeckx, O.P.

Professor at Nijmegen in Holland, Edward Schillebeeckx went to Rome to meet with Cardinal Joseph Ratzinger, prefect of the SCDF,

---

21. The text is in NCCB Committee on Doctrine, *The Küng Dossier* (Washington: USCC, 1980), pp. 92-93. This book contains extensive documentation on the Küng case.

22. Ibid., pp. 200-201 gives the full text.

23. The apostolic constitution *Sapientia christiana* (April 19, 1978) was issued by John Paul II and deals with ecclesiastical universities and faculties. Article 27, 1 states: "Those who teach disciplines concerning faith or morals, must receive, after making their profession of faith, a canonical mission from the Chancellor or his delegate, for they do not teach on their own authority but by virtue of the mission

between December 13–15, 1979. Schillebeeckx's purpose was to defend his book, *Jesus: An Experiment in Christology* (New York: Seabury, 1979), which was originally published in 1974. The major points of disagreement concerned the divinity of Christ, his awareness of being the Messiah and the Son of God, and the objective reality of his resurrection. In 1980, the Congregation announced that it had found no "errors" in his writings and that it was satisfied with the "clarifications" that he had made.[24] He agreed to incorporate these in his future writings.[25]

His problems with Rome, however, were not over. In 1982, the Congregation began to investigate his theology of ministry contained in his book *Ministry: Leadership in the Community of Jesus Christ* (New York: Crossroad, 1981), which was originally published in 1980. Finally, on June 13, 1984, the SCDF informed Schillebeeckx that it found unacceptable his teaching that under extraordinary circumstances someone other than an ordained priest could preside at the eucharist.[26] Furthermore, it asked that he indicate his adherence to the teaching contained in the letter on the sacramental priesthood, *Sacerdotium ministeriale* (August 6, 1983), sent earlier by the SCDF to the bishops.[27] Schillebeeckx agreed to this demand and said that his new book on ministry would be in accord with *Sacerdotium ministeriale*. He published this book in 1985: *The Church with a Human Face: A New and Expanded Theology of Ministry* (New York: Crossroad, 1985).

Rome was still not satisfied. In a notification from the SCDF on September 15, 1986, the Congregation said that the ideas of Schillebeeckx on the ministry remain "out of harmony with the teaching of the Church." It noted that although he does not reject *Sacerdotium ministeriale*, neither does he clearly affirm it. In addition, the Congregation said that he continues to understand apostolicity in such a way that "apostolic succession through sacramental ordination repre-

---

they have received from the Church." English translation from *On Ecclesiastical Universities and Faculties* (Washington: USCC, 1979), pp. 24–25. Full Latin text of the constitution in *Acta apostolicae sedis* 71 (1979):469–499.

24. *Origins*, January 29, 1981, vol. 10, no. 33:523–524.

25. The documentation between 1976 and 1980 is found in Ted Schoof, ed., *The Schillebeeckx Case* (New York: Paulist, 1984).

26. *Origins*, January 24, 1985, vol. 14, no. 32:523, 525–526.

27. Text in *Origins*, September 15, 1983, vol. 13, no. 14:229, 231–233.

sents a nonessential element for the exercise of ministry." This position, according to the Congregation, opposes the doctrine of the Church.[28]

Leonardo Boff, O.F.M.

The writings of Leonardo Boff, a Brazilian professor of theology at Petrópolis and a well-known exponent of liberation theology, had been under Vatican scrutiny since 1982. The major criticism focused on his book *Church: Charism and Power: Liberation Theology and the Institutional Church* (New York: Crossroad, 1985), which was first published in 1981. In September 1984, he met in Rome with Cardinal Ratzinger of the SCDF and defended his teaching. After studying his oral and written replies, the Congregation issued a notification dated March 11, 1985, that provided a detailed critique of his book.[29] The main points raised were Boff's ecclesiological relativism, his understanding of the sacraments as part of a pattern of production and consumption, and his severe critique of the Church's hierarchy and institutions. It concluded that these views "endanger the sound doctrine of the faith." Boff's now famous reaction to the Vatican statement was: "I prefer to walk with the Church rather than to walk alone with my theology."[30] In May 1985, the Vatican ordered Boff to maintain "a period of respectful silence" to allow him time for "serious reflection." He was told to give up his editorship of the *Revista eclesiástica brasileira* and not to teach or publish. A little less than a year later, the Vatican lifted the ban.[31]

The Boff case took place in the midst of the continuing debate on liberation theology. In the early 1980's, the SCDF also investigated two other leaders in the movement: Gustavo Gutiérrez from Peru, and Jon Sobrino, a Spanish-born theologian now living in El Salvador. No public charges were made. The Congregation also issued two

---

28. For full text of the notification see *Origins*, October 23, 1986, vol. 16, no. 19: 344.

29. *Origins*, April 4, 1985, vol. 14, no. 42:683, 685-687.

30. Ibid., 686.

31. For full documentation of the Boff case see *Roma locuta: Documentos sobre o livro "Igreja: Carisma e poder, Ensaios de eclesiologia militante" de Frei Leonardo Boff* (Petrópolis: Vozes and Rio Branco: Servicio de Intercâmbio Nacional do Movimento Nacional das Entidades de Defesa dos Direitos Humanos, 1985).

major documents on liberation theology: "Instruction on Certain Aspects of the Theology of Liberation" (August 6, 1984) and "Instruction on Christian Freedom and Liberation" (March 22, 1986).[32]

Anthony Wilhelm

A catechism for adults written by Anthony Wilhelm, *Christ Among Us*, was first published by Paulist Press in 1967. It received an *imprimatur* from Archbishop Thomas A. Boland of Newark in 1971 and later from his successor, Archbishop Peter L. Gerety. By 1984, more than 1.6 million copies of the book had been sold. Archbishop Gerety was in close contact with the SCDF from its first inquiry about the book in January 1982. Gerety established a committee of theological advisors and, with the full cooperation of the author and the publisher, they suggested corrections in response to the SCDF criticisms.

Cardinal Ratzinger, in a letter dated February 28, 1984, said that even a corrected version "would not be suitable as a catechetical text." He requested that Gerety withdraw his *imprimatur* and that Paulist Press not reprint the book.[33] Both the archbishop and Paulist Press acceded to these demands. Some of the inadequacies mentioned by the SCDF included the way the author discussed the following issues: the teaching authority of the Church and Vatican II, the value of biblical imagery, the indissolubility of marriage, contraception, masturbation, and homosexuality. The Congregation insisted that its decision was based on substantive reasons and not because of pressure from extremist groups.[34]

Other catechetical works have also received the attention of Rome.[35] The Dutch catechism, *De Nieuwe Katechismus*, was published in 1966.[36] After some Dutch traditionalists protested to Rome

---

32. The text of these instructions can be found in *Origins*, September 13, 1984, vol. 14, no. 13:193-204, and *Origins*, April 17, 1986, vol. 15, no. 44:713-728.

33. *Origins*, April 26, 1984, vol. 13, no. 46:762.

34. The letter of Archbishop Gerety to Bishop James M. Malone, president of the National Conference of Catholic Bishops, which explains the entire matter was published in *Origins*, March 7, 1985, vol. 14, no. 38:619, 621-622.

35. A very useful discussion of this issue can be found in the joint committee report, "The Approval of Catechisms and Catechetical Materials," *Proceedings of the Catholic Theological Society of America* 41 (1986):181-204.

36. Translated in English as *A New Catechism: Catholic Faith for Adults* (New York: Herder and Herder, 1969).

about certain teachings in this work, an international commission of cardinals and theologians was appointed to study the catechism. It suggested several clarifications.[37] A French catechism, published under the direction of the French bishops' conference in 1981,[38] was reviewed by the SCDF, and that body ordered several changes to be made.[39]

Philip S. Keane, S.S.

At the request of the SCDF, Archbishop Raymond Hunthausen of Seattle announced on April 24, 1984, that he had withdrawn his *imprimatur* from the book, *Sexual Morality: A Catholic Perspective* (New York: Paulist, 1977), written by Philip S. Keane, professor of moral theology at St. Mary's Seminary in Baltimore. The book had sold some thirty thousand copies. Archbishop Hunthausen explained that Rome informed him that the *imprimatur* can be given only to those works which agree completely with the official teaching of the Church. Even though Keane presented the Church's teaching on controversial moral questions, he departed in some points from official nondefined doctrine. Hunthausen said: "I am bound in conscience to withdraw my *imprimatur* . . . because it does not meet the necessary requirements as these are presently set forth by the Congregation."[40] Paulist Press was not asked to stop publishing the book but only to remove the *imprimatur* in all future printings.

Charles E. Curran

In 1979, the SCDF began its investigation of Charles E. Curran, professor of moral theology at The Catholic University of America in Washington, D.C. For the next seven years Curran and the SCDF

---

37. Text in *Acta apostolicae sedis* 60 (1968):655–691. A theological explanation of the text, written by Edouard Dhanis and Jan Visser on behalf of the commission of cardinals, is a supplement in the most recent English version of the catechism: *A New Catechism: Catholic Faith for Adults* (New York: Crossroad, 1986), pp. 511–574. Also see Aldo Chiaruttini, ed., *Il dossier del catechismo olandese* (Verona: Arnoldo Mondadori, 1968).

38. *Pierres vivantes* (Paris: "Catéchèse 80," 1981).

39. See René Marlé, "La réfonte de Pierres vivantes," *Etudes* 363 (1985):533–540.

40. *Origins*, May 17, 1984, vol. 14, no. 1:15.

were in correspondence. Curran defended the right of legitimate dissent from noninfallible teachings. He repeatedly asked, without success, that the SCDF indicate what are the norms governing such dissent and how he has violated those norms. On September 17, 1985, Cardinal Ratzinger informed Curran that he had dissented from the teaching of the magisterium on several moral doctrines: artificial contraception, direct sterilization, abortion, euthanasia, masturbation, premarital intercourse, homosexual acts, and the indissolubility of sacramental and consummated marriage. The Congregation, as it did in the case of Hans Küng, referred to the canonical mission (*Sapientia christiana*, art. 27, 1) and to the incompatibility of having someone who is supposed to teach in the name of the Church deny her teaching. It concluded: "The Congregation now invites you to reconsider and to retract those positions which violate the conditions necessary for a professor to be called a Catholic theologian."[41]

On March 8, 1986, Curran—at his own request and not as part of the formal procedures of the Congregation—went to Rome and met with Cardinal Ratzinger and other members of the SCDF. On April 1, 1986, Curran wrote Ratzinger that "in conscience at the present time I cannot and do not change the theological positions I have taken."[42] He also repeated his request for a compromise: that he be allowed to remain a tenured professor of theology at Catholic University on his agreement not to teach the course on sexual ethics and that the Congregation could issue a document indicating that his teachings differ from those of the official Church.

The final decision of the SCDF, which was approved by John Paul II, was communicated to Curran on August 18, 1986. It declared that because of his "repeated refusal to accept what the Church teaches," he is no longer "suitable nor eligible to exercise the function of a professor of Catholic theology."[43] Curran subsequently decided to use the due-process procedures of Catholic University that are

---

41. *Origins*, March 27, 1986, vol. 15, no. 41:668. This issue of *Origins* has the Ratzinger letter, a statement by Curran, and some of the correspondence between Curran and the SCDF. Also see *Origins*, April 3, 1986, vol. 15, no. 42:691–694. Father Curran himself has published extensive documentary material in *Faithful Dissent* (Kansas City, Mo.: Sheed and Ward, 1986).

42. *Origins*, May 8, 1986, vol. 15, no. 47:771.

43. *Origins*, August 28, 1986, vol. 16, no. 11:203. This issue contains the decision of the SCDF and a response by Curran.

available to faculty members whose canonical mission may be withdrawn.

The university's academic senate established a special committee to carry out the procedures. Archbishop Hickey, chancellor of the university, in January 1987, suspended Curran, who had been on sabbatical during the calendar year of 1986, from teaching in the Department of Theology pending the outcome of the proceedings. Curran, claiming that the suspension violated his contractual rights, filed a civil suit in March 1987 against the university in the Superior Court of the District of Columbia. In April 1987, he said that he would not continue the suit unless the board of trustees of the university failed to reach a decision concerning the withdrawal of his canonical mission in its fall 1987 meeting.

Priests and Religious

In the years since Vatican II, some fifty thousand priests and one-hundred and fifty thousand nuns throughout the world have left the active ministry. Western Europe and North America have been the most severely affected; many seminaries have closed and the number of priestly and religious vocations has declined dramatically. Rome is concerned with this depressing statistical picture and is exercising closer control over the formation, governance, and activities of clerics and religious. The following material indicates some of the actions Rome has taken with the intention of clarifying the identity of religious and clerical life.

Religious Congregations

In the first instance, John Paul II intervened in the life of the twenty-six thousand-member Society of Jesus—the largest order of male religious in the world. In October 1981, a few months after Pedro Arrupe, Superior General of the Jesuits, was disabled by a severe stroke, the Pope appointed eighty-year-old Paolo Dezza, S.J., as his personal delegate and Giuseppe Pittau, S.J., as coadjutor. Dezza's mandate was "to superintend the government of the Society until the election of a new superior general."

Immediate reaction to these appointments was mostly negative.

Was the Pope rebuking the Jesuits because they were too "political" in their social activism or too "secular" in their understanding of religious life? Was he using his authority to bring the Jesuits under control and to give warning to other religious? Although the Society of Jesus has always defined itself in terms of service to the universal Church and to the Pope, the action of the Pope was without precedent. Never before had a Pope acted independently of the Society's constitution, which determines how a superior general should be replaced. Arrupe would become the first superior general not to die in office.

Much apprehension had developed by the time the Pope met with 104 of the order's leaders in Rome on February 27, 1982. To the relief of his audience, there was not only no confrontation but a warm endorsement of the contribution Jesuits have made to the life of the Church. Yet the Pope reminded his audience of the need for fidelity to the magisterium and to the Roman Pontiff and of the necessity of genuine priestly spirituality.[44] It was also announced that a general congregation would be held in 1983 to elect a new superior general. On September 13, 1983, the delegates on the first ballot elected as the twenty-ninth superior general a Dutch priest, Peter-Hans Kolvenbach, rector of the Pontifical Oriental Institute in Rome.

A second example of Vatican intervention concerns the Discalced Carmelite nuns. In 1977, the Vatican approved an experimental constitution for these thirteen thousand contemplative nuns who live in seventy-two countries. Some 80 percent of the nuns favored the new charter with its moderate reform elements. They considered it a genuine expression of the spirit of their foundress, St. Teresa of Avila. A traditionalist faction, however, opposed the experimental rule. This minority, which is very strong in Spain, desired a stricter constitution based on the constitution of 1581. It communicated its desires to Rome.

The Vatican sided with the traditionalists. In October 1984, Cardinal Agostino Casaroli, Vatican Secretary of State, wrote to Felipe Sainz de Baranda, Father General of the female and male Discalced Carmelites.[45] He said that the Holy See must take action to resolve this "grave and difficult problem." In an unusual step, he said that the Vatican itself, through the Sacred Congregation for Religious

---

44. *Origins*, March 11, 1982, vol. 11, no. 39:624–628.
45. Letter in *Acta ordinis carmelitarum discalceatorum*, Anno 29, 1984:26–31.

and Secular Institutes, would prepare a definitive text of a new constitution to be based on the 1581 version. In 1986, the completed constitution was sent to the nuns for their reaction. It is uncertain when the new constitution will be promulgated.

A third instance concerns the Franciscan Order of Friars Minor, which held its general chapter at Assisi in May 1985. Present were some two hundred delegates representing twenty thousand male Franciscans in 120 countries. John Paul II sent the delegates a letter instructing them to take steps to revise "the theories and practices" that have been an obstacle to the authentic Franciscan tradition. Although the Pope did not specify the unacceptable "theories and practices," he did stress that Franciscanism was an "established way of life" and not a "movement open to new options continually substituted by others in the insistent search for an identity, as if this identity had not been found."[46] In addition, the Pope, in an unusual though not unprecedented move, appointed Archbishop Vincenzo Fagiolo, secretary of the Sacred Congregation for Religious and Secular Institutes, as his personal delegate to preside over all the sessions of the chapter. The chapter reelected the American Franciscan, John Vaughn, as minister general.

Political Activity

John Paul II has made it clear from the first days of his pontificate that partisan politics and the life of priests and religious are incompatible. In Puebla, Mexico, in 1979, he told the bishops that it is wrong to view Christ as a political or revolutionary figure, and he reminded priests that they are not political leaders. In Zaire, a year later, he instructed priests "to leave political responsibilities to those who are charged with them."[47] These views are reflected in the 1983 Code of Canon Law. Two canons are pertinent: canon 285, 3, states that clerics are forbidden to hold any public office that entails participation in civil power, and canon 287, 2, states that clerics may take an active role in political parties only if the competent ecclesiastical authority considers this necessary to defend the Church or to promote the common good. These restrictions are applied to members of religious orders by canon 672, and to members of societies of

---

46. *Osservatore romano*, May 14, 1985, p. 7.
47. *Origins*, May 22, 1980, vol. 10, no. 1:11.

apostolic life by canon 739.[48] The four examples that follow show how Rome has interpreted and applied these laws.

1. *Robert Drinan, S.J.* The Jesuit priest, Robert Drinan, a Massachusetts Democrat, had served five terms in the United States House of Representatives. In 1980, he was told by his Jesuit superiors, at the direction of the Vatican, not to run for reelection. He accepted that decision.

2. *Agnes Mary Mansour, R.S.M.* This case was quite complex, since it involved several meetings and conversations as well as correspondence between Sister Agnes Mary, Archbishop Edmund Szoka of Detroit, Archbishop Pio Laghi of the Apostolic Delegation, and members of the Sisters of Mercy administrative team.[49] I have summarized here the most critical moments.

On December 29, 1982, Sister Agnes Mary Mansour, who had been a Sister of Mercy for thirty years, was appointed director of the Department of Social Services for the state of Michigan. Archbishop Szoka insisted that, since her agency would administer $5.7 million a year for abortions, she should state publicly her opposition to such expenditures. Although she was personally opposed to abortion, she refused to accept Szoka's demand. On February 23, 1983, the archbishop announced that because of her refusal, she should immediately resign as director of social services. On March 10, Szoka reported the matter to the Vatican by way of the apostolic-delegate.

On April 25, 1983, Auxiliary Bishop Anthony Bevilacqua of Brooklyn, was informed by the Congregation for Religious and Secular Institutes, that at the direction of the Holy Father he had been appointed an ad hoc delegate to deal with this case. On May 9, 1983, Bevilacqua met with Sister Agnes Mary and asked that she resign as director and that if she refused he would have to initiate a canonical trial that could lead to her dismissal from the order. She requested a dispensation from her vows, and it was granted. Three years later, at the end of 1986, she

---

48. See James H. Provost, "Clergy and Religious in Political Life: Canonical Comments in the American Context," *The Jurist* 44 (1984):276-303.

49. For extensive documentation see *Origins*, March 10, 1983, vol. 12, no. 39:621-622; March 31, 1983, vol. 12, no. 42:676-680; May 26, 1983, vol. 13, no. 2: 34-36; and September 1, 1983, vol. 13, no. 12:197-206. The Mansour dossier is also found in Madonna Kolbenschlag, ed., *Authority, Community, and Conflict* (Kansas City, Mo.: Sheed and Ward, 1986).

left her state-government post to work for the Mercy Health Services in Detroit.

3. *Arlene Violet, R.S.M.* On January 19, 1984, Sister Arlene Violet, who had entered the Sisters of Mercy in 1961, announced that she had resigned from her congregation and had petitioned for a dispensation from her vows. She made this decision after she was informed by Bishop Louis E. Gelineau of Providence, Rhode Island, that he would not grant her an exemption from canons 285 and 672, which would have allowed her to run for the office of Rhode Island attorney general in the 1984 election.[50] She subsequently ran for office as the Republican candidate and was elected. She failed to win reelection in 1986.

4. *Four Nicaraguan Priests.* Four priests have held high positions in the Nicaraguan government since the Sandinistas came to power in 1979; Miguel d'Escoto Brockmann, a Maryknoll priest and foreign minister; Ernesto Cardenal, a Trappist and minister of culture; Fernando Cardenal, a Jesuit and minister of education; and Edgardo Parrales, priest of the Diocese of Estelí and representative to the Organization of American States. After months of negotiation, they were given an ultimatum by the Vatican in August 1984: they must resign their government positions, since they were in violation of canon 285, or face disciplinary action. By February 1985, all four rejected the Vatican request and decided to keep their posts. Rome's response was to suspend them *a divinis*; that is, to forbid them from celebrating the eucharist or administering the other sacraments. A few months earlier, Fernando Cardenal had been dismissed from the Jesuits, and Edgardo Parrales had revealed his desire to leave the priesthood and said that he had petitioned for laicization.

Papal Study of Seminaries

In September 1981, John Paul II ordered a study of the seminaries in the United States. Similar studies were being undertaken in Brazil, Italy, and the Philippines. The Pope appointed Bishop John A. Marshall of Burlington, Vermont, as the representative of the Holy See to act as coordinator.[51] Bishop Marshall is directly responsible to the Holy See

---

50. For the statement of Bishop Gelineau see *Origins*, February 2, 1984, vol. 13, no. 34:570–571.

51. See *Origins*, October 8, 1981, vol. 11, no. 17:263–264.

—the Sacred Congregation for Catholic Education—although he works closely with the National Conference of Catholic Bishops and the Conference of Major Superiors of Men.

The purpose of the study is twofold: to promote the renewal of seminary training in the United States and to provide information that can help seminary administrators make the best use of their personnel and resources. The study, therefore, involves an extensive evaluation of the current status of priestly formation in American seminaries in terms of administration, faculty, libraries, academics, spiritual life, liturgy, pastoral formation, community life, and discipline. One of the major tasks of the visiting teams is to determine whether the theology being taught in the seminaries is in conformity with the teaching of the Church. The visits are guided by conciliar and postconciliar documentation on priestly formation.[52]

The Congregation for Catholic Education made three significant interpretations of the existing norms. First, responsibility for formation in the essentials of priesthood always rests with the priest-members of the faculty. Religious brothers, religious sisters, or lay persons may be appointed to teach certain disciplines but only to a limited degree. Second, the spiritual directors of seminarians must be priests. Laity and nonpriest religious are not to be appointed to this task. Third, students other than seminarians are generally not to be admitted to the academic programs of the seminary. At most, only a small number of nonseminarians may be allowed in the seminary courses, provided that the purpose for which the seminary exists is not weakened.

The Marshall committee developed instruments of evaluation to be used in the visitations to freestanding theologates, seminaries of religious communities, theological unions, consortia, and clusters, Eastern Rite seminaries, college-level seminaries, and houses of formation.

Visitation teams, which were composed of bishops, religious superiors, and seminary personnel, began their first series of five-day visits in March 1983. By the end of 1986, all theologates, unions, and seminaries in the United States had been visited, and by the end of 1987, the visits to the college-level seminaries and houses of formation are to be completed. The confidential report of each visitation is sent to

---

52. The norms are contained in two volumes: *The Program of Priestly Formation,* 3rd ed. (Washington, NCCB, 1982), and *Norms of Priestly Formation* (Washington: NCCB, 1982).

the Congregation for Catholic Education in Rome for review, and the final report sent to the ordinary of the diocese and the head of the institution.

Cardinal William W. Baum, prefect of the Congregation for Catholic Education, issued a report on the visitations of the thirty-eight freestanding theologates in October 1986.[53] His overall assessment was that the seminaries are serving the Church well in preparing the candidates for the priesthood. He commended seminary staffs for the balanced way in which they have integrated the spiritual, academic, and pastoral dimensions of priestly training. Dissent, he reported, is not a major characteristic of these seminaries. A more common phenomenon is confusion about the teaching of the magisterium, especially in courses of moral theology.

Papal Study of Religious

Some one-hundred and fifty thousand sisters, brothers, and priests belong to religious institutes in the United States. John Paul II, in a letter to the bishops of the United States in 1983, expressed grave concern over the marked decline in the number of religious vocations.[54] The letter contained two requests. It asked the bishops to render special pastoral services to the religious in their dioceses, and it asked that a study be made of the reasons why young people are not entering religious life in greater numbers. To carry out these mandates the Pope appointed Archbishop John R. Quinn of San Francisco as his personal delegate to head a special commission of three bishops. The two other episcopal members were Archbishop Thomas C. Kelly, O.P., of Louisville, Kentucky, and Bishop Raymond W. Lessard of Savannah, Georgia.

Archbishop Quinn appointed a committee of six religious (four women and two men) and two consultors (a woman and a man) to assist the commission. The commission worked closely with the episcopal conference, the two conferences of major superiors, and the Sacred Congregation for Religious and Secular Institutes. It followed the document of the Congregation, "Essential Elements of Religious

---

53. *Origins*, October 16, 1986, vol. 16, no. 18:313, 315–325.
54. *Origins*, July 7, 1983, vol. 13, no. 8:129, 131–133.

Life," that was made public at the same time as the Pope's letter.[55] This document, which was approved by John Paul II, gave the salient features of the Church's teaching on religious life.

Archbishop Quinn insisted that the Pope was not calling for an investigation of religious life in the United States or even asking for an elaborate study as in the case of the seminaries. "Rather," he said, "there is a personal call to the bishops to encourage and strengthen religious life in its own authentic renewal."[56] The Quinn commission engaged in extensive consultation between bishops and religious. Each bishop was asked to meet twice with the religious (both men and women) in his diocese: once in order to listen to their views and a second time to engage in dialogue with them. Over one hundred bishops conducted these listening and dialogue sessions and sent personal letters to the Pope evaluating their results and indicating their judgment about the state of religious life in their dioceses. A long, final report of the commission's work was sent to the Pope in October 1986.

A summary of the final report was published in November 1986.[57] It suggested some reasons for the decline in vocations: cultural factors, the impact of Vatican II, and the development of the Church in the United States. The report also referred to some personal causes for the numerical decline: identity crises for some religious and for some communities, the lack of sufficient interiorization of religious life, improved selection processes, and the demands of celibacy and permanence. The commission noted that it is unlikely that there would be a significant increase in vocations in the foreseeable future, since it is a systemic problem and not the fault of individuals nor the lack of religious spirit. It concluded, nevertheless, that "religious life in the United States is in good condition."[58]

---

55. The full title is "Essential Elements in the Church's Teaching on Religious Life as Applied to Institutes Dedicated to the Works of the Apostolate," Text in *Origins*, July 7, 1983, vol. 13, no. 8:133–142. Also see Sharon L. Holland, "The Code and *Essential Elements*," *The Jurist*, 44 (1984):304–338, and Patrick Granfield, "Changes in Religious Life: Freedom, Responsibility, Community," *America*, September 15, 1984, pp. 120–123.

56. *Origins*, July 7, 1983, vol. 13, no. 8:145.

57. *Origins*, December 4, 1986, vol. 16, no. 25:467–470.

58. Ibid., 470.

Signers of the Abortion Advertisement

In the midst of the 1984 United States presidential election in which abortion was a major political issue, a full-page advertisement appeared in the October 7, 1984, Sunday edition of the *New York Times*. This advertisement, paid for by Catholics for a Free Choice, declared:

> A diversity of opinions regarding abortion exists among committed Catholics. Statements of recent Popes and of the Catholic hierarchy have condemned the direct termination of prenatal life as morally wrong in all instances. There is a mistaken belief in American society that this is the only legitimate Catholic position.

Among the ninety-seven signers of the advertisement there were twenty-seven religious: twenty-four nuns and three male religious. On November 30, 1984, the Sacred Congregation for Religious and Secular Institutes sent letters to the superiors of the religious signatories.[59] It said that the view expressed in the advertisement was contrary to the teaching of the Church and that the signers were "seriously lacking in 'religious submission of will and mind' to the magisterium." To stop this "flagrant scandal," each superior was to direct each signer "to make a public retraction." If the relegous refused and remained "obstinately disobedient," then, in accordance with canons 696, 1, and 697, the superior was to warn the religious that they faced dismissal from the institute.

In August 1985 Cardinal Jérôme Hamer, prefect of the Congregation for Religious and Secular Institutes, made a further statement. The language of "retraction" was avoided or at least put in another way. Hamer referred to the competency of the Congregation in this question, the clear teaching of the Church on abortion, and the scandal that had been given. In order to repair the scandal, the religious superiors of the signers should secure statements from them indicating their "adherence to the teaching of the Church" on abortion.[60]

The three male religious issued public retractions almost immediately. The twenty-four nuns, however, delayed. Gradually most of the nuns were able to satisfy the demands of their superiors and the Congregation. Jérôme Hamer announced on July 21, 1986, that

---

59. *Origins*, January 17, 1985, vol. 14, no. 31:515–516.
60. *Origins*, September 5, 1985, vol. 15, no. 12:188–189.

twenty-five of the signers had made "public retractions of adherence to Catholic doctrine on abortion."[61] Two sisters of Notre Dame de Namur refused to make such a declaration. Their cases are still pending. Eleven of the twenty-four nuns, whose cases were supposedly closed, responded to the July 21 announcement and "categorically denied" that they had made any public declaration of adherence to the Church teaching on abortion.[62]

Reports surfaced early in 1985 that the Committee of Concerned Catholics was organizing a new signature campaign and planning to run another advertisement in the *New York Times*. The *National Catholic Reporter* advised its readers: "Don't sign the abortion ad" and described it as "a deceitful, dishonest, and divisive effort by a small, single-issue group."[63] The second advertisement appeared in the *New York Times* on Sunday, March 2, 1986. It noted that, since many of the signers of the earlier statement had been penalized in various ways for their actions, "We affirm our solidarity with all Catholics whose right to free speech is under attack." It listed some one thousand signatories, including an indeterminate number of sisters and priests. The Vatican has taken no further action in this matter.

Bishops

Bishops have not been exempt from close scrutiny by the Pope and the curial congregations. They often receive inquiries from various Vatican offices about reported abuses in their dioceses concerning liturgical innovations and pastoral approaches to moral problems. The following examples, however, reveal a more direct exchange between Rome and the diocesan bishops.

The Tridentine Mass

Here is a vivid illustration of the problem of papal and episcopal interaction, even when there is collegial participation. In 1980, the Congregation for the Sacraments and Divine Worship surveyed the

61. *Origins*, July 31, 1986, vol. 16, no. 9:170, and *New York Times*, July 22, 1986, p. A11.

62. See *National Catholic Reporter*, August 15, 1986, p. 1.

63. Ibid., September, 27, 1985, p. 12.

Latin Rite bishops on the question of the Tridentine Mass. Ninety-eight percent of the 1,750 bishops who responded said that the absence of the Tridentine Latin Mass was not a problem for the whole Church but only the concern of "a tiny—but very active—minority that makes itself heard with much noise."[64] The majority of the bishops were clearly against any concession allowing the celebration of the Tridentine Mass.

In October 1984, the Congregation for Divine Worship announced that, because the problem still perdures, the Pope had granted an indult allowing bishops under specific conditions to permit the Latin Tridentine Mass to be celebrated in their dioceses.[65] A few weeks later, a group of English-speaking liturgical experts from thirty-two episcopal conferences (including twenty-seven bishops) were in Rome as part of a conference marking the twentieth anniversary of the *Constitution on the Liturgy* of Vatican II. They expressed "grave concern, regret, and dismay" that the permission to celebrate the Tridentine Mass had been granted. They said that the concession "appears to be a movement away from the ecclesiology of the Second Vatican Council" and "seems to violate the collegial sense of the world-wide episcopate" whose opinion was given in the 1980 survey.[66]

The 1983 *Ad Limina* Visits

Every five years each diocesan bishop has to submit to the Pope a report on the state of his diocese and to make an *ad limina* visit to Rome: to venerate the tombs of Saints Peter and Paul and to visit the Holy Father (cans. 399 and 400). In the late summer and early fall of 1983, a steady stream of American bishops went to Rome for their *ad limina* visits. They met with the Pope in private audiences, at meals in the papal apartments, and in small groups. In his addresses to them the Pope discussed, among other things, the priesthood, the eucharist, the ministry of bishops, and the religious life.

On September 5, in speaking to a group of twenty-three bishops, the Pope insisted that they proclaim "without fear or ambiguity" the moral doctrine of the Church concerning the indissolubility of mar-

---

64. *Origins*, February 11, 1982, vol. 11, no. 35:558.
65. *Origins*, October 25, 1984, vol. 14, no. 19:290.
66. *Origins*, November 8, 1984, vol. 14, no. 21:335.

riage and explain the reason for the Church's opposition to artificial contraception, homosexual activity, and premarital sex. A bishop, he said, is expected to oppose all discrimination against women by reason of sex and to show that the exclusion of women from ordination is not discrimination but part of Christ's plan for the priesthood. He continued: "A bishop must give proof of his pastoral ability and leadership by withdrawing all support from individuals or groups who in the name of progress, justice, or compassion, or for any other alleged reason, promote the ordination of women to the priesthood."[67]

The press, predictably, viewed the *ad limina* visits as a severe rebuke of the American bishops and an attack by the Vatican on the American Church. Some of the bishops, likewise predictably, saw it in another light. Archbishop John Roach, for example, in his presidential address to the National Conference of Catholic Bishops on November 14, 1983, said that according to the press "there was a confrontation under way between a rebellious American Church, led by its bishops, and a stern pontiff bent on taking us to task."[68] That was not true, he said. It was not harsh confrontation nor criticism but collegial encouragement and support. He called it "collegiality in action." Cardinal Joseph Bernadin's reaction was similar. He said: "He [the Pope] is saying basically that we must fulfill our roles with integrity. Has he lost confidence in us? I think not. Rather, he has taken a real interest in us because of the importance of the Church in the United States."[69]

The Visitation of Episcopal Sees

It is not without precedent but it is unusual for one bishop to investigate another. In 1983 two American dioceses were investigated by Rome. The first investigation received relatively little public notice. Archbishop John May of St. Louis, at the request of the Apostolic Delegate, Archbishop Pio Laghi, conducted a visitation of the Richmond, Virginia, diocese of Bishop Walter Sullivan. Complaints had reached Rome about liturgical abuses and the life-style of some of the priests in the diocese. Archbishop May visited Richmond in

---

67. *Origins*, September 15, 1983, vol. 13, no. 14:239.
68. *Origins*, November 24, 1983, vol. 13, no. 24:401.
69. *New York Times*, October 31, 1983, p. A17.

June 1983 and talked with Bishop Sullivan and several other people "to find out the situation of the diocese overall" and "to ask whether the bishop's requests for an auxiliary was well-founded."[70] He sent his confidential report to Rome. An auxiliary bishop was appointed for Richmond in May 1985.

The second investigation received much publicity. In June 1983 the Holy See appointed Archbishop James A. Hickey of Washington, D.C., to conduct an apostolic visitation of the Archdiocese of Seattle and of its ordinary, Archbishop Raymond G. Hunthausen. Although Archbishop Hunthausen had supported unilateral disarmament, refused to pay part of his income tax as a protest, and denounced a nearby nuclear submarine base, Archbishop Hickey said that these political questions were not the focus of the visitation.[71] Rather, his mandate was to investigate allegations against Hunthausen and his episcopal ministry made by some Seattle Catholics concerning liturgical and doctrinal irregularities. Archbishop Hickey visited Seattle, November 2–8, 1983, conferred with more than seventy members of the clergy, religious, and laity, and had thirteen hours of discussion with Archbishop Hunthausen.

Two years later, on November 14, 1985, Archbishop Pio Laghi wrote Hunthausen to say that the visitation "has been concluded and is considered closed."[72] He praised Hunthausen for his efforts in renewal, for his support and encouragement of priests, laity, and religious in the life of the archdiocese, and for his devotion and obedience to the Holy Father. He noted that "you and your collaborators have suffered from exaggerated and mean-spirited ciriticism."[73] Yet Laghi urged Hunthausen to attend to several specific concerns: to present more clearly and to uphold the teachings of the Church concerning the indissolubility of marriage, contraceptive sterilization, and homosexuality; to follow the universal norms of the Church in regard to the celebration of the eucharist and the proper sequence of first confession before first communion; to review seminary formation and the continuing education of the clergy; and to make it clear that laicized priests are excluded from certain roles in the Church.

70. *National Catholic Reporter*, November 4, 1983, p. 23.

71. See remarks of Hickey in *National Catholic Reporter*, November 4, 1983, pp. 1, 23.

72. *Origins*, December 26, 1985, vol. 15, no. 28:457.

73. Ibid., 459.

On December 3, 1985, the Holy See appointed Donald W. Wuerl as auxiliary to Hunthausen. In accordance with canon 403, 2, Wuerl had "special faculties." Nine months later, on September 4, 1986, Hunthausen issued a public statement saying that he had not initially understood the nature and extent of Bishop Wuerl's role as his auxiliary. He thought that Wuerl would only assist him by assuming a general responsibility in specific areas. Rome, he said, later clarified it: he should delegate Wuerl to have complete and final decision-making power in five areas: tribunal staff and operation, seminary formation and continuing education of the clergy, priests leaving the ministry and laicized priests, and moral issues in institutions of health care and in the ministry to homosexuals.

A few weeks before the bishops were to meet in Washington for their annual meeting in November 1986, confusion abounded. Archbishop Pio Laghi (by then apostolic pronuncio) sent, on the authority of the Holy See, a chronology of the events to all the American bishops.[74] It noted that the Holy See considered Hunthausen "lacking in the firmness necessary to govern the archdiocese." Hunthausen responded to the Vatican report with his own chronology.[75] The two chronologies offered different versions of the facts and different interpretations.

At the meeting of the bishops, Hunthausen addressed the bishops, saying that he found the situation in Seattle "all by impossible, even to the point of being unworkable."[76] In closed executive session the bishops discussed the Seattle controversy. Their final statement expressed concern for the pain suffered by the parties involved, but said that an episcopal conference has no authority to intervene in this dispute and could not review, much less judge, a case involving the Holy See and a diocesan bishop. It also declared that the U.S. bishops "affirm unreservedly their loyalty to and unity with the Holy Father."[77]

In January 1987, the Vatican announced the appointment of a three-member ad hoc commission to assess the current situation in the Seattle archdiocese. Named to the commission were Cardinal Joseph L. Bernardin of Chicago, Cardinal John J. O'Connor of New York, and Archbishop John R. Quinn of San Francisco.*

---

74. Text in *Origins*, November 6, 1986, vol. 16, no. 21:361, 363–364.

75. Found in *Origins*, November 20, 1986, vol. 16, no. 23:406–408.

76. Ibid., 405.

77. Ibid., 400.

* For the most recent developments in the Hunthausen case, see the addendum on page 196.

Conclusion

In this chapter we have documented the extensive exercise of primatial authority in the last decade. Rome has acted frequently and decisively in the activities of theologians, priests, religious, and bishops. Catholics in the United States and elsewhere have reached no consensus about these events. In fact, there exists a broad range of opinion.

At one end of the spectrum, there are those Catholics who have reacted to the recent Roman interventions with enthusiastic approval, considering them predictable, reasonable, and commendable. They see such actions as long overdue and absolutely necessary if the purity of the faith and the uniqueness of Catholicism is to be preserved. For them, literal loyalty to the Holy See is the touchstone of orthodoxy, and anyone dissenting from the teaching of the Church must be corrected. At the other end of the spectrum, there are Catholics who are profoundly disturbed by the present situation. They view the Roman actions as unjustified, ill-timed, and detrimental to the vitality of Catholic life; they insist that such events weaken the high hopes generated by Vatican II and point to excessive centralization in the Church.

A simple global judgment on the events of the last ten years is difficult, because each individual case that we have described is complex and has its own inner dynamics. Yet the evident increase in the use of papal authority raises some fundamental ecclesiological issues. The most basic one is the limitation of papal power. To unpack this concept, it is necessary first to examine the claims of papal primacy and then, using the principles of limitation, to examine how the Pope is related to the bishops, local Churches, the faithful, and other Christians.

·II·

The Claims of Primacy

*The Pope is the meeting point
between God and man ... who can
judge all things and be judged by no
one.*

—Innocent III*

In the drama of world history, the papacy has played a major role.
It is a venerable institution—complex, daunting, an object of
both love and contempt, but always fascinating. With remarkable re-
siliency, it has survived catastrophic internal and external upheavals
for nearly two millennia. Although the papacy is unique because of
its divine origins, it remains a human social reality, shaped by culture
and confronted by persistent challenges. The history of the papacy
reveals a circuitous path toward self-identity marked by moments of
glorious accomplishment as well as by those of humiliating disgrace.
Historically, debates about the papacy and its exercise by individual
Popes have focused on one large concern: What is the nature, extension, and limitation of the supreme primatial authority claimed by
the Bishop of Rome as successor of St. Peter? From the first century of
the Christian era until today, this issue continues to dominate the
discussion.

To understand the various dimensions of the theological issue of
limitation, it is first necessary to recognize the full range of prerogatives that have been claimed for the papacy throughout history. It is
only against such a background that the question of limitation can be
understood. For that reason, in this chapter we shall explore historically and canonically the claims of papal primacy. Only the broad
picture is given here; a fuller theological analysis will appear in subsequent chapters.

---

* Sermo 2. *Patrologia latina* 217:658.

The Theological Development

For the first three centuries, the Christian Church differed greatly from the well-organized international community we know today. Rather, it functioned as a relatively loose federation of local Churches united in a common faith. Only from the middle of the second century can one speak of the "Bishop" of Rome. But even in the Church's earliest days, Rome enjoyed a unique position: the place of the martyrdom of Peter and Paul, the capital of the empire, and the only Apostolic See in the West. The Roman Church, "presiding in love," to use a phrase from Ignatius of Antioch, symbolized the center of orthodoxy, its bishops often settling doctrinal and disciplinary conflicts.

The jurisdiction of the Bishop of Rome developed gradually. Pierre Batiffol spoke of "three zones of papal power" in the Church of the first three centuries.[1] The first zone was Italy where the Bishop of Rome exercised full and immediate authority over all local Churches. The second zone was the West — Gaul, Spain, and to some extent Africa — where Churches were eventually organized into provinces that recognized Rome as the center of communion and the final arbiter in disputes. The third zone was the East where the Churches enjoyed greater autonomy; interventions from Rome were limited to only the most serious cases. Hilaire Marot has suggested a fourth zone: Churches in Persia and Abyssinia whose acceptance of the great councils was a sign of their communion with the universal Church but whose relationship to Rome was tenuous.[2]

Not until the end of the fourth century did the Bishops of Rome begin to assert vigorously their universal primatial claims. The theoretical foundation for primacy took shape in the century between Damasus I (366–384) and Leo I (440–461). It was Leo who was the first to claim the fullness of power (*plenitudo potestatis*).[3] He also developed the theory of the Peter-Pope identity. Another seven hun-

---

1. *Cathedra Petri: Etudes d'histoire ancienne de l'Eglise* (Paris: Cerf, 1938), pp. 41-79.

2. "L'unité de l'Eglise et diversité géographique aux premiers siècles," in Yves Congar and Bernard-Dominique DuPuy, eds., *L'épiscopat et l'Eglise universelle* (Paris: Cerf, 1962), pp. 565-590.

3. This idea was developed even further in the Middle Ages. See Gerhard B. Ladner, "The Concepts of '*Ecclesia*' and '*Christianitas*' and their Relation to the

dred years would pass before these claims were fully operative in Western Christendom; after the disastrous tenth century, Gregory VII (1073–85) and his successors managed, by exerting strong papal control, to restore prestige and integrity to the papal office.

The Medieval Period

In the Middle Ages there was no ambiguity about the papal prerogative of primacy, at least in the minds of the Popes themselves. The *Dictatus papae* of Gregory VII is a good example. It gives twenty-seven propositions, which originally may have been chapter headings for a now lost canonical treatise. The affirmation of Roman authority is extensive and detailed with the Pope claiming near absolute power in his governance of the Church. All bishops, clerics, and lay persons, including emperors, are subject to his authority. Gregory declared:

1. That the Roman Church was founded by God alone.
2. That the Roman Pontiff alone is rightly to be called universal.
3. That he alone can depose or reinstate bishops.
4. That his legate, even if of lower grade, takes precedence in a council of all bishops and may render a sentence of deposition against them.
5. That the Pope may depose the absent.
6. That, among other things, we also ought not to stay in the same house with those excommunicated by him.
7. That for him alone is it lawful to enact new laws according to the needs of the time, to assemble together new congregations, to make an abbey of a canonry and, on the other hand, to divide a rich bishopric and unite the poor ones.
8. That he alone may use the imperial insignia.
9. That the Pope is the only one whose feet are to be kissed by all princes.
10. That his name alone is to be recited in churches.
11. That his title is unique in the world.
12. That he may depose emperors.
13. That he may transfer bishops, if necessary, from one see to another.

Idea of Papal '*Plenitudo Potestatis*' from Gregory VII to Boniface VIII," *Miscellanea historiae pontificiae* 18 (1954):49–77, and William D. McCready, "Papal *Plenitudo Potestatis* and the Source of Temporal Authority in the Late Medieval Papal Hierocratic Theory," *Speculum* 48 (1973):654–674.

14. That he has the power to ordain a cleric of any church he may wish.

15. That he who has been ordained by him may rule over another church, but not be under the command of others; and that such a one may not receive a higher grade from any bishop.

16. That no synod may be called general without his order.

17. That no chapter or book may be regarded as canonical without his authority.

18. That no sentence of his may be retracted by anyone; and that he, alone of all, can retract it.

19. That he himself may be judged by no one.

20. That no one shall dare to condemn a person who appeals to the Apostolic See.

21. That to this See the more important cases of every church should be submitted.

22. That the Roman Church has never erred, nor ever, by the witness of Scripture, shall err to all eternity.

23. That the Roman Pontiff, if canonically ordained, is undoubtedly sanctified by the merits of St. Peter; of this St. Ennodius, Bishop of Pavia, is witness, many Holy Fathers are agreeable and it is contained in the decrees of Pope Symmachus the Saint.

24. That, by his order and with his permission, subordinate persons may bring accusations.

25. That without convening a synod he can depose and reinstate bishops.

26. That he should not be considered a Catholic who is not in conformity with the Roman Church.

27. That the Pope may absolve subjects of unjust men from their fealty.[4]

During the pontificate of Innocent III (1198–1216), the idea of a world-wide papal theocracy embracing both the faithful and the unbeliever reached its peak.[5] He referred to the Pope not only as the Vicar of Christ but also the Vicar of God.[6] At the end of the thirteenth

---

4. English translation from S. Z. Ehler and J. B. Morrall, *Church and State Through the Centuries* (Westminster, Md.: Newman, 1954), pp. 43–44. Latin text in E. Caspar, ed., *Das Register Gregors VII*, in *Monumenta germaniae historica, Epistolae selectae*, II:55a, 201–208.

5. For further information on this point see Brian Tierney, *Foundations of the Conciliar Theory* (Cambridge: Cambridge University, 1955).

6. See Jean Rivière, "Sur l'expression '*Papa-Deus*' au Moyen Age," in *Miscellanea*

century, Boniface VIII (1294–1303) continued to foster a grandiose conception of papal sovereignty. His most famous statement appeared in the dogmatic bull *Unam sanctam*: "We declare, state, and define that it is absolutely necessary for the salvation of all that they submit to the Roman Pontiff."[7] Boniface VIII, disregarding the facts of history, also asserted that Rome had established all the patriarchal, metropolitan, and episcopal sees.[8] A further step was taken by Clement VI (1342–52) who required from Armenian Catholics the belief that the Pope, as the Vicar of Christ on earth, possesses the same full power of jurisdiction that Christ himself possessed during his human life.[9]

The Church, according to the ecclesiology of the Middle Ages, was often viewed, in the formal treatises at least, more as a legal corporation than as the living body of the risen Christ. From the eleventh century onward, the ideas and trappings of the imperial court influenced the development of papal authority. The Pope was portrayed in terms of a monarchical ideology.[10] This approach is evident in the conciliar definitions of papal primacy. Among theologians and ca-

---

F. Ehrle, *Scritti di storia e paleografia*, vol. 2: *Per la storia di Roma* (Rome: Biblioteca apostolica Vaticana, 1924), 276–289.

7. H. Denzinger and A. Schönmetzer, *Enchiridion definitionum et declarationum de rebus fidei et moribus*, 36th ed. (Freiburg: Herder, 1973), p. 875. Hereafter cited as DS. English translation from Josef Neuner and Heinrich Roos, *The Teaching of the Catholic Church* (Staten Island, N.Y.: Alba House, 1967), no. 342. Hereafter cited as TCC. George Tavard has argued that this proclamation is not an infallible definition according to the norms established by Vatican I: "The Bull *Unam Sanctam* of Boniface VIII," in Paul C. Empie and T. Austin Murphy, eds., *Papal Primacy and the Universal Church: Lutherans and Catholics in Dialogue V* (Minneapolis: Augsburg, 1974), pp. 105–119.

8. Pontificia commissio ad redigendum codicem iuris canonici orientalis, *Fontes, Acta romanorum pontificum ab Innocentio V ad Benedictum XI*, ed. F. M. Delorme and A. L. Tautu (Vatican City: Typis Polyglottis Vaticanis, 1954), series III, vol. V, tom. II, p. 204, no. 456.

9. Ibid., *Acta Clementis PP. VI*, A. L. Tautu, ed. vol. IX, p. 304, no. 641.

10. St. Bernard of Clairvaux opposed the imperial trappings of the papacy as is evident in his remarks to Pope Eugene III (1145–53): "When the Pope, clad in silk, covered with gold and jewels, rides out on his white horse, escorted by soldiers and servants, he looks more like Constantine's successor than St. Peter's." *De consideratione*, IV, 3, 6. *Patrologia latina* 182:776. Quoted in Yves Congar, *Power and Poverty in the Church* (Baltimore: Helicon, 1965), p. 125. Congar has also written on this point in *L'Eglise de saint Augustin à l'époque moderne* (Paris: Cerf, 1970), and "The

nonists there were also strong episcopal and "conciliarist" views. Ecumenical councils, such as Lyons II (1274)[11] and Florence (1438-45),[12] proclaimed the primacy of the Pope, but it was in *Pastor aeternus* of Vatican I (1869-70) that we find the most detailed and definitive teaching.

Vatican I

The definition of the primacy at Vatican I was occasioned by two factors. First, the Council sought to reject the conciliarist errors of Gallicanism, Febronianism, and Josephinism that evidenced a strong antipapal bias, even though these movements were quite weak by the middle of the nineteenth century. Second, the Council felt impelled to affirm the spiritual authority of the Pope because his temporal power had been weakened by the rise of Italian nationalism and the impending loss of the Papal States. The following four canons from *Pastor aeternus* reveal how strongly Vatican I envisioned the papal office:

> In any one, therefore, shall say that Blessed Peter the Apostle was not appointed Prince of all the Apostles and the visible head of the whole Church Militant; or that he directly and immediately received from the same Lord Jesus Christ a primacy of honor only, and not of true and proper jurisdiction—*let him be anathema*.[13]

Historical Development of Authority in the Church. Points for Reflection," in John M. Todd, ed., *Problems of Authority* (Baltimore: Helicon; London: Darton, Longman & Todd, 1962), pp. 136-144.

11. "The same holy Roman Church also has supreme and full primacy and jurisdiction over the universal catholic Church, which she recognizes in truth and humility she received with full powers from the Lord himself in Blessed Peter, prince or head of the Apostles, whose successor the Roman Pontiff is. And as she above others is obliged to defend the truth of faith, thus if any questions are raised about faith they must be decided by her judgment" (DS 861; TCC 848).

12. "We decree that the Holy Apostolic See and the Roman Pontiff have primacy in the whole world, and that this Roman Pontiff is the successor of blessed Peter, Prince of the Apostles, and true Vicar of Christ, head of the whole Church and father and teacher of all Christians; that to him in blessed Peter was given by our Lord Jesus Christ the full power of feeding, ruling, and governing the universal Church" (DS 1307; TCC 349).

13. DS 3055; TCC 374.

If, then, any one shall say that it is not by the institution of Christ the Lord, or by divine right, that Blessed Peter should have a perpetual line of successors in the primacy over the Universal Church; or that the Roman Pontiff is not the successor of Blessed Peter in this primacy — *let him be anathema.*[14]

If, then, any one shall say that the Roman Pontiff has the office merely of inspection or direction, but not full and supreme power and jurisdiction over the Universal Church, not only in things pertaining to faith and morals, but also in things that relate to the discipline and government of the Church spread throughout the world; or that he possesses merely the principal part, and not all the fullness of this supreme power; or that this power which he enjoys is not ordinary and immediate, both over each and all the Churches and all the pastors and the faithful— *let him be anathema.*[15]

Finally, the Council also defined the doctrine of papal infallibility as a divinely revealed dogma.

We teach and define that it is a dogma divinely revealed: that the Roman Pontiff, when he speaks *ex cathedra*, that is, when in discharge of the office of Pastor and Doctor of all Christians, by virtue of his supreme apostolic authority he defines a doctrine regarding faith or morals to be held by the Universal Church, by the divine assistance promised him in Blessed Peter, is possessed of that infallibility with which the Divine Redeemer willed that his Church should be endowed for defining doctrine regarding faith or morals: and that therefore such definitions of the Roman Pontiff are irreformable of themselves and not from the consent of the Church. But if anyone, which God forbid, presume to contradict this Our definition— *let him be anathema.*[16]

In the conciliar discussions, some of the Council Fathers tried to temper the obvious legal and political connotations of the declarations on the Pope by placing them in a scriptural and pastoral context. The German Bishop Krementz of Ermland, for example, insisted that the notion of *plenitudo potestatis* is rooted in the constitution that Christ

---

14. DS 3058; TCC 377.
15. DS 3064; TCC 382.
16. DS 3074, 3075; TCC 388.

gave to his Church, and that "the government of this Church cannot be adequately compared to a monarchy, whether absolute or limited, or to an aristocracy or any such thing."[17]

Other Fathers were concerned with the ecumenical impact of the definition. Thus, Bishop Wiery of Gurk, Austria, asked his colleagues to be more moderate in describing the papal office, lest other Christians say: "You Catholics, papists, you look for your savior at Rome and not from heaven; you expect salvation from the Pope and not from Christ."[18]

The French-born Sulpician, Jean-Pierre Augustin Vérot, of Savannah, Georgia, brought up the question of the limits of papal authority. One of the few real Gallicans at the Council and the *enfant terrible* among the bishops, he made a provocative intervention. Arguing that earlier councils had always declared that the Pope exercises his supreme power according to the canons, he suggested a new canon: "If anyone says that the authority of the Roman Pontiff over the Church is so complete that he can dispose of everything he wishes, let him be anathema."[19] His suggestion, proposed perhaps more as a pleasantry than as a serious contribution, drew murmurs and laughter from the audience. Cardinal Capalti, one of the presidents of the Council, rebuked him for his buffoonery and absurd behavior.

Pastor aeternus taught that the primacy of jurisdiction of the Pope is supreme and full, universal, ordinary, immediate, and truly episcopal. Each of these characteristics deserves comment. They show how extensively the Council detailed the papal prerogatives but without raising the question of limits to any significant degree.

First, the Pope has supreme and full jurisdiction. The term "jurisdiction," derived from the Roman canon law tradition, means the public power of ruling with the consequent obligation of obedience. The Pope is subject to no superior human power in the Church because his authority lacks nothing. The papacy is not simply an office of inspection or direction nor is the Pope's power only a part, however important, of supreme power. Rather the Pope, as the Vicar of Christ and head of the Church, enjoys the complete fullness of supreme

---

17. J. D. Mansi, ed., *Sacrorum conciliorum nova et amplissima collectio* (Arnhem and Leipzig: Welter, 1927), 52:683 B. Hereafter cited as Mansi.

18. Mansi 52:503 A.

19. Mansi 52:591 C.

power (*tota plenitudo potestatis*) not only in faith and morals but also in the discipline and government of the Church throughout the world. The Pope, moreover, is the supreme judge of the faithful in the Church; his decisions are subject to review by no one, not even an ecumenical council.

The Pope also has the supreme power of teaching. By the assistance of the Holy Spirit, he guards and faithfully explains the revelation that was handed down by the Apostles. As the pastor and teacher of all Christians the Pope possesses the infallibility of the Church when he defines doctrines of faith or morals. His *ex cathedra* definitions are irreformable "of themselves and not from the consent of the Church."

Second, the Pope has universal power of jurisdiction. All the faithful—bishops, clergy, religious, and laity—are subject to the Pope. No one is exempt. He is the head of the universal Church and his authority extends to all particular Churches, whatever their rank, and to all rites in communion with him. It is not limited to Rome or even to the Western Church but embraces the entire globe.

Third, the Pope has the ordinary power of jurisdiction. The term "ordinary" is used in the narrow canonical sense to mean the power that is not delegated but belongs to the Pope properly in virtue of his office. He exercises this power in his own name and not in the name of another. This issue was hotly debated by the Council Fathers.[20] They agreed that the Pope could exercise his power at any time, but they rejected the idea that ordinary meant the daily, continuous, habitual exercise of authority in individual dioceses. Bishop Ketteler of Mainz pointed out that it would be impossible for the Pope to exercise this kind of quotidian authority.[21] Since the episcopate is also of divine right, the Council, in one of its few references to bishops, affirmed that supreme papal jurisdiction does not interfere with the ordinary and immediate episcopal jurisdiction but rather asserts, confirms, and strengthen it.[22] *Pastor aeternus* did not give a precise and satisfactory answer to the relationship between respective competencies of the Pope and the bishops. The debates, as we shall see in later chapters, are helpful, but they are somewhat ambiguous.

---

20. See Gustave Thils, "'*Potestas ordinaria*,'" in Y. Congar and B.-D. Dupuy, eds., *L'épiscopat et l'Eglise universelle*, pp. 689–707.

21. Mansi 51:934 C.

22. DS 3061; TCC 380.

Fourth, the Pope has immediate power. He can exercise his authority directly without having to go through any intermediary—civil or ecclesiastical. The Council affirmed the right of the Pope to communicate freely with all the faithful and repudiated the idea that the authority of the Apostolic See "cannot have force or value unless it be confirmed by the assent of the secular power."[23] Likewise, the Pope does not have to go through the local bishop if he wishes to perform certain episcopal functions in his diocese. Bishop Zinelli of Treviso, speaking for the Deputation on the Faith—the theological commission at Vatican I—addressed the question of whether the Pope needed the permission of the local bishop to confirm or hear confessions in his diocese. He responded rhetorically: "As often as it was asked by one of the most reverend speakers whether the Pope needed permission, laughter broke out in the group."[24]

Fifth, the Pope has truly episcopal power.[25] The Pope has the same pastoral authority of teaching, sanctifying, and governing in the entire Church that the bishop has in his own diocese. Episcopal authority has its source in the sacrament of episcopal consecration. In that sense, as Bishop Zinelli pointed out, both Pope and bishops share in the same reality: "Episcopal power resides in the bishops and supreme episcopal power in the sovereign pontiff."[26] Yet there is a difference: "Episcopal authority in the Pope is supreme and independent; in the bishops it is immediate and ordinary but dependent."[27]

One glaring omission in Vatican I is the almost total absence of any practical limits to the jurisdictional authority of the Pope and his relationship to the episcopate. The minority members of the Council wanted the traditional canonical limitations of authority expressed in the text. The majority, however, resisted, arguing that such limi-

---

23. DS 3062; TCC 380.

24. Mansi 52:1105 C.

25. Good textual analysis and historical background can be found in two articles by Wilfrid F. Dewan: "'*Potestas vere episcopalis*' au premier Concile du Vatican," in Y. Congar and B.-D. Dupuy, *L'épiscopat et l'Eglise universelle*, pp. 661-687, and "Preparation of the Vatican Council's Schema on the Power and Nature of the Primacy," *Ephemerides theologicae lovanienses* 36 (1960):23-56. Also see Gustave Thils, *La primauté pontificale. La doctrine de Vatican I. Les voies d'une révision* (Gembloux: Duculot, 1972).

26. Mansi 52:1104 D.

27. Mansi 52:1115 A B.

tations are obvious and that their explicit inclusion in the text would be interpreted as a restriction on the Pope and would diminish the teaching that the Pope enjoys the fullness of power.

In the years following Vatican I, there was an evident preoccupation with the papacy. The militant Ultramontanism of the nineteenth century was refined, but its main themes were preserved. Some of the hopes of Joseph de Maistre (d. 1821) seemed to have been realized. He believed that the restoration of Catholicism after the French Revolution had to be built on the twin truths of papal supremacy and infallibility. In his words: "No European religion without Christianity, no Christianity without Catholicism, no Catholicism without the Pope, no Pope without the supremacy that belongs to him."[28] In accord with these ideas an ecclesiology "from above" took shape that viewed all ecclesial power flowing from the Pope. Reinforced by the 1917 Code of Canon Law, centralization and uniformity increased in the Church.

Vatican I also occasioned a cult of the Pope and an exaltation of papal prerogatives as is evident in theological and catechetical texts, devotional literature, and in preaching. Bishop Gaspard Mermillod of Geneva (d. 1892), a renowned preacher and pioneer in the Catholic social movement, gave a sermon in 1870 in which he referred to three sanctuaries: the crib, the tabernacle, and the Vatican, as containing God, Jesus Christ, and the Pope. Today, he said, Jesus Christ is in the form of the Pope. In another moment of homiletic excess, he spoke of the three incarnations of the Son of God: in the womb of the Virgin, in the eucharist, and in the Pope.[29] Bishop Alexis Lépicier (d. 1936) spoke of Abyssinia as a country with great devotion to "the three white things," ("*les trois blancheurs*"): the host, the Virgin Mary,. and the Pope.[30] In more recent times, the traditionalist Archbishop Marcel Lefebvre has also used this same imagery.[31]

---

28. *Correspondence* IV, p. 428. Quoted in Y. Congar, "L'ecclésiologie de la révolution française au Concile du Vatican, sous le signe de l'affirmation de l'autorité," in M. Nédoncelle et al., *L'ecclésiologie au XIX siècle* (Paris: Cerf, 1960), p. 82.

29. Referred to by Yves Congar, *I Believe in the Holy Spirit* (New York: Seabury, 1983), I:161. Congar considered the words in the homily on the "three sanctuaries" as "perfectly ridiculous, which excuses them from being blasphemous."

30. Idem.

31. Idem. St. John Bosco was even more effusive in his devotion to the Pope: "The Pope is God on earth. Jesus has set the Pope above the prophets, above his precursor, above the angels. Jesus has placed the Pope on a level with God." *Meditazioni*, vol. 1,

Vatican II

The Second Vatican Council (1962-65), not surprisingly, reaffirmed the teaching of Vatican I on the institution, the perpetuity, and the nature of papal primacy and its infallible teaching authority (*Lumen gentium*, art. 18). Since later chapters will explore in detail the major themes of papal and episcopal authority in Vatican II, at this juncture we will present only some general observations about the Council's understanding of ecclesial authority.

First, there was a profound shift in both style and substance in the way Vatican II treated the hierarchical structure of the Church. This change is evident in the terminology employed. *Pastor aeternus* used the term "jurisdiction" six times, while *Lumen gentium* used it only twice (arts. 23 and 45) and the *Nota praevia* once.[32] Compared to Vatican I, Vatican II was more scriptural than juridical, more ecumenical than polemical, more pastoral than dogmatic. It portrayed hierarchical ministry not as dominion but as service and encouraged all the People of God to work together in pursuit of the common goal of salvation.

Second, Vatican II, unlike Vatican I, began its description of the hierarchical structure not with the Pope but with the College of Bishops as successor of the college of the Apostles under the leadership of the Pope, the successor of Peter. In so doing it deepened the theological understanding of ecclesial authority and gave us the fundamental idea of the doctrine of collegiality. The Pope, then, is placed within the College of Bishops; he himself is a fellow bishop and head of the college. The College of Bishops is the subject of supreme authority in the Church, but it must always be understood in rela-

---

2nd ed., pp. 89-90. Quoted in René Laurentin, "Peter as the Foundation Stone in the Present Uncertainty," in Edward Schillebeeckx and Bas van Iersel, eds., *Truth and Certainity, Concilium* no. 83 (New York: Herder and Herder, 1973), 103. For further references to this kind of papal adulation before and after Vatican I see Roger Aubert, *Le pontificat de Pie IX, 1846–1878*, rev. ed. (Paris: Bloud & Gay, 1963); Cuthbert Butler, *The Vatican Council, 1869–1870*, ed. Christopher Butler (Westminster, Md.: Newman, 1962), pp. 44–62; and Claude Gerest, "Le pape au XIX siècle: histoire d'une inflation," *Lumière et vie* 26 (1977):70–86.

32. See Giuseppe Alberigo, "La jurisdiction: Remarques sur un terme ambigu," *Irénikon* 49 (1976):167–180, and Gérard Fransen, "Réflexions sur la jurisdiction ecclésiastique," *Revue théologique de Louvain* 2 (1971):129–144.

tionship to the Pope who, as "pastor of the universal Church" has full, supreme, and universal power that he can exercise freely.

Episcopal consecration confers the offices of sanctifying, teaching, and governing; the exercise of the powers of teaching and governing, however, depends on the maintaining of hierarchical communion with the head and members of the college. Furthermore, each individual bishop, as a member of the college, is obliged to exercise pastoral solicitude for the whole Church. This solicitude involves the duty to promote the unity of faith and discipline and to instruct the faithful to love the entire Body of Christ, especially its poor and suffering members.

Third, Vatican II emphasized the catholicity and apostolicity of authority in the Church. By stressing the sacramental and collegial qualities of Church leadership, it provided a more cohesive understanding of how the Pope and the bishops, each with a particular ministry, function within the community of believers. Moreover, in the doctrine of collegiality we have a new perspective by which to examine the limits of papal sovereignty. The question is: What precisely are the norms governing the cooperation between the College of Bishops and its head, the Pope, who together share in the governance of the universal Church? Vatican II did not fully answer that question.

The Canonical Expression

The 1983 Code of Canon Law is the Church's principal legislative document. In promulgating the Code, John Paul II said that his act was "an expression of pontifical authority and therefore is invested with a primatial character."[33] The Code reflects the major themes and ideas found in Vatican II and in postconciliar documents; they form the theological basis for Church law. Our interest in the Code is specific: What does it say about the authority of the Pope? What rights and privileges does it assign to the papal office?

The Code uses several titles to refer to the Pope: Roman Pontiff, Supreme Pontiff, Successor of Peter, supreme authority, and the

---

33. Apostolic constitution *Sacrae disciplinae leges. Acta apostolicae sedis* 75, 2 (1983):x.

Bishop of the Church of Rome (once only, in can. 331). It also uses the expressions Apostolic See and Holy See. Canon 361 explains that in the Code the terms "Apostolic See" or "Holy See" apply not only to the Pope but also to other curial offices, unless the nature and context make the contrary evident. On this point the apostolic constitution *Regimini ecclesiae universae* (1967) gives us two important norms. First, "nothing important and out of the ordinary is to be done unless it has first been made known to the Supreme Pontiff by the head of the congregation or department."[34] Second, "all decisions require pontifical approval" with the exception of those for which special faculties have been given by the Pope and the decisions of the Rota and the Apostolic Signatura.[35] What follows is an examination of the Code in terms of the Pope's ministry as ruler, teacher, and judge. It treats both the canons that refer to the Pope explicitly and the canons that use the expressions "Apostolic See" or "Holy See."

The Pope's primatial authority in regard to the lay Christian faithful is, of course, included under the Pope's supreme power that extends to each and every member of the Church. The Code explicitly treats the obligations and rights of the Christian faithful in book II, part I. Other sections of the Code, such as those dealing with marriage legislation, have special relevance for the laity.

The Pope as Ruler and Teacher

The Code gives the Pope a broad range of rights in his office as ruler and teacher of the universal Church. Some of the more important ones are as follows.

The Roman Pontiff

The Code declares that the Bishop of the Church of Rome is head of the College of Bishops, Vicar of Christ, and pastor of the universal Church; he enjoys supreme, full, immediate, and universal ordinary power in the Church, which he can always exercise freely (can. 331). As supreme pastor he has the right to determine, according to the needs of the Church, the way he will exercise his power, either per-

---

34. Ibid., 59 (1967):928.
35. Idem.

sonally or collegially (can. 333, 2). The College of Bishops, under the leadership of the Pope, is also the subject of supreme and full power over the universal Church (can. 336). Bishops, especially the Synod of Bishops, cardinals, and other persons and institutions—papal legates and the Curia—assist the Pope, and, in so doing, they fulfill their duties in his name and by his authority (can. 334). The Pope and the College of Bishops have the supreme direction and coordination of missionary work (can. 782).

The supreme authority of the Church—the Pope and the College of Bishops—alone can approve or define those things required for the validity of the sacraments (can. 841). The Pope can hear the confessions of the faithful anywhere (can. 967). The Roman Pontiff is the supreme administrator and steward of all ecclesiastical goods (can. 1273), and those who exercise the right of ownership over temporal goods of the Church do so always under his authority (can. 1256).

The Pope determines when and how he will exercise his primatial authority (can. 333, 2). He cannot be forced to act, and any use of ecclesiastical power that stems from force or fear is null (can. 125, 1). Nor is the Pope to be prevented from acting legitimately. No human authority can legitimately impede papal action; any attempt to do so would be a crime (can. 1375).

The duty of proclaiming the Gospel has been especially committed to the Pope and the College of Bishops (can. 756, 1). In virtue of his office, the Pope also possesses infallible teaching authority when, as supreme pastor and teacher, "he proclaims with a definitive act that a doctrine of faith or morals is to be held as such" (can. 749, 1). The assent of faith is required for those truths proposed as divinely revealed by the solemn magisterium of the Church or by its universal and ordinary magisterium (can. 750). Religious submission of intellect and will is due the teaching on faith or morals proposed by the Pope or the College of Bishops even when they do not proclaim it with a definitive act (can. 752). All the Christian faithful are obliged to observe the constitutions and decrees issued by the Church, especially those that come from the Pope or the College of Bishops (can. 754).

The Pope freely selects men to be cardinals (can. 351, 1) and presides over consistories (can. 553, 1). Cardinals are obliged to cooperate assiduously with the Roman Pontiff; those who hold any office in the Curia and are not diocesan bishops must reside in Rome (can.

356). The Pope usually conducts the business of the universal Church by means of the Roman Curia, which fulfills its duty in his name and by his authority for the good and service of the Churches (can. 360). Finally, the Pope alone can convoke an ecumenical council, preside over it, transfer, suspend or dissolve it, and approve its decrees (can. 338, 1). The decrees of an ecumenical council do not have obligatory force unless they are approved by the Pope together with the Fathers of the council and are confirmed by the Pope and promulgated by his order (can. 341, 1).

The Code also gives the Pope broad authority over particular or local Churches. He has a primacy of ordinary power over all particular Churches (can. 333, 1). The supreme authority in the Church has the sole competency to erect particular Churches (can. 373) and, after the bishops have been consulted, to establish, suppress, or change ecclesiastical provinces (can. 431, 3).

Bishops too fall under the primatial authority. The Pope freely appoints bishops or confirms their elections (can. 377, 1) and no rights or privileges of election, nomination, presentation, or designation of bishops are hereafter granted to civil authorities (can. 377, 5). It pertains to the supreme authority of the Church to erect, suppress, or change the conferences of bishops, after consultation with the bishops concerned (can. 449, 1).

The Pope can in some cases limit the authority of the bishops (can. 381, 1). Diocesan bishops, at the completion of their seventy-fifth year, must submit their resignation to the Pope who then decides what action to take (can. 401, 1). Every five years the diocesan bishop is to submit a report on the state of his diocese (can. 399); the same year the report is submitted the bishop is to go to Rome on his *ad limina* visit to venerate the tombs of Peter and Paul and to appear before the Pope (can. 400, 1). A Synod of Bishops is directly under the authority of the Roman Pontiff. It is he who convokes a synod, ratifies the election of its elected members, determines the topics for discussion and the agenda, and presides over it (can. 344). He also ratifies its decisions (can. 342).

Clerics are bound by special obligation to show reverence and obedience to the Pope (can. 273). Religious, too, by reason of their special bond of obedience, are bound to obey the Supreme Pontiff as their highest superior (can. 590, 2). The Pope can exempt religious institutes from a bishop's authority (can. 591).

The Apostolic See and the Holy See

"Apostolic See" and "Holy See," as we mentioned earlier, are terms that apply to both the Pope and the curial congregations, offices, and tribunals. The rights of the Apostolic See and the Holy See represent, then, a further level of universal control by Rome. Nothing important and extraordinary is to be done by the Curia without the knowledge and approval of the Pope. A good illustration is the form used in many of the decisions of the Sacred Congregation of the Doctrine of the Faith that were mentioned in Chapter One. At the end of most of those documents there is a formula stating that the Pope had approved the final decision. Thus Cardinal Ratzinger's letter of July 25, 1986, to Father Charles E. Curran contained the following paragraph: "This decision was presented to His Holiness in an audience granted to the undersigned prefect on the 10th of July of this year, and he approved both its content and the procedure followed."

Concerning prospective bishops, the Apostolic See makes the definitive judgment of their suitability (can. 378, 2). The designation of bishops is usually handled by the Congregation for Bishops. If it involves missionary Churches, the Congregation for the Evangelization of Peoples is competent. The Council for the Public Affairs of the Church deals with those cases where episcopal designation entails negotiations with civil governments. The Congregation for Bishops operates in the following instances. Only the Apostolic See can erect personal prelatures (can. 294). The acts of plenary and provincial councils can be promulgated only after they are reviewed by the Apostolic See (can. 446). Statutes of an episcopal conference are to be reviewed by the Holy See (can. 451), and the erection, change, or suppression of a cathedral chapter is reserved to the Apostolic See (can. 504).

The erection of interdiocesan seminaries and their statutes need the approval of the Apostolic See (can. 237, 2) and the program for priestly formation drawn up by the episcopal conference of a country needs approval of the Holy See (can. 242, 1). The Holy See alone can establish ecclesiastical universities and faculties; it approves its statutes and maintains a supervisory role (can. 816). The Congregation for Catholic Education has competency in the above matters.

All associations of the Christian faithful are subject to the vigilance of the Holy See (can. 305, 2), and it alone has the authority to establish and suppress public associations of the Christian faithful that are universal and international (can. 312, 1 and 320, 1). Religious institutes of pontifical right are erected by the Apostolic See (can. 589), and they are immediately and exlusively subject to it in internal governance and discipline (can. 593). Mergers, unions, federations, and confederations of religious institutes are reserved to the Apostolic See alone (can. 582) as is the suppression of any institute (can. 584, 1). The Apostolic See alone can approve new forms of consecrated life (can. 605).

The liturgy and certain publications also come under the purview of Rome. The Apostolic See and, in accord with the law, the diocesan bishop are responsible for the supervision of the liturgy (can. 838, 1). To the Apostolic See is reserved the right to publish liturgical books for the universal Church, to review translations, and to see that liturgical ordinances are faithfully observed everywhere (can. 838, 2). The conference of bishops may publish catechisms with prior approval of the Apostolic See (can. 775, 2). The Holy See alone can establish new sacramentals, authentically interpret those already established, and abolish or change any of them (can. 1167, 1).

The Pope as Judge

As part of his universal governance the Pope also exercises a judicial function. The Pope is the supreme judge of the entire Catholic world; he tries cases either personally or through the ordinary tribunals of the Apostolic See (the Rota and the Apostolic Signatura) or through judges delegated by himself (can. 1142). Because of the primacy of the Pope, anyone of the faithful is free to bring a contentious or penal case before the Holy See in any grade of judgment and at any stage of litigation (can. 417, 1).

Canon 1404 repeats the ancient canonical maxim: "The First See is judged by no one." This phrase originated as a forgery at the time of Pope Symmachus (498–514) and was later included in the *Decretum* of Gratian. The Code does not add the second part of Gratian's passage: "unless he is found straying from the faith." Gelasius I (492 –496) held that the See of Rome had supreme jurisdiction, which included the "right to loose what has been bound by the sentence of any bishop, because it has the authority to judge all the Churches and can be judged by no one."[36] Gregory VII, in number 19 of the *Dictatus papae*, also used a similar expression.

No appeal nor recourse is allowed for any decision or decree of the Pope (can. 333, 3). Likewise, no appeal is possible against a sentence of the Pope or of the Apostolic Signatura (can. 1629, 1). Decrees of the Pope are not subject to administrative recourse (can. 1732). The Pope alone has the right to judge heads of states, cardinals, legates of the Apostolic See, bishops in penal cases, and other cases that he has reserved to himself (can. 1405, 1). In those cases the incompetence of other judges is absolute (can. 1406, 2). A judge cannot review an act or instrument explicitly confirmed by the Pope without his prior mandate (can. 1405, 2). The Pope alone can grant dispensations from a ratified and nonconsummated marriage (cans. 1142 and 1698, 2), and he can dispense persons from private vows (can. 1196).

The Apostolic See also has judicial powers. Certain crimes that incur automatic excommunication are reserved to the Apostolic See (cans. 1370, 1378, 1382). It can also dispense from various irregularities and impediments for orders and marriage (cans. 1047, 1078). To the Apostolic See is reserved the right to dispense the perpetual vows of religious in institutes of pontifical right (can. 691, 2). It can also dispense deacons and priests (can. 290, 3), but the dispensation from the obligation of clerical celibacy is granted by the Pope alone (can. 291).

Conclusion

The two Vatican Councils and the Code of Canon Law leave no doubt that the Pope has the fullness of executive, legislative, and judicial power. Papal authority, either directly or through the Curia, touches the lives of every Catholic—bishops, clerics, religious, and laity. No one is exempt and no aspect of Catholic life is unaffected. Moreover, as we saw in Chapter One, this power is not a museum piece but is continually being exercised. Are there any limits to this wide-ranging and ubiquitous power? Are there any principles of limitation that apply to the papacy and its seemingly extravagant claims? The next chapter will address this issue.

---

36. Ep. 10, 5. P. Jaffé and F. Kaltenbrunner, *Regesta pontificum*, reprint (Graz: Akademische Druck-u. Verlagsanstalt, 1956), I:622.

·III·

The Possibility of Limitation

The problem of the limits of the primacy and of the teaching authority forces itself upon us. Its investigation is, to my mind, one of the most urgent tasks to be undertaken by modern theology.

—*Wilhelm De Vries**

The Pope may determine his own competence, define the scope of his power, and judge all cases, even those in which he is involved. The history of the Church reveals, as Gustave Thils has noted, "the imperturbable movement towards the same point —the concentration of everything in the papacy."[1] The expansion of papal power may be understandable in view of historical circumstances, but to many it seems far removed from the scriptural ideal of authority as humble service within and for the People of God. Catholics and non-Catholics inevitably ask about the limits of papal authority. What are the boundaries that determine the legitimate exercise of papal authority? This chapter attempts to address this issue. It will first present a brief historical survey and then discuss the major factors that affect the exercise of primatial authority.[2]

---

* "Limits of Papal Primacy," in P. S. Achútegui, ed., *Cardinal Bea Studies II: Dublin Papers on Ecumenism* (Manila: Ateneo University, 1972), p. 162.

1. "The Theology of the Primacy: Towards a Revision," *One in Christ* 10 (1974): 24.

2. Two works have been especially helpful in writing this chapter: Wilhelm De Vries, "Limits of Papal Primacy," pp. 162–199, and Gustave Thils, *La primauté pontificale. La doctrine de Vatican I. Les voies d'une révision* (Gembloux: J. Duculot, 1972).

The Past Attempts at Limitation

Without making an exhaustive and detailed study, we can see that history is filled with examples of opposition to ecclesial authority and of attempts to limit it. The strong-willed St. Paul reported his disagreement with St. Peter over the issue of table fellowship with the Gentiles: "When Cephas came to Antioch, I opposed him to his face, since he was manifestly wrong" (Gal. 2:11). It took a long time before Rome clearly emerged as the institutional center of the Christian community. During the first three centuries, the Churches in the West outside of Italy enjoyed considerable autonomy from Rome but not without conflict. Cyprian of Carthage in North Africa, for example, disagreed with Pope Stephen I (254–257) over the baptism of heretics, and a Carthaginian synod (418) forbade any appeal to Rome.[3] Even after the Edict of Milan (313), which facilitated the increase of papal power, Rome faced difficulties in exercising its authority.[4]

In the ninth century, Archbishop Hincmar of Rheims (d. 882) opposed several Popes—Nicholas I (858–867), Adrian II (867–872), and John VIII (872–882)—although he was ultimately obedient. He advocated greater authority for metropolitans over their suffragan sees; neither Rome nor the suffragan bishops accepted his ideas. Although he held that the Pope was "the patriarch of patriarchs" and "the first primate of all the provinces," Hincmar did not consider the Church to be a pontifical monarchy.[5]

The Church in the East from its earliest days had an uneasy relationship with Roman authority, even though the first eight ecumenical councils were all held in the Eastern part of the empire. Eastern Christians for a millennium acknowledged that the Bishop of Rome had a spiritual primacy in the universal Church, but they resisted the claims of Rome that is was the sole judge in doctrinal matters or that it possessed full jurisdictional authority. By the middle of the

---

3. Mansi 3:922. Cited in De Vries, "Limits of Papal Primacy," p. 178, n. 94.

4. On this period see Michele Maccarrone, "La dottrina del primato papale dal IV all' VIII secolo nelle relazioni con le chiese occidentali," in *Settimane di studio del Centro Italiano di Studi sull' atto medioevo* (Spoleto, 1960), vol. 7, 633–742.

5. An analysis of Hincmar's ecclesiology is found in Yves Congar, *L'ecclésiologie du haut Moyen-Age* (Paris: Cerf, 1968), pp. 166–77.

eleventh century the Byzantine Church had formally rejected the Roman primacy. The debates between the Popes and the Patriarchs of Constantinople—Photius and Michael Cerularius—are legendary.[6]

In the Middle Ages there were bitter disputes over the extent of papal jurisdiction.[7] Two dramatic examples are the controversies between Gregory VII (1073-85) and Emperor Henry IV and between Boniface VIII (1294-1303) and King Philip the Fair of France. The *imperium* and the *sacerdotium* engaged in intense conflicts over such issues as lay investiture and benefices. Popes affirmed their authority, but they were often ignored; reform movements met fierce opposition.

In 1179, the cardinals were made the sole electors of the Pope; the participation of the clergy and the laity was reduced to a mere formality. Many theologians and canonists in the Middle Ages and even later held that the cardinalate was of divine institution.[8] Power struggles between the Pope and his cardinals increased and various steps were taken to resolve them. The constitution *Ubi periculum* of the Second Council of Lyons (1274), for example, prohibited all pacts, conventions, or treaties made by cardinals during a papal election; they were declared null and void, even if they were made by oath.[9] Clement V (1305-14), in a further effort to curb the power of the cardinals, affirmed that the College of Cardinals does not exercise papal jurisdiction during a vacancy.

During the residency of the Popes at Avignon (1308-78), the cardinals made a concerted effort to reduce the power of the Pope by

6. See Francis Dvornik, *The Photian Schism: History and Legend* (Cambridge: Cambridge University, 1948), and Wilhelm De Vries, *Orient et occident: Les structures ecclésiales vues dans l'histoire des sept premiers conciles oecuméniques* (Paris: Cerf, 1971).

7. See Walter Ullmann, *The Growth of Papal Government in the Middle Ages*, 3rd ed. (London: Methuen, 1970), and Brian Tierney, *Foundations of the Conciliar Theory* (Cambridge: Cambridge University, 1955).

8. John of Torquemada affirmed it in his *Summa de ecclesia* (1448), and M.-D. Bouix in his *Tractatus de curia romana* (1859) considered it to be *saltem probabile*. Yet F. X. Wernz in his *Ius decretalium* (1899) said it was *plane improbabile*. For a full analysis of the cardinalate see Giuseppe Alberigo, *Cardinalato e collegialità: Studi sull'ecclesiologia tra l'XI et il XIV secolo* (Florence: Vallecchi, 1969).

9. Text in G. Albergio et al., eds. *Conciliorum oecumenicorum decreta* (Freiburg: Herder, 1962), pp. 290-294.

increasing their own.[10] They were convinced that the cardinalate was of divine institution and that the Church consisted of cardinals and Pope and not just the Pope alone; they were bent on establishing an oligarchic form of government in the Church.

In their efforts to establish what they considered their constitutional right to participate in Church government, the cardinals resorted to papal electoral pacts or capitulations—agreements made by the electors of the Pope to limit the authority of the person eventually chosen. Despite the prohibition of capitulations by *Ubi periculum*, the cardinals were not deterred.[11].

The first recorded capitulation took place in 1352, at the election of Innocent VI (1352-62). At his election the cardinals, in clear violation of *Ubi periculum*, drew up a pact that included the following items: the future Pope could not under any circumstances create any new cardinals until their number had fallen to sixteen; he could depose or excommunicate a cardinal only with the unanimous consent of the rest of the other cardinals; and he should give the cardinals one-half of the papal revenues.[12] After his election, Innocent VI, appealing to *Ubi periculum*, declared in the bull *Sollicitudo pastoralis* that the pact threatened his monarchical power and was therefore void.[13]

Subsequent Popes also prohibited capitulations, but still they were made in the papal elections of 1431, 1458, and 1464, with provisions similar to the 1352 pact. Pius IV (1559-65) and Gregory XV (1621-23) proscribed all pacts and promises made by cardinals during papal elections. The present legislation governing papal elections, issued by Paul VI (1963-78) in 1975, condemned any form of electoral agreements: "We likewise forbid the cardinals to enter into any compromise before the election or to undertake commitments of common accord to which they agree to be bound should one of them be ele-

---

10. For a study of the Avignon papacy see Guillaume Mollat, *The Popes at Avignon*, trans. from the 9th French ed. (London: Thomas Nelson and Sons, 1963).

11. See Walter Ullmann, "The Legal Validity of the Papal Electoral Pacts," *Ephemerides iuris canonici* 12 (1956):246-278.

12. Text of this pact in Raynaldus, *Annales ecclesiastici*, ed. A. Theiner (Bar-le-Duc, 1874), XXV, 540, ad annum 1352, no. 26. Also see Guillaume Mollat, "Le sacré collège de Clement V à Eugène IV," *Revue d'histoire ecclésiastique* 46 (1951): 99ff.

13. Text in Raynaldus, *Annales ecclesiastici*, ad annum 1353, no. 29.

vated to the pontificate. These promises too, should any in fact be made, even under oath, we declare null and void."[14]

The theory of conciliarism, developed by theologians and canonists in the twelfth and thirteenth centuries, deeply affected papal sovereignty. It was fundamentally a reform movement, which opposed corrupt practices in papal government and exaggerated papal claims. The conciliarists, critical of the Popes for their failure to preserve the unity of the Church, sought to limit papal authority by asserting the supremacy of the general council over the Pope. Their goal was to ensure a reformation *in capite et in membris*.

In the early fifteenth century the Church faced a constitutional crisis with the coexistence of three claimants to the papal throne: Gregory XII (1406-15) of Rome, Benedict XIII (1394-1423) of Avignon, and John XXIII (1410-15) of Pisa. The Great Western Schism was finally resolved at the Council of Constance (1414-18), which appealed to conciliarist principles in its decree *Haec sancta*. The Council elected Martin V (1417-31), and unity was restored.[15] Several Popes condemned conciliarism in the centuries after Constance, but the debate has continued over the dogmatic validity of the decree *Haec sancta* issued at Constance.[16]

In the late medieval period two major events took place that directly touched the papacy and its limitation: the Catholic reform movement and the Protestant Reformation. The Catholic movement sought to control the excesses of papal power by promoting radical reform in head and members.[17] Many Catholic reformers were sympathetic to the admonition of the Italian bishop Zaccaria Ferreri to Adrian VI (1522-23): "*Purga Romam, mundus purgatur*"

---

14. *Romano pontifici eligendo, Acta apostolicae sedis* 67 (1975):642. Partial English text in *Origins*, November 27, 1975, vol. 5, no. 23:366.

15. See Robert E. McNally, "Conciliarism and the Papacy," *Proceedings of the Catholic Theological Society of America* 25 (1970):13-30, and August Franzen and Wolfgang Müller, eds., *Das Konzil von Konstanz* (Freiburg: Herder, 1964).

16. For two different views on this point see Paul de Vooght, *Les pouvoirs du concile et l'autorité du pape au concile de Constance* (Paris: Cerf, 1965), and Joseph Gill, "The Fifth Session of the Council of Constance," *Heythrop Journal* 5 (1964):131-143.

17. See John C. Olin, *The Catholic Reformation: Savonarola to Ignatius Loyola. Reform in the Church 1495-1540* (New York: Harper & Row, 1969).

("Cleanse Rome and the world will be cleansed").[18] Some notable ecclesiastics, such as Cardinals Capranica and Nicholas of Cusa, and Bishop Domenico Domenichi suggested elaborate programs for the reform of the Church. Domenichi (d. 1478), Bishop of Torcello, in 1456 wrote a lengthy treatise on papal authority.[19] Such reform plans, however, had little practical effect. "Nothing was accomplished, nothing changed," writes John Olin. "In fact, the papacy itself in the later decades of the fifteenth century . . . entered into a period of moral disintegration which culminated in the most scandalous venality and secularization."[20] It was not until after the Council of Trent that the Catholic Counter-Reformation movement began to make an impact on the life of the Church.

The Protestant reformers—Zwingli, Calvin, and Luther—objected strenuously to papal and curial abuses, claiming that the Roman Church violated the spirit of the Gospel and distorted the faith tradition of the past. Eventually, although it was not the original intention of the Reformers, a separate Church was created that totally rejected the jurisdictional supremacy of the Pope.[21] At the Council of Trent (1545–63), the Roman Church, somewhat belatedly, responded to the Protestant upheaval.

From the seventeenth to the twentieth century, other movements appeared in opposition to papal primacy. These included Gallicanism, Febronianism, Josephinism, the French Revolution, and the *Kulturkampf*. Gallicanism, a seventeenth-century version of conciliarism, attempted to limit the control of Rome over the French Church. The Four Gallican Articles, composed in 1682 by Jacques Bénigne Bossuet, Bishop of Meaux, give its major tenets: complete independence of the French king from Roman control over temporal matters; the superiority of general councils over the Pope; the inviolability of the rights and customs of the Gallican Church; and the consent of the universal Church to validate papal judgments on faith

---

18. *Concilium Tridentinum: Diariorum actorum epistularum tractatum nova collectio* (Freiburg: Herder, 1930), vol. XII, pars prior, p. 27, no. 8.

19. For a critical edition of this text with commentary see Heribert Smolinsky, *Domenico de' Domenichi und seine Schrift "De potestatae pape et termino eius": Edition und Kommentar* (Münster: Aschendorff, 1976).

20. *The Catholic Reformation*, p. xxi.

21. For Luther's view of the papal office see Scott H. Hendrix, *Luther and the Papacy: Stages in a Reformation Conflict* (Philadelphia: Fortress, 1981).

and morals. Although condemned by several Popes, Gallicanism was supported by many Catholics—bishops, priests, and laity— throughout the eighteenth century. By the middle of the nineteenth century Gallicanism was not a major force in the Catholic Church.

Febronianism, a kind of Gallicanism-across-the-Rhine, advocated the establishment of a national German Church subject to the local ruler and not to Rome. Josephinism, named after Emperor Joseph II of Austria, also tried to bring the Church under the control of the state. The French Revolution rejected the traditional papal prerogatives; Napoleon's disputes with Pius VI (1775-99) and Pius VII (1800-23) had devastating effects on the Catholic Church in Europe during the nineteenth century. Finally, the *Kulturkampf* (1871-90), initiated by Bismarck, was hostile to the Church and to any semblance of Roman control. *Pastor aeternus* of Vatican I, with its strong declarations on papal primacy and infallibility, responded to many of the principal ideas found in these movements.[22]

This brief historical survey shows that in nearly every era debates over the nature and extent of papal authority took place. The issue has not yet been fully resolved. It is agreed, however, that every individual who exercises power—king, president, or Pope—is restricted in some way, since only God has unlimited authority. "No visible, earthly body, however idealistically planned, can ever be safe from the corruption of human folly, ignorance or sin," observed the Consultation on Church Union.[23] This principle also applies to the papacy.

What then are the limitations on papal authority, which is so extensive? The sections that follow attempt to answer that question. We shall examine the following limits: official, legal, dogmatic, and practical.

The Official Limits

By official limits we mean those that emerge from the office of the papacy itself. Catholic tradition has consistently taught that the

---

22. See Derek Holmes, *The Triumph of the Holy See: A Short History of the Papacy in the Nineteenth Century* (London: Burns & Oates; Shepherdstown, West Virginia: Patmos, 1978).

23. *Consultation on Church Union 1967* (Cincinnati: Forward Movement, 1967), p. 66.

mandate or purpose of the primatial office provides the most fundamental limitation on the Pope. Since the papacy exists within the
Church, and the Pope is a member of the Church, to understand
the purpose of the papacy and its possible limits it is necessary first
to understand the purpose of the Church.

The Church is a unique combination of several elements: human
and divine, visible and invisible, temporal and transcendent. It is
both a mystery, a part of God's "hidden plan" (Eph. 1:19), and a
social institution. The most important element in every institution is
the directing idea of the work to be realized. The directing idea is
the principle of both unity and purpose in a social body. The Church,
then, from an institutional perspective, can be defined as a stable
communion of persons in an idea for the shaping of values through a
pattern of practices.[24]

The Christ event is the directing idea of the Church; it determines
its purpose and shapes its identity. The Church, remaining permanently dependent on God's saving acts in Jesus Christ, preserves its
character and authenticity insofar as it is faithful to its mission. The
unity and continuity of the Church are maintained as long as Jesus
Christ is the center of its memory and meaning. Believers, by actively participating in the faith, form a stable communion. They share
ideas and operations for the development and integration of values
that are intimately linked to their deep, personal, and subjective appropriation of the Christ event.

The ultimate purpose of the Church is transcendent: that of
reaching God himself and achieving sanctification and salvation.[25]
Vatican II calls the Church a "sign of intimate union with God and
of the unity of all humanity" (*Lumen gentium*, art. 1). As servant
and prophet it proclaims the Gospel message of peace and social
justice (*Gaudium et spes*, arts. 11 and 57).

The Church, however, is a society with no counterpart because of
its unique origin, means, patterns of interaction, and goals. Yet it is
still a society, and its purpose is determinative of its nature and
operation. The venerable canonical maxim that "*societates sunt ut
fines*" ("societies are determined by their purpose") is still valid.

---

24. I have developed this concept in "The Church as Institution," *Journal of
Ecumenical Studies* 16 (1973):425-447.

25. Yves Congar discusses this theme in "The Idea of the Church in St. Thomas
Aquinas," in *The Mystery of the Church* (Baltimore: Helicon, 1960), pp. 97-117.

There exists a correlative relationship between the means and the purpose of a society. Alfredo Ottaviani explained: "If the means proposed have no relation with the purpose, the members are bound by no obligation; anything that is foreign to the purpose is not consonant with the norm of reason and hence is not binding."[26]

The purpose of the papacy functions as a principle of limitation. The Pope should use all necessary or useful means to achieve the purpose of his office and avoid anything that hinders it. The Pope tries to make the directing idea of the Christ event a living reality. "The institution," according to Eric Voegelin, "is successfully perfected when the ruler has become subordinate to the idea. . . . The power of a ruler has authority insofar as he is able to make his factual power representative of an idea."[27] Papal authority has its specific mission or purpose that, in an overarching sense, determines and delineates all its actions.

What is the mission and purpose of the papacy? According to Vatican I, the Pope is the "perpetual principle" and "visible foundation" of the unity of the Church (DS 3051). His mission is to preserve all believers in the unity of faith and communion (DS 3051, 3060), to maintain the perpetual welfare and lasting good of the Church (DS 3056), and to ensure that the episcopate is one and undivided (DS 3051). By fulfilling this mandate, the Pope strengthens the bonds of communion with the Church of Rome and enables the members of the Church to form a unified body (DS 3057).

The mandate of the Bishop of Rome, therefore, is to maintain and safeguard the visible unity of the Church and to show solicitude for all the local Churches that belong to the *communio*. The idea of the *sollicitudo omnium ecclesiarum* has a long tradition going back to St. Paul who referred to "my daily pressing anxiety, the care of all the churches" (2 Cor. 11:28). Many of the early Popes also used the idea of solicitude to describe their mission as successors of Peter: Siricius (384-399);[28] Innocent I (401-417);[29] Celestine I (422-432);[30] and Leo I (440-461).[31]

---

26. *Institutiones iuris publici ecclesiastici*, 3rd ed. (Vatican City: Typis Polyglottis Vaticanis, 1947), I:43. Ottaviani's juridical treatment, though dated, is still useful in some aspects.

27. *The New Science of Politics* (Chicago: University of Chicago, 1952), p. 48.

28. *Patrologia latina* 13:1138.

29. PL 20:590.

30. PL 50:485.

31. PL 54:152.

The Pope is the symbol of ecclesial unity. He expresses the unity of all Churches as he functions uniquely as the universal authority. He should vigorously promote peace and justice in the world. By facilitating communication, mutual help, and solicitude, the Pope is less a lawgiver than a focal point of inspiration and support. "The basic function of the Pope in the Church," writes Ludwig Hertling, "is not his performance of certain official duties, but simply that he be present."[32] This does not mean that the Pope is simply "a lifeless rock or an abstract principle,"[33] but rather that he plays a sacramental and symbolic role as the center of the *communio* of the Churches. The Pope is an effective and a juridically empowered symbol.

Another aspect of the mandate of the papacy that relates to limitation is the traditional idea that papal authority should build and not destroy the Church (*ad aedificationem et non ad destructionem*). It is taken from St. Paul:

> Maybe I do boast rather too much about our authority, but the Lord gave it to me for building you up and not for pulling you down, and I shall not be ashamed of it (2 Cor. 10:8).

Bishop Zinelli referred to this idea several times at Vatican I.[34] It was also used by Nicholas of Cusa (d. 1464) and John (Quidort) of Paris (d. 1306). John of Paris wrote: "God did not give Peter or ecclesiastical ministers the power to act indiscriminately but to act in good faith—and to build and not to destroy."[35] Using the same passage in Paul, he explained the limitation of the Pope's power over the use of external ecclesiastical goods: the material possessions of the Church. The Pope cannot freely use ecclesiastical goods in any way he wants, since he is not God. As dispenser of the goods of

---

32. *Communio: Church and Papacy in Early Christianity*, Introduction by Jared Wicks (Chicago: Loyola University, 1972), p. 71.

33. Ibid., p. 72.

34. Mansi 52:1105 C D, and 1116 A. Also see J. M. R. Tillard, "The Horizon of the 'Primacy' of the Bishop of Rome," *One in Christ* 12 (1976):5-33.

35. *Tractatus de potestate regia et papali*, cap. 20 in Jean Leclercq, ed., *Jean de Paris et l'ecclésiologie du XIIIe siècle* (Paris: J. Vrin, 1942), p. 240. English in Arthur P. Monahan, *John of Paris on Royal and Papal Power* (New York: Columbia University, 1974), p. 106.

the Church, "the only power he possesses . . . relates to their being necessary or useful for the churches as a whole."[36]

All papal actions, therefore, can be judged according to this Pauline ideal. Papal power should build up and not destroy, and, as Joseph Lecler warns, "Christendom must be watchful that it remains so."[37] Any exercise of papal authority that does not contribute to the good of the Church but leads to its destruction is reprehensible. The purpose and mission of the office of the papacy, then, limit papal authority. The legislative, executive, and judicial actions of the Pope should contribute to the unity of faith and communion.

This principle, because of its generality, is admittedly vague. It is difficult, if not impossible, to establish specific norms that apply to every concrete situation. The principle, however, is still important as an objective norm of limitation. It serves as a constant reminder to the Pope that in sanctifying, teaching, and governing his flock he is accountable for his actions. The papacy exists in order to strengthen the Church, to ensure the salvation of humanity, and to allow the Spirit to animate its members. Any action that violates these goals is blameworthy and may even be invalid.

The Legal Limits

In the past, theologians have sought to compare Church government to civil government. Although they recognized that the Church is unique and that any comparison to forms of civil authority is analogous, many argued that the Church is a monarchy. Robert Bellarmine (d. 1621), for example, felt that a pure monarchy was the ideal form of government, but "because of the corruption of human nature" a form of government that has elements of monarchy, aristocracy, and democracy is preferable.[38]

Vatican I did not use the term "monarchy," but, in fact, it did give a monarchical description of the papal office. There are sound theological reasons to avoid calling the Church a monarchy: the idea

---

36. Cap. 6, Leclercq, p. 188; Monahan, p. 26.

37. *Le pape ou le concile? Une interrogation de l'Eglise médiévale* (Lyons: Le Chalet, 1973), p. 177.

38. *Opera omnia, De controversiis christianae fidei. De summo pontifice*, ed. J. Fèvre (Paris: L. Vivès, 1870), liber I, cap. 1, 461. Also liber I, cap. 5, 469.

seems to foster unilateralism in decision making, triumphalism in style, and excessive centralization in government. Papal monarchism tends to stress the juridical at the expense of the spiritual, isolate the Pope from the rest of the Church, and neglect the charismatic gifts in the Church at large.

But if the Church is called a monarchy, then it is a unique one. It is not hereditary nor absolute but constitutional. At Vatican I, Gregory II, Youssef, the Melkite Patriarch of Antioch, recommended unsuccessfully that *Pastor aeternus* state clearly that the Church is not an absolute monarchy.[39] Bishop Joseph Papp-Szilagyi of Hungary said that Orthodox Christians considered heretical the idea of an absolute and unrestricted monarchy of the Pope.[40] The Pope is not an absolute monarch because he does not have unlimited authority. He is bound by the constitution of the Church and by certain doctrinal and structural restraints. The German episcopate, responding to Bismarck in 1875, clearly stated this position: "The title of absolute monarch cannot be rightly applied to the Pope even in purely ecclesiastical affairs, for he is subject to divine law and bound by the dispositions made by Christ for his Church."[41]

Two important texts emphasize this point and in so doing give us a starting point for our discussion of the legal limitations of the papal primacy. The first text is from Vatican I. Bishop Zinelli of the Deputation on the Faith declared:

> From all the sources of revelation it is clear that full and supreme power in the Church was conferred upon Peter and his successors, full in the sense that it cannot be limited by any greater human power but only by the natural and divine law.[42]

The second text is from Vatican II. In the discussion of the papacy in chapter three of *Lumen gentium*, Paul VI suggested that the phrase "accountable to the Lord alone" ("*uni Domino devi[n]ctus*") be added to the text describing the exercise of papal primacy. The Theological Commission rejected this amendment for the following reasons:

---

39. Mansi 52:1096 C.
40. Mansi 52:310 B.
41. DS 3114.
42. Mansi 52:1108 D-1109 A.

It is an oversimplified formula. The Roman Pontiff is also bound to revelation itself, to the fundamental structure of the Church, to the sacraments, to the definitions of earlier councils, and other obligations too numerous to mention. Since such a formula would also require long and complicated explanations, the Commission has decided that it is better not to use it. There is also a psychological reason, lest in appeasing some we cause anxiety among others, especially in our relations with the East, as is clear in the history of another formula "*ex sese et non ex consensu ecclesiae.*"[43]

These two texts, even though they do not possess formal conciliar authority, are significant. They clearly indicate that it was the mind of the two Vatican Councils that the Pope does not have absolute power but is limited by the very constitution of the Church. It is necessary, then, for us to examine the limitations on papal actions dictated by natural, divine, and ecclesiastical law.

Natural Law

Popes, like the rest of humanity, are bound by fundamental norms of conduct, which have their source in human reason. God makes possible this natural wisdom by giving human beings the ability to ask and answer questions. These answers lead to more and more perfect generalizations binding on all men and women. The Pope, for example, must act according to the precepts of the natural law, such as to do and pursue good and avoid evil, to give to each his own, to use his faculties reasonably, and to avoid such sins as idolatry, murder, lying, and theft. The more concrete the precepts, the more subject to differences of opinion. Ultimately, however, the

---

43. Text in *Acta synodalia sacrosancti concilii oecumenici Vaticani II* (Vatican City: Typis Polyglottis, 1973), vol. III, part 1, 247. Also see Giuseppe Alberigo and Franca Magistretti, eds., *Constitutionis dogmaticae "Lumen gentium" synopsis historica* (Bologna: Istituto per le scienze religiose, 1975), pp. 432, 456. Cardinal Franjo Šeper, Prefect of the Congregation for the Doctrine of the Faith, made a similar observation in Rome during the 1969 Synod of Bishops. Speaking of the exercise of papal primacy, he said that it does not mean "that the task of the primacy must be carried out only according to subjective and arbitrary rules, but certainly according to objective norms based on fidelity to revelation and tradition and adapted to the changing needs of the times" (*Osservatore Romano*, October 13–14, 1969).

test is following one's conscience, that is, bringing one's doing into harmony with one's knowing.

It is surprising to find statements by learned and saintly figures that at first glance seem to deny some natural-law limits to papal power. In rule 13 of the "Rules for Thinking with the Church" in the *Spiritual Exercises,* Ignatius of Loyola wrote: "If we wish to proceed securely in all things, we must hold fast to the following principle: What seems to me white, I will believe black if the hierarchical Church so determines it."[44] Robert Bellarmine stated: "If the Pope errs by commanding vices or forbidding virtues, the Church must believe that vices are good and virtues bad, unless it wishes to sin against conscience."[45] These two passages cannot be taken literally as categorical determinations; they can be interpreted as figures of speech—examples of florid and excessive language common at that time. Despite the unfortunate phrasing, the authors wanted to indicate that Christians should be fully open and disposed to obey the Pope and the Church.

Obviously, the Pope is also bound by the laws of nature: he is neither above them, exempt from them, nor in control of them. Because he is not God, he cannot alter the structure and laws of the physical universe, control the weather, heal the sick, or confer immortality. Yet the medieval canonist Panormitanus (Nicolaus de Tudeschis), who died in 1453, said: "Whatever God can do, the Pope can do."[46] A more realistic view, long before Ignatius or Bellarmine, was given by Guilemus de Lauduno (d. 1343) who held that not even the Pope can turn black into white.[47]

---

44. George E. Ganss gives the following commentary on Rule 13: "If the hierarchical Church should define something to be black which the exercitant privately and perhaps too hastily sees as white, as a lover he would be disposed to admit humbly that the error might lie in his own deficient perception and still believe in the Church" ("Thinking with the Church: The Spirit of St. Ignatius's Rules," *The Way Supplement* 20 [August 1973]:81).

45. *De summo pontifice,* liber IV, cap. 5, 87. Despite this text, Bellarmine did not advocate absolute papalism. He taught that the Pope can fall into heresy (liber II, cap. 30, and liber IV, cap. 6); that unjust laws of the Pope do not bind in conscience (liber IV, cap. 15); that the Pope is neither the temporal ruler (*dominus*) of the whole world (liber V, cap. 2) nor even of the whole Christian world (liber V, cap. 3); and that the Pope has supreme temporal power only indirectly (liber V, cap. 6).

46. *Commentaria decretalium librum* (Venice: Iuntas, 1588), lvi, 34.

47. Cited in Brian Tierney, *Foundations of the Conciliar Theory,* p. 200, n. 3.

Divine Law

The Pope is also limited by the divine positive law, which is a law not derived from natural law but from revelation. The meaning and application of divine law is a complex theological problem and admits of many interpretations.[48] It is difficult to delineate precisely what is *ius divinum* in the sacraments and structures of the Church and what is simply *ius humanum*. Piet Fransen noted that the term "*ius divinum*" has a potential for misinterpretation. It becomes, he said, "the atom bomb of the reactionary" when it is extended to "matters where no such evidence is to be found."[49] My purpose here is not to unravel the complexities of the meaning of divine law, but to indicate how it relates to the papacy as a factor of limitation.

Magisterial documents use the terms "divine law" ("*ius divinum*") or similar terms (e.g., "divine institution") most often in relationship to something instituted by Christ himself, thus connoting permanence and irreversibility. The Council of Trent, for example, declared that all the seven sacraments were instituted by our Lord Jesus Christ (DS 1601) and that sacramental confession was instituted by divine law and is necessary for salvation according to the same law (DS 1706). Trent also taught that it is necessary by divine law to confess each and every moral sin we remember, even secret sins, and to confess the circumstances that change the species of a sin (DS 1707).

The Pope can approve or define elements related to the validity of the sacraments, but he cannot abolish them because they are divinely established. Not even the Pope, for example, can dispense from marriage impediments that come from the divine positive law, such as consanguinity in the direct line or in the second degree of the collateral line (can. 1078, 3).

Vatican I taught that it is by divine law that Peter has perpetual successors in the primacy over the whole Church (DS 3058). Vatican

---

48. Karl Rahner, "Reflections on the Concept of '*Ius Divinum*' in Catholic Thought," *Theological Investigations* (New York: Crossroad, 1976), XIV: 3–23; Carl J. Peter, "Dimensions of *Ius Divinum* in Roman Catholic Theology," *Theological Studies* 34 (1973):227–250; and Avery Dulles, "*Ius Divinum* as an Ecumenical Problem," *Theological Studies* 38 (1977):681–708.

49. "Criticism of Some Basic Theological Notions in Matters of Church Authority," *Journal of Ecumenical Studies* 19 (1982):67.

II did not use the expression "divine law," but it did refer to the "divine institution" ("*divina institutio*") of the episcopate (*Lumen gentium*, art. 20), the Church (*Lumen gentium*, art. 32), and papal authority (*Christus Dominus*, art. 2).

At Vatican I there was much discussion about divine law, especially in relationship to the status of the episcopate. Many bishops, reacting to the emphasis given by the Council to the sovereign powers of the Pope, desired that the Council state unambiguously that the episcopate is of divine right. Bishop Zinelli responded that this was not necessary since "no sane person could suppose that the Pope or a Council could destroy the episcopate or other divinely established rights in the Church."[50] He also said that the "vain and futile cries" of those who imagined that the plenary power of the Pope could destroy the episcopate were "hard to take seriously" because the episcopate is of divine law.[51] The Pope cannot, therefore, suppress the entire episcopate, but he can, of course, restrict, suspend, or excommunicate individual bishops for cause.

Ecclesiastical Law

This limitation is not as stringent as the other legal limitations we have considered, but it is still an important factor. The Pope is expected to observe the positive laws of the Church and its established customs. Even though he is the supreme legislator and free to change any law, it does not mean that he need not follow the laws of the Church. He may not be bound legally to do so or risk having his "illegal" acts invalidated but, according to the mission and purpose of his office, he is per se morally obliged, though he may make prudent exceptions. The harmony, unity, and good of the Church require—unless there is a sufficient reason to the contrary—that he observe the procedures and practices instituted by custom or ecclesiastical law.

Bishop Zinelli at Vatican I responded to those who feared that supreme papal power would have no limits. He rejected the view that the Pope could annul "all canonical decisions enacted with wisdom and piety by the Apostles and the Church." His principal reason was

50. Mansi 52:1114 D.
51. Mansi 52:1109 A.

that "moral theology teaches that the legislator is subject to his own laws if not by coercive power at least in the manner of a directive."[52] He also noted that precepts that are unjust, null, and harmful do not require obedience, except for the sake of avoiding scandal.[53]

Many papal prerogatives, which are now part of the Church's law or custom, originally belonged to the local Church. Dispensations, benefices, reservations, appeals, and other rights were progressively reserved to the Bishop of Rome. In the future, the Pope may wish to return many of these rights to diocesan bishops or to episcopal conferences. The nomination of bishops is a good example.

For a thousand years the Pope did not intervene in the nomination of bishops, except for those in his own region and later in the West. When the papacy, because of urgent political and ecclesiastical reasons, sought to reserve all episcopal nominations to itself, it met strong resistance from the East. Eventually, the right of nomination, which had initially been exercised by the Pope because of specific circumstances, began to be considered an exclusive papal right. Thus, in this century, F. X. Wernz said that "the personal right of instituting bishops belongs by nature to the Roman Pontiff."[54] Wernz did not give convincing historical and theological reasons to support his point. It is one thing to say that it may be useful and even necessary for the Pope to nominate bishops, but another to say that this belongs by its very nature to his primacy and thus is of divine institution.[55]

At Vatican II, Maximos IV, Patriarch of Antioch, spoke from an Eastern Catholic perspective. In the Eastern tradition the synod of bishops of the patriarchate appoints new bishops who are confirmed by the Pope. He said:

> It must be clear that neither the designation of bishops nor their canonical mission are reserved by divine law to the Roman Pontiff alone. What has been a contingent fact of the Western Church should not be made a doctrine or a rule for the entire Church.[56]

---

52. Idem. Similar to Bellarmine, *De summo pontifice*, liber IV, cap. 27.

53. Idem.

54. *Ius canonicum* (Rome: Gregoriana, 1943), I: 578, 725.

55. See Gustave Thils, *La primauté pontificale*, p. 197, and Gérard Philips, *L'Eglise et son mystère au IIe Concile du Vatican* (Paris: Desclée, 1967), I: 278.

56. *Acta synodalia sacrosancti concilii oecumenici Vaticani II* (Vatican City: Typis Polyglottis Vaticanis, 1972), vol. II, part 2, 240.

The Dogmatic Limits

In exercising his teaching ministry, the Pope is limited by revelation.[57] He cannot reject the "deposit of faith" and repudiate everything in Scripture and tradition. Nor can the Pope define something that is in no way related to revelation. Papal definitions of doctrine are, according to Vatican I, consonant with Holy Scripture and apostolic tradition (DS 3069). They are not new revelations, but rather articulations of what has already been revealed (DS 3070). Vatican II taught that the magisterium has the exclusive right of authentically interpreting the Word of God, but it added that "the magisterium is not above the Word of God, but serves it, teaching only what has been handed on" (*Dei verbum*, art. 10).

Vatican I clearly indicated that even infallibility is subject to specific limits and conditions.[58] A passage from the official *relatio* of Bishop Gasser of Brixen on infallibility is worth repeating:

> Absolute infallibility belongs only to God, the first and essential truth who can never deceive or be deceived in any way. All other infallibility, by the fact that it is communicated for a certain end, has limits and conditions by which it is judged to be present. This is true also of the infallibility of the Roman Pontiff.[59]

An obvious general condition for a legitimate *ex cathedra* definition is that the Pope act freely without violence, fear, or coercion. In addition, severe mental illness would be an obstacle to authentic teaching, since the Pope would be incapable of making a genuine and free human act. Vatican I gave more formal conditions (DS 3074). The Pope who intends to define something *ex cathedra* must act according to the following four conditions:

---

57. For some references by canonists and theologians on this topic see Yves Congar, *Tradition and Traditions* (New York: Macmillan, 1967), pp. 221-225.

58. See Avery Dulles, "Infallibility: The Terminology" and "Moderate Infallibilism" in Paul C. Empie, T. Austin Murphy, and Joseph A. Burgess, eds., *Teaching Authority and Infallibility in the Church: Lutherans and Catholics in Dialogue VI* (Minneapolis: Augsburg, 1978), pp. 69-100, and Gustave Thils, *L'infallibilité pontificale* (Gembloux: J. Duculot, 1969).

59. Mansi 52:1214 A.

a) The Pope must speak as the supreme pastor and teacher of all Christians. He is not infallible as a private theologian or even as the Bishop of Rome, but only when he acts as the universal pastor of the Church.

b) He must act in virtue of his supreme apostolic authority as the successor of Peter.

c) He must teach in the area of faith or morals.

d) He must propose the defined doctrine as something to be held by the universal Church.

The Code of Canon Law adds one more requirement: "No doctrine is understood to be infallibly defined unless it is clearly established as such" (can. 749, 3).

Vatican I, rejecting the Gallican tenet, did not list the consent of the Church as a condition. Rather it said that the definitions of the Pope are irreformable, "of themselves and not from the consent of the Church" ("*ex sese non autem ex consensu ecclesiae*," DS 3074). "Consent" here means that infallible definitions do not need subsequent juridical verification by the bishops or by the Church at large to establish their legitimacy. They are authenticated by the very act of defining. The term "irreformable" can be misleading. It means that the doctrine defined is true and cannot be denied; it does not preclude the possibility of further understanding and development of that truth.[60]

Papal infallibility, then, is not a blank check that gives the Pope unlimited teaching authority; formal conditions carefully circumscribe its use. Furthermore, papal infallibility is rooted in the infallibility of the entire Church (DS 3074). Bishop Gasser rejected the idea that infallibility was first given to the Pope and then shared by him with the rest of the Church.[61]

Popes are also limited by previous doctrinal decisions.[62] The Catholic Church has always exhibited a reverence for the past. The early creeds, the *regulae fidei*, and the professions of faith show the Roman concern with fidelity to apostolic teaching. Popes have frequently expressed their acceptance of the binding force of the coun-

---

60. See Heinrich Fries, "Das Lehramt als Dienst am Glauben," *Catholica* 23 (1969):165–166.

61. Mansi 52:1216 B C.

62. See Congar, *Tradition and Traditions*, pp. 225–229.

The Limits of the Papacy

cils and canons. Leo I (440–461), for example, recognized the councils as established by the Holy Spirit and hence inviolable.[63] Martin I (649–655) expressed a typical sentiment among early Popes: "We cannot transgress the ecclesiastical canons; on the contrary, we are their defender and protector, not their violator."[64] Likewise, Gregory I (590–604) declared: "I confess that I accept and honor the four councils as I do the four books of the Holy Gospel."[65]

Every Pope, then, is obliged to adhere to the dogmatic canons of the councils and to all previous dogmatic articulations of the faith. He is not free to reject them or declare them as nonbinding; he may neglect them, but he cannot deny them. This norm, however, must not be understood simplistically. When the Church or a council defines a truth of faith, it is doing so through the assistance of the Holy Spirit. Dogmas are irrevocably true, but they give only limited insights into the mystery of divine truth; deeper understanding and development are possible and necessary.

Dogmas must be interpreted; they are not isolated, ahistorical events. Piet Fransen, in his discussion of the authority of ecumenical councils, gives three fundamental norms of interpretation: (a) Only the central assertion in a dogmatic decree or canon is defined. The reasons, arguments, or illustrations used to support a particular dogma do not have the same authority as the decree or the canon. (b) One must distinguish between teachings that are addressed to the universal Church and those that are addressed to one or several local Churches. Dogmatic definitions bind the entire Church, but some disciplinary norms or ecclesiastical laws may apply only to certain Churches. A particular law does not automatically have universal application. (c) The text must be read in the spirit in which it was written.[66]

---

63. Ep. 106, *Patrologia latina*, 54:1003.

64. Ep. 9, Mansi 10:823.

65. A synodal letter of February 591. *Monumenta germaniae historica*, Epp. I, 36. Much later in the Middle Ages, John of Torquemada (d. 1468), a papalist, said that if a Pope alone holds an opinion contradictory to a council, then he must yield to its unanimous teaching. Such a situation—the Pope *alone* opposed to the rest of the Fathers of a council—would obviously be most unusual but not theoretically impossible. In E. Candal, ed., "Ioannis de Torquemada, O.P. *Oratio synodalis de primatu*," in *Concilium Florentinum. Documenta et scriptores*, series B, vol. 4, 2 (Rome: Pontificium institutum orientalium studiorum, 1954), p. 58.

66. "The Authority of the Councils," in John M. Todd, ed., *Problems of Authority* (Baltimore: Helicon; London: Darton, Longman & Todd, 1962), pp. 60–72.

This last rule, which emphasizes the importance of the historical dimension of dogmatic truths, was developed in the 1973 declaration *Mysterium ecclesiae* from the Congregation for the Doctrine of the Faith.[67] It stated that all statements of the faith are affected in four ways by the historical situation because of (a) the restricted expressive power of language; (b) the growth of faith and human knowledge; (c) the specific purpose and context of a particular dogma (its *Sitz-im-Leben*); and (d) the time-conditioned quality of certain concepts.

What happens if a Pope unambiguously and publicly denies a truth of the faith, repudiates Scripture and tradition, rejects the sacraments, attempts to suppress the very office of the papacy and episcopate, or dismisses the dogmatic teachings of previous Popes and councils? John of Torquemada answered this question: "Were the Pope to command anything against Holy Scripture, or the articles of faith, or the truth of the sacraments, or the commands of the natural or divine law, he ought not to be obeyed, and in such commands he is to be disregarded."[68]

A more canonical response was given by Gratian in the first half of the twelfth century. In the *Decretum*, an immense compendium of canon law, he stated: "No mortal shall presume to rebuke his [the Pope's] faults, for he who is to judge all is to be judged by no one, unless he is found straying from the faith."[69] The principle—"The First See is judged by no one"—was effectively incorporated in the teachings of Lyons II, Florence, Vatican I, Vatican II, and in the present Code of Canon Law (can. 1404). The exception—unless the Pope deviates from the faith—has been a source of unending controversy. Although never defined nor included in the current Code of Canon Law, it would seem to be still valid. But what action can the Church take with a Pope who denies the faith? Can he be legitimately deposed?[70]

Medieval canonists argued that the Pope, unless he is a heretic, can be judged by no one. Some suggested that the concept of heresy

---

67. *Acta apostolicae sedis* 65 (1973):396–408.

68. *Summa de ecclesia* (Venice: M. Tramezinum, 1561), lib. II, c. 49, p. 163 B.

69. *Decretum Gratiani*, Dist. 40, c. 6. Text in *Corpus iuris canonici*, I, E. Friedberg, ed. (Leipzig: B. Tauchnitz, 1879), col. 146.

70. I have discussed this topic at length in *The Papacy in Transition* (Garden City, N.Y.: Doubleday, 1980), pp. 166–174.

also included schism and other crimes, such as fornication or simony, since they were then considered equivalent to heresy. Later canonists took a narrower view: only notorious or manifest heresy or schism deprives a Pope of his jurisdictional power. They also applied this norm to a Pope who was clearly insane, since mental illness may render a person incapable of acting in a free, human way. What procedures are used to depose a heretical Pope?

Two main solutions have been proposed. Some theologians (John of Torquemada and Robert Bellarmine) said that a Pope who denies the faith cuts himself off from the Church; he is no longer a Christian and no longer the Pope. He does not have to be formally deposed by the Church, since he is already deposed by divine law, that is, by God himself. If a Church council does judge the case, it simply makes a declaratory judgment of what in fact has already taken place. Others (Cardinal Cajetan, Francis Suarez, and John of St. Thomas) said that a deposition by the Church is necessary. A heretical Pope, they argued, does not automatically cease to be Pope until some judicial body in the Church—the cardinals or an ecumenical council—establishes his guilt and declares him a heretic.

Vatican I discussed the possibility of an incorrigibly heretical Pope or one who is habitually insane. Bishop Zinelli referred to these as "hypothetical cases" that, in all probability, would never happen. But if God would permit such evils to occur, he would give sufficient means to deal with them. In any event, he continued, these hypothetical possibilities do not weaken the doctrine of the universal power of the Roman Pontiff.[71]

The present Code of Canon Law has no articles of impeachment or procedures for dealing with an heretical Pope. But, as Patrick J. Burns has noted, prophetic protest rather than juridical process has been the primary Catholic response to abuses of the papacy. He suggests that public criticism within the Church is "ultimately a much more effective protection against the abuse of papal power than any conceivable juridical system."[72] In the unhappy event that a future Pope would fall into heresy, the Church, under the guidance of the

---

71. Mansi 52:1109 A B.

72. "Communion, Councils, and Collegiality: Some Catholic Reflections," in Paul C. Empie and T. Austin Murphy, eds., *Papal Primacy and the Universal Church: Lutherans and Catholics in Dialogue V* (Minneapolis: Augsburg, 1974), p. 170.

Spirit, would have to deal with the situation in a manner that is most beneficial to ecclesial unity and good order.

The Practical Limits

Whatever theoretical power a Pope may have, in the practical realm there are limits to what he can do. These limitations are of two kinds. Speaking pragmatically, there are those over which he has little control and those over which he has greater control. In the first group, we look at his person, office, and social context.

Every human being has personal limitations, physical, mental, and moral; the Pope is no exception. The Church, however, tries to select the least limited person to hold the office of Supreme Shepherd. Neither tradition nor the law of the Church provides a formal list of qualifications for a papal candidate. We do, however, get suggestions in canon 378, which deals with bishops in general and so also applies to the Bishop of Rome. Accordingly, a suitable candidate for the episcopal office should have solid faith, good morals and reputation, zeal for souls, wisdom, prudence, and human virtues. He must also have a doctoral or licentiate degree in Scripture, theology, or canon law or be an expert in these disciplines.

A more expanded version of the qualities required of a bishop was given in the March 1972 norms on the selection of bishops issued by the Council for the Public Affairs of the Church.[73] They add that the candidate should be even-tempered and of stable character, impartial, and faithful to the magisterium. He should also have an aptitude for governing, a social sense, a spirit of dialogue and cooperation, and openness to the signs of the times.

The papal office itself with its manifold contingencies and responsibilities also limits the Pope's ability to exercise his authority directly and concretely. Consequently, the Pope must rely on the assistance of cardinals, bishops, and other members of the Church's central administration in Rome. Speaking to the Curia, Paul VI said: "The Roman Curia is the instrument which the Pope needs and which the Pope uses to develop his own divine mandate."[74] The Curia, however,

---

73. *Acta apostolicae sedis* 64 (1972):386-391.
74. *Acta apostolicae sedis* 55 (1963):796.

is "an organ of immediate adherence and absolute obedience to the Pope."[75]

The social context also restricts the exercise of papal authority. Within his own Church the Pope may find that his authority is not accepted. In some cases this may be simply selective noncompliance or neglect of papal teaching; in other cases it may lead to schism or heresy. The break with the East, the Great Western Schism, and the Protestant Reformation are dramatic illustrations of severe limitations on the extent and acceptance of papal leadership.

In the wider world, a Pope may face opposition on several fronts: hostile secular governments may deny his rights, interfere with his authority, refuse to allow him to communicate with the faithful, and seek to bring the Church fully under the control of the state. History is filled with examples of secular rulers who rejected primatial claims and took steps to prevent Popes from exercising power within their realms. Popes have been imprisoned, exiled, deposed, and killed.

In addition to the limitations implicit in the person, office, and social context of the papacy, the Pope can voluntarily limit his exercise of power through resignation, delegation, or negotiation.

Resignation is the ultimate example of voluntary limitation; the Pope willingly gives up all his authority.[76] The last undisputed example is that of Celestine V (1294) who was elected when he was eighty-five and resigned less than five months later. The present Code of Canon Law states that if the Pope resigns his office, it is required for validity not that it be accepted by anyone but that it be made freely and be properly manifested (can. 332, 2). Since the election of the Pope is confirmed by no authority, so too papal resignation needs no acceptance. A Pope is free to resign, but he has to make this known, presumably to the cardinals who are responsible for electing his successor. The resignation takes effect immediately, but a resigned Pope could be eligible for reelection.

Delegation, a more realistic possibility, is another example of voluntary limitation. A Pope can freely delegate some of his powers to other bodies—the Synod of Bishops, the College of Cardinals, epis-

---

75. Idem.

76. Papal resignation was a controversial issue during the Middle Ages. I have discussed it in *The Papacy in Transition*, pp. 151-166.

copal conferences, curial congregations. He cannot, of course, delegate all his primatial powers, such as the personal prerogative of infallibility.

Finally, negotiation is a strategy often used by the Popes in dealing with governments and rulers who have threatened the independence of the Church. Although Popes have condemned and even deposed emperors and kings, one of the most successful ways of resolving disputes with civil society and of maintaining peaceful relations with them has been the concordat—a public bilateral agreement between the Holy See and a sovereign state on matters of common concern. This is a voluntary limitation of the exercise of papal authority.

The first genuine concordat was the Concordat of Worms (1122) between Callistus II (1119-24) and Emperor Henry V that resolved the investiture controversy. In the nineteenth century there were about thirty concordats. Many of them concerned Catholic schools, marriage legislation, the establishment or suppression of dioceses and ecclesiastical provinces, and the appointment of bishops, pastors, and military chaplains. In some instances the Church made concessions in order to obtain formal commitments that the Church could freely exercise its spiritual power. The Code of Canon law does not abrogate existing concordats (can. 3).

Many concordats deal with the appointment of bishops. The present law of the Church states that the Pope freely appoints bishops or confirms their election and that hereafter no rights and privileges of election, nomination, presentation, or designation will be granted to civil authorities (can. 377, 1, 5). *Christus Dominus*, article 20, of Vatican II asked civil authorities to renounce voluntarily any rights or privileges they have by treaty or custom concerning episcopal appointments.

In several countries concordats still in effect allow different practices.[77] In the dioceses of Basel and St. Gallen in Switzerland, for example, the cathedral chapter elects the bishop who is then confirmed by the Pope. Several dioceses in Germany and the Diocese of Salzburg

---

77. See Jean-Louis Harouel, *Les désignations épiscopales dans le droit contemporain* (Paris: Presses Universitaires de France, 1977), and "The Method of Selecting Bishops Stipulated by the Church-State Agreements in Force Today," in Peter Huizing and Knut Walf, eds., *Electing Our Own Bishops, Concilium* no. 137 (New York: Seabury, 1980):63-66.

in Austria elect the bishop from a list of names that comes from Rome. In Bavaria, every three years and when a see becomes vacant the bishops and the cathedral chapter send a list of potential bishops to Rome. The Pope is obliged to make his choice from these two lists. In a few cases the bishop is nominated by the state (Paraguay, Peru, Haiti, and Monaco) or by the diocese (Metz and Strasbourg).

A more common practice is the *droit de regard*, or right to consultation, which does not violate the right of the Pope to select his own candidate but allows the state to make known its objections. Although the state does not have a right of veto, Rome carefully considers the state's responses. The following countries have, on the basis of concordats or similar accords, the *droit de regard*: France, Austria, West Germany, Ecuador, Portugal, Dominican Republic, Poland, Venezuela, Argentina, El Salvador, Colombia, and probably Hungary.

Conclusion

The office of the papacy, granting its extensive prerogatives, is not a pure example of unfettered or absolute power. The Pope's actions are limited by the purpose of his ministry; the natural, divine, and ecclesiastical law; revelation, defined doctrine; and practical circumstances. The examples of limitation described above give us only broad norms; they must be seen in detail. The first and most obvious issue is how the Pope relates to the College of Bishops in his role as the pastoral minister of unity within the Church. The next chapter will deal with that topic.

·IV·

The Experience of Collegiality

*Remember above all things that the
Holy Roman Church, over which God
has established you as head, is the
mother and not the mistress of the
other churches, and that you are
not the lord of the bishops but one
of their number.*

—*St. Bernard**

E piscopal collegiality as taught by the Second Vatican Council may well be the most far-reaching and revolutionary teaching in the entire history of ecclesiology. It has profound implications for the theology of the papacy and its limitations. Like all doctrines, collegiality is destined to be modified and interpreted as it is gradually received by the Church; the complex process of reception involves all the People of God. Since the Council, there has been an intense discussion of both the theory and practice of collegiality in the life of the Church. It is appropriate to assess the development of collegiality over the last two decades and to relate it to the question of the limits of the papacy.

The term "collegiality" will be used in two senses, as effective and as affective collegiality.[1] Narrowly speaking, *effective collegiality*

* To Pope Eugene III (1145-53). *De consideratione*, liber iv, 23. *Tractatus et opuscula Sancti Bernardi opera*, ed. J. Leclercq and H. M. Rochais (Rome: Editiones cistercienses, 1963), III: 465–466.

1. Although the terms "effective and affective collegiality" are not found as such in the documents of Vatican II, they are substantially present. *Lumen gentium*, article 22 refers to "a true collegial act" (*"actus verus collegialis"*) that is equivalent to effective collegiality. Article 23 refers to the "collegial spirit" (*"affectus collegialis"*) which is equivalent to affective collegiality. John Paul II often uses this distinction. In his address to the German bishops, for example, he said: "I understand effective

77

refers to the world-wide solidarity of the bishops who, through their sacramental consecration and hierarchical communion with one another and with their head, the Pope, possess full and supreme authority in relation to the universal Church. The fullest expression of this kind of collegiality is an ecumenical council. Broadly speaking, *affective collegiality*, or the collegial spirit, refers to mutual cooperation, collaboration, and fraternal interaction among the bishops and the Pope on the national, regional, and international levels.

In presenting collegiality in the contemporary Church as a possible limitation on papal primacy, it should be noted that the episcopal college is not external to the papacy; it is a conditioning environment which helps define the nature of the papal role. I shall describe, first, the negative shift that has occurred in its evaluation over the last two decades. Second, I shall elaborate the main ecclesiological principles that must be operative if collegiality is to have a productive future. Third, I shall discuss the status of the Synod of Bishops and episcopal conferences, two major instruments of collegiality.

The Shift in the Evaluation of Collegiality

The formulation of the doctrine of collegiality found in chapter three of *Lumen gentium* did not have an easy passage. There were several drafts of the *Constitution on the Church*, heated debates in the conciliar aula, and much lobbying behind the scenes. It is the only document of the Council for which the Theological Commission issued, at the request of "a higher authority" (presumably the Pope), a special explanatory and prefatory note before the final voting on chapter three. This document, *Nota explicativa praevia*, was intended to clarify the relationship between the Pope and the bishops and to

---

and affective collegiality of the bishops as a weighty help to my own service" (*Origins*, December 4, 1980, vol. 10, no 25:387). The "Final Report" of the 1985 Synod of Bishops also used this terminology. *Extraordinary Synod of Bishops, Rome, 1985: A Message to the People of God and the Final Report* (Washington: NCCB, 1986), p. 19. Some of the material in this chapter is taken from my article, "The Uncertain Future of Collegiality," *Proceedings of the Catholic Theological Society of America* 40 (1985):95–106.

show that collegiality was compatible with primacy. It used, in explaining the meaning of college and hierarchical communion, more juridical concepts than *Lumen gentium*.

The uncertainty among several of the Fathers over the meaning of collegiality during the course of the deliberations was also reflected in the number of votes that were *placet iuxta modum*—a basically favorable vote to which some reservation or *modum* is attached. One Father, it was reported, became so cautious that in signing his attendance card one morning he wrote *Adsum* ("present"), automatically adding *iuxta modum*.

Some of the Fathers opposed the very idea of collegiality and spoke out against it. They feared that, if it were accepted, it would mean the evisceration of papal primacy, the independence of the bishops from the Pope, and the elimination of the monarchical Church. Cardinal Alfredo Ottaviani, for example, was clearly opposed. He said: "I am astonished at all those who insisted so much on the question of collegiality from which they would deduce a diminution of the primacy of the Roman Pontiff, at least in its exercise."[2] Cardinal Michael Browne came right to the point. Shaking his hand dramatically at the Fathers, he declared: "Collegiality does not agree with Vatican I. Venerable Fathers, beware!"[3] Bishop Antonio de Castro Mayer said: "The notion of collegiality is neither adequately demonstrated nor sufficiently studied."[4] Finally, one Council Father argued, and the report may well be apocryphal, that he had carefully studied the New Testament, and that, besides the Council of Jerusalem, the only other example of collegial action he could find in the Scriptures was in Matthew 26:56, which says that at the arrest of Jesus, "all the disciples deserted him and ran away."[5]

Other Fathers, however, spoke out strongly in favor of collegiality. Incisive interventions were made by Cardinals Joseph Frings, Paul Emile Léger, Franziskus König, Léon-Joseph Suenens, Albert Mayer,

---

2. *Acta synodalia sacrosancti concilii oecumenici Vaticani Secundi* (Vatican City: Typis Polyglottis Vaticanis, 1972), vol. II, part 4, 625.

3. Ibid., 627.

4. Ibid., 631.

5. This story appears to be a gloss on Cardinal Ottaviani's intervention. He said that the report of a biblical expert whom he has asked for scriptural evidence on collegiality was that "there are no arguments from Sacred Scripture to deduce the collegiality of the Apostles" (ibid., 625).

and others. They argued that the Council was not inventing episcopal collegiality, because it already had a secure foundation in Scripture, Church teaching, and theology. As Hervé Coathalem later observed: "It is obvious that Vatican II did not create collegiality any more than Vatican I created primacy."[6] The supporters of collegiality insisted that the Council revive or rediscover this important ecclesial concept, give it greater clarity, and articulate it more thoroughly. The Council was finally able to arrive at a consensus and to approve the doctrine on collegiality. In so doing it presented us with a classic example of compromise: a formulation broad enough to satisfy the various factions and ambiguous enough to allow for further clarification.

Theologians enthusiastically welcomed the definition of collegiality. Karl Rahner, for example, referred to it as "one of the central themes of the whole Council";[7] Michael Novak asserted: "No issue is so important to the Second Vatican Council: episcopal collegiality will characterize Vatican II as papal infallibility characterized Vatican I";[8] and Bishop Christopher Butler called it "one of the outstanding contributions to the Church today."[9] Other Christian theologians were just as positive. Anglican Bishop John Moorman said that collegiality was "one of the greatest achievements of Vatican II,"[10] and Eugene Fairweather noted that "new paths have been opened up which could scarcely have been imagined a decade ago."[11]

In the years immediately after the Council, collegiality was introduced into the life of the Church. Paul VI, in his efforts at implementing the Council, established the Synod of Bishops, which met regularly and gave the national episcopal conferences a new and dynamic role. John Paul II, in his first address as Bishop of Rome in 1978, announced as one of the priorities of his pontificate a deeper reflection on the meaning of collegiality, and noted that "the bond

---

6. "Un horizon de Vatican II. L'autorité suprême du pontife romain et celle des évêques," *Nouvelle revue théologique* 92 (1970):1014, note 20.

7. In Herbert Vorgrimler, ed., *Commentary on the Documents of Vatican II* (New York: Herder and Herder, 1967), I: 195.

8. *The Open Church: Vatican II, Act II* (New York: Macmillan, 1964), p. 104.

9. "The Bishop of Rome," *The Tablet* (London), March 6, 1982, p. 222.

10. In B. C. Pawley, ed., *The Second Vatican Council: Studies by Eight Anglican Observers* (London: Oxford University, 1967), p. 88.

11. Ibid., p. 77.

of collegiality closely links the bishops to the successor of Peter and to each other."[12] The spirit of collegiality was also reflected in the local Churches or dioceses with the establishment of presbyteral and pastoral councils. It seemed that the collegial vision was firmly taking root.

The initial euphoria about collegiality, however, has now given way in some quarters to a more pessimistic outlook. In the last ten years especially a probing and in some quarters quite negative evaluation of collegiality has emerged. Many worry that the very notion of collegiality is threatened and that we are seeing the return to a monarchical exercise of Church authority. They point to an atmosphere of repression triggered by the frequent and recent Roman interventions: the severe censuring of theologians, the removal of *imprimaturs*, the study of seminaries and religious orders, and the visitation of individual episcopal sees. These and other actions of the Holy See have diminished the hopes of many that Vatican II had fundamentally affected the Roman Catholic Church and caused them to wonder about Rome's commitment to collegiality. Some have interpreted these events as a disturbing indication of a growing tendency toward centralization in the Church.

Certain questions arise. Are there signs of a new Ultramontanism in the Church today? Are we seeing a return to a view of ecclesial authority that is quite different from the doctrine of collegiality — a view that reflects an authoritarian concept of the papacy and looks to Rome for the answer to all questions, essential or peripheral? Ultramontanism is hardly passé, but neither is collegiality fully alive. As Gabriel Daly has observed:

> The collegial ideal which might have been the queen of Vatican II's achievements is now a sleeping princess. Some day her prince will come, but on present showing he will need to be a man of unusual qualities, not indeed in order to awaken her . . . but to occupy the fortress where she has been placed in suspended animation.[13]

It is important, therefore, for us to reexamine collegiality: to look at the issues as yet unresolved and the principles still dormant.

---

12. *Origins*, October 26, 1978, vol. 8, no. 19:292.

13. "Faith and Theology: The Ultramontane Influence," *The Tablet* (London), April 18-25, 1981, p. 381.

Above all, it is necessary to study the relationship between collegiality and the limits of the papacy.

The Principles of Collegiality

The term "collegiality," made popular by Yves Congar in the 1950's in his writings on the theology of the laity, was not used in the documents of Vatican II. The Council spoke rather of the *collegium, ordo, corpus,* or *coetus* of bishops. It was, however, later adopted by theologians and by the magisterium itself to describe the unique relationship that exists within the College of Bishops under the leadership of the Pope. The concept of collegiality involves theological, pastoral, canonical, and ecumenical ramifications. To understand what collegiality is depends, to a large extent, on the recognition and appropriation of certain fundamental truths connected with it. Here are three essential principles of collegiality.

Collegiality Is a Theological Concept

The first principle is that collegiality is primarily a theological and evangelical reality and not a juridical structure. The comment by Joseph Ratzinger is appropriate:

> Collegiality must not be taken in a secular juridical sense, much less may it be reduced to the meaninglessness of a mere ornament. It expresses an aspect of the juridical structure of the Church that arises from the communion and community of the individual churches and the harmonious plurality of the bishops representing them.[14]

Collegiality rests on the idea of communion. The Church is a *communio*—a people united in faith, sharing the grace of God in Christ and the Spirit, and celebrating this unity most visibly through the eucharist. The 1985 Synod of Bishops also emphasized this point: "The ecclesiology of communion provides the sacramental

---

14. "The Pastoral Implications of Episcopal Collegiality," in E. Schillebeeckx, ed., *The Church and Mankind, Concilium* no. 1 (Glen Rock, N.J.: Paulist, 1965): 48.

foundation of collegiality. Therefore, the theology of collegiality is much more extensive than its mere juridical aspect."[15]

Vatican II stressed the unity and cooperation between the papal and episcopal offices. It sought to explain how these two offices are related. The College of Bishops is in continuity with the apostolic college, and the Pope is in continuity with Peter. Both the Pope and the bishops are essential to the Church; the papacy and episcopate exist by divine right. Although they have different functions, together they form one communion. It is not a question of comparing the Pope with three thousand bishops in a confrontational situation, but rather of seeing the Pope within the college as its head and as working together with his fellow bishops to promote the salvific message of Christ. The College of Bishops needs the Pope and the Pope needs the college; one cannot exist without the other.

The body of bishops under the leadership of the Pope forms a collegial body of teachers and pastors that exercises supreme and full authority in the Church (*Lumen gentium*, arts. 18 and 22). As a member of the college, a bishop is responsible not only for the care of his own particular Church but also, in a nonjuridical way, for the whole Church (*Lumen gentium*, arts. 22 and 23). Each bishop shares in the college's universal responsibility for the evangelization of the world. As Origen put it: "He who is called to the office of bishop is not called to dominate but to serve the whole Church."[16] This same theme is also found in other patristic writers: Ignatius of Antioch, Clement of Rome, Dionysius of Corinth, and Polycarp.

One becomes a member of the college through episcopal consecration and enters into a hierarchical communion with the head and members of the college (*Lumen gentium*, art. 21 and *Nota praevia*, no. 2).[17] Consecration confers the fullness of orders with the threefold office of sanctifying, teaching, and ruling. Although bishops need, by a canonical mission, papal permission to exercise their ministry in a particular territory, they do not receive their episcopal authority from

---

15. *Extraordinary Synod*, p. 19.

16. *In Isaiam hom.*, 6, 1. *Patrologia graeca* 13:239.

17. See Gianfranco Ghirlanda, "*Hierarchica communio*": *Significato della formula nella Lumen Gentium* (Rome: Gregoriana, 1980). Also see Oskar Saier, "*Communio*" *in der Lehre des zweiten Vatikanischen Konzils* (Munich: M. Hueber, 1973). For a critique of Ghirlanda, see Yves Congar, *Revue des sciences philosophiques et théologiques* 66 (1982):93–97.

the Pope; it is given to them directly by God in the sacrament of orders. Apostolic authority, therefore, is not a personal possession of the Pope who then dispenses it to the other bishops; it is a common possession of the College of Bishops who are united with the Pope. The juridical dimensions of collegiality flow from the sacramental nature of the episcopal office. Collegiality arises from sacramentality.

Collegiality Depends on the Papacy

The second principle is that collegiality has both a theoretical and practical dependency on the papacy. On the theoretical level it means that the College of Bishops cannot exist without the Pope, since he is both fellow member and head. The college exists with its head and never without it. Vatican II taught that the supreme and plenary power in the Church belongs to the united episcopate with and under the Pope. The critical text on collegiality is found in article 22 of *Lumen gentium:*

> Together with its head, the Roman Pontiff, and never without this head, the episcopal order is the subject of supreme and full power over the universal Church. But this power can be exercised only with the consent of the Roman Pontiff.[18]

Vatican II stated the principle of collegiality but did not define the precise relationship between the Pope as the "chief pastor of the whole Church" and the Pope as "head of the college." Theologians have debated this question since the Council, using as sources both *Lumen gentium* and the *Nota praevia.*

Some theologians hold that there are two inadequately distinct subjects of supreme authority in the Church: the Pope as head of the Church and the Pope with the episcopal college. Referring to the *Nota praevia* they argue that, as pastor of the universal Church, the Pope can decide to use his supreme power either personally or collegially. As head of the college, he can perform certain actions that do not belong to the other bishops, such as convoking and directing the college.[19]

---

18. Also see *Nota praevia*, nos. 3 and 4.

19. William F. Bertrams, Michael Browne, Avery Dulles, and others hold this view. The 1985 Synod of Bishops seemed to make a similar distinction (*Extraordinary Synod*, p. 19).

Other theologians, and I agree generally with their position, affirm that there is only one subject of supreme authority in the Church: the episcopal college under papal leadership which can operate in two ways: through a strictly collegial act or through a personal act of the Pope as head of the college.[20] Thus every primatial action is collegial. This view, however, does imply a broadening of the meaning of "collegial" to include actions *of* the full college and also actions *pertaining to* the college. The calling of an ecumenical council by the Pope, for example, may be a collegial action, since the Pope is the head of the college. It may also be said to pertain to the college, even though it is not directly initiated by the college.

On a theoretical level, at least, collegiality does not jeopardize papal authority. If there is one thing that the Council is clear about it is that the Pope can always exercise his supreme power freely (*Lumen gentium*, art. 22). The *Nota praevia* states that the Pope, in view of the welfare of the Church, can "according to his own discretion . . . always exercise his authority as he chooses" (*Nota praevia*, nos. 3 and 4). Canon 333, 2 makes a similar statement. Gustave Thils remarks that such phrases "add, in defense of a free exercise of legitimate rights, a nuance applied to the *Ancien Régime* or to discretionary power which are badly suited to Christian authority."[21] At any rate the *libertas papae* is preserved.[22]

Papal primacy is not opposed to episcopal collegiality, because it is a primacy of service fostering the unity of the communion of the Churches in faith and love. The Pope should be viewed neither as a dictator arbitrarily imposing his will on the bishops nor as an executor simply carrying out the wishes of the bishops. The bishops, for their part, are not vicars of the Pope but Vicars of Christ who exercise an authority that is proper to them. "Their power, therefore, is not destroyed by the supreme and universal power" (*Lumen gentium*, art. 27).

---

20. This position is held by Karl Rahner, Yves Congar, Richard McBrien, Christopher Butler, Otto Semmelroth, and others.

21. *La primauté pontificale. La doctrine de Vatican I. Les voies d'une révision* (Gembloux: J. Duculot, 1972), p. 225.

22. Antonio Acerbi has shown that the postconciliar institutions have in no way limited the liberty and authority of the Pope. See his "L'ecclesiologia sottesa alle istituzioni ecclesiali postconciliari," in Giuseppe Alberigo, ed., *L'ecclesiologia del Vaticano II: Dinamismi e prospettive* (Bologna: Dehoniane, 1981), pp. 203-234.

On a practical level, collegiality is also dependent on the Pope. The Pope, for example, is under no obligation, at least no canonical one, to convene an ecumenical council or a synod of bishops. If Popes simply ignored the collegial principle, it would become a quaint doctrinal heirloom — of historical interest but without practical effect. The Pope ultimately determines the success or failure of collegiality. Given the complexity of today's world, it is unthinkable that collegiality would not be necessarily operative in the Church.

The universal primate does not exercise his office in isolation but in cooperation with the bishops. This sharing of authority requires considerable forbearance and flexibility for both the Pope and the bishops. The words of Cardinal Suenens are appropriate: "Collegiality is an art that must be learned in common or not at all."[23] The doctrine of collegiality may well introduce modifications in the exercise of the primacy but it cannot reject it.

Collegiality Is Dialogic

The third principle is that collegiality is essentially dialogic. Dialogue is the indispensable vehicle of collegiality. We sometimes overlook this dialogic dimension of revealed truth, categorizing dialogue as a mere social technique. Actually dialogue permeates our Christian faith. God's inner Trinitarian life is preeminently dialogic in the community of the Father, Son, and Spirit. "The divine persons are not only in dialogue, they are dialogue," observed Walter Kasper.[24] Jesus of Nazareth manifested this threefold dialogue in his active ministry and in his death and resurrection. The Church must engage in dialogue with both believers and unbelievers. It would be discordant indeed if the Pope, the Vicar of Christ, were not continually in dialogue with the rest of the Church, especially with his fellow Vicars of Christ, the bishops. A united episcopate in dialogue constitutes authentic Church governance; collegiality is its name.

Dialogue is fundamentally communication. Paul VI in *Ecclesiam suam* noted: "Before speaking, it is necessary to listen. The Spirit of dialogue is friendship and, even more, service."[25] Like any other

---

23. José de Broucker, *The Suenens Dossier: The Case for Collegiality* (Notre Dame, Ind.: Fides, 1970), p. 36.

24. *The God of Jesus Christ* (New York: Crossroad, 1984), p. 290.

25. *Paths of the Church* (Washington: NCWC, 1964), no. 87.

human dialogue, collegiality is a process—lengthy, trying, but ultimately rewarding—of persons attempting to arrive at consensus. The Pope and the bishops, attentive to the developments in theology and sensitive to the lived experience of the People of God, must share accumulated insights with charity, humility, and trust in their mutual search for truth.

Collegiality challenges bishops and believers to enter into dialogue with each other and with the Pope. It is necessary for them to seek acceptable ways to communicate the validity of their experience, to correct false impressions, and to be open to change and reconciliation. Collegiality is also a challenge to the Pope, as Archbishop John R. Roach observed in his presidential address at the 1983 meeting of the National Conference of Catholic Bishops. He called collegiality a two-way street. Part of the task of the American hierarchy, he explained, "is to interpret the teaching of the Holy Father to the Church in the United States"; another part, "is to interpret the experience and insights of the Church in the United States to the Holy Father and those who collaborate with him in Rome."[26] He candidly admitted that both interpretive tasks need to be done better and more effectively by the American bishops.

Practical implementation of dialogue may become a delicate and even onerous task, since bishops are members of the hierarchy as well as pastors of their own local Churches. And tensions do occur between bishops and Rome. On occasion, bishops find themselves caught between papal directives and diocesan expectations.[27] At times, however, individual bishops or perhaps the more persuasive voice of a conference of bishops may have no other choice than to react negatively—though with respect and charity—to what they consider to be misapprehensions or misguided efforts on the part of Rome. The dialogic interaction, a kind of mutual fraternal correction, between the Pope and the bishops may be the critical test of the collegial principle, demanding wisdom and courage as well as tact and creativity. When genuine fraternal dialogue between the Pope and the bishops is taken as the accepted climate of opinion in ecclesial governance, then collegiality will have come of age.

---

26. *Origins*, November 24, 1983, vol. 13, no. 24:403.

27. Daniel E. Pilarczyk, Archbishop of Cincinnati, discussed this relationship in "Domestic Manners of the American People," *America*, May 25, 1985, pp. 425–427.

The Synod of Bishops

As a most important instrument of collegiality, the Synod of Bishops may also be an indirect limitation or restraint on absolute papal power. Pope Paul VI formally established the Synod of Bishops on September 15, 1965, by the *motu proprio Apostolica sollicitudo*, which explained the nature and authority of the synod and laid down norms for its operation.[28] According to Paul VI, the synod has a threefold purpose: to foster a close association between the Pope and the bishops of the entire world; to ensure that firsthand and accurate information is available concerning problems facing the Church and the course of action it should adopt; and to facilitate agreement (*concordia*) at least in regard to essential points of doctrine and procedural policy in the life of the Church. The Pope, through the establishment of the synod, wished to develop a closer relationship with the bishops and to share their common solicitude for the universal Church. He wished, he said, to avail himself "of the consolation of their assistance, the help of their prudence and experience, the support of their counsel, and the benefit of their authority."[29]

Historical Background

Current legislation speaks of three kinds of synodal meetings. Ordinary sessions deal with any important matter that requires the attention and advice from the Catholic episcopate. Extraordinary sessions address subjects that affect the entire Church and need immediate consideration. The distinction between ordinary and extraordinary synods is not precise. Special sessions are designed to discuss matters affecting one or other specific region in the Church. Through 1987, eleven synods have been held: seven ordinary, two extraordinary,

---

28. *Acta apostolicae sedis* 57 (1965):775-780. The Code of Canon Law—canons 342-348—draws heavily on this document. For a commentary on these canons see James H. Provost in J. A. Coriden, T. J. Green, and D. E. Heintschel, eds., *The Code of Canon Law: A Text and Commentary* (New York: Paulist, 1985), pp. 281-286.

29. *Acta apostolicae sedis* 57 (1965):775. These words were first said by Paul VI at the closing of the third period of the Council on November 21, 1964 (Ibid., 56 [1964]:1011).

and two special. The synods have all taken place in Rome and, with the exception of the special ones, they have each had some two hundred participants and have lasted anywhere from two weeks to a month.

The seven ordinary synods dealt with the following topics: 1969—dangers to the faith, revision of the Code of Canon Law, seminaries, mixed marriages, and liturgy; 1971—ministerial priesthood and justice in the world; 1974—evangelization; 1977—catechetics; 1980—the role of the family; 1983—penance and reconciliation; and 1987—the laity.

The first extraordinary synod was held in 1967 and explored the relationship between the episcopacy and the primacy; the second extraordinary synod in 1985 was called to celebrate the twentieth anniversary of the close of Vatican II and to review, evaluate, and further the goals of the Council. In 1980, John Paul II convoked two special synods with bishops of a particular region or rite: one dealing with the Church in the Netherlands and another concerned with Ukrainian Catholics.

The most controversial synod was the special synod with the bishops of the Dutch Church, which had as its theme: "the pastoral work of the Church to be exercised in the Netherlands in the present situation, so that the Church will reveal itself more as a communion."[30] It was held in the Vatican in a frescoed room known, ominously, as the Hall of Broken Heads; it lasted sixteen days.

Although the Dutch synod appears to have followed the letter of the *motu proprio*, some ecclesiologists complained that it violated the spirit of the law and its particular or regional character. They noted the presence of a Belgian archbishop who acted as a copresidential delegate of the Pope, and that of a large number of prefects from the curial congregations.[31]

The results of the synods have been communicated to the Church at large in several ways. Only two of the ordinary and extraordinary synods have issued an official report on their proceedings with the

---

30. *Origins*, January 17, 1980, vol. 9, no. 31:593.

31. On this second point, Giuseppe Alberigo says that the basis of the papal decision to invite curial prefects was "once again the sovereign will of the Pope in dealing with a collegial organ" ("Istituzioni per la communione tra l'episcopato universale e il vescovo di Roma," in *L'ecclesiologia del Vaticano II*, p. 244).

permission of the Pope: the ordinary synod of 1971, and the extraordinary synod of 1985. The practice of the ordinary synods of 1974, 1977, 1980, and 1983 varied slightly, but there was a common pattern: the bishops at the end of the synod issued a short "message" to the People of God rather than a formal document. They also submitted their recommendations or "propositions," which were not made public, to the Pope who used them as the basis for his own public statement in the form of an apostolic constitution. The following apostolic exhortations from the Pope, supposedly based on the discussion of the synods, have appeared: *Evangelii nuntiandi* (1974 synod), *Catechesi tradendae* (1977 synod), *Familiaris consortio* (1980 synod), and *Reconciliatio et paenitentia* (1983 synod).

An interesting theological exercise is to try to determine how closely the apostolic exhortations accurately reflect the deliberations of the synod—not an easy task considering the aura of secrecy that surrounds much of the proceedings. A more pressing task, however, is to compare the apostolic exhortations with the developing theology since the Council. Have these documents advanced the topic under consideration or have they merely repeated the obvious? The 1980 synod has been carefully analyzed in terms of its relationship to both the deliberations of the synod itself and to the current state of theological thought on the question. "One searches desperately for something in *Familiaris consortio*," write Jan Grootaers and Joseph A. Selling, "that emanated specifically from the synod and was not already part of presynodal teaching or practice."[32]

Theological Basis

It is difficult to determine the precise collegial character of the Synod of Bishops.[33] Jan Grootaers is correct when he says that the synod "is part of the fundamental ambiguity of postconciliar eccle-

---

32. *The 1980 Synod of Bishops on "The Role of the Family": An Exposition and an Analysis of Its Texts* (Leuven: University Press, 1983). A critical evaluation of the 1983 synod is given by James Dallen in *"Reconciliatio et paenitentia:* The Postsynodal Apostolic Exhortation," *Worship* 59 (1985):98–116.

33. See Charles M. Murphy, "Collegiality: An Essay Toward Better Understanding," *Theological Studies* 46 (1985):38–49.

siology."[34] Although theologians agree that the synod is an instrument or organ of collegiality, they disagree on whether it can perform a "true collegial act" (*actus verus collegialis*) as described in *Lumen gentium*, article 22 and canon 337.

According to Vatican II and the Code, the College of Bishops clearly exercises supreme authority in the universal Church in an ecumenical council, but this is not the only way it may so function. A true collegial act is also possible through the united action of the bishops dispersed throughout the world, provided that such "action has been inaugurated or has been freely accepted by the Roman Pontiff" (can. 337, 2).[35] Does the Synod of Bishops perform a true collegial act or only a collective act?

Some theologians have argued vigorously that the synod is an example of a legitimate, nonconciliar, strictly collegial action of the bishops united with the Pope.[36] Citing the *motu proprio* that the synod is "representative of the entire Catholic episcopacy" ("*partes agens totius catholici episcopatus*"), they contend that the bishops attending the synod act not as delegates of the Pope but as representatives of the entire College of Bishops. The synod, they hold, satisfies the requirements for a strictly collegial act as long as the Pope accepts its counsels or, if it is granted a deliberative vote, ratifies its final decisions.

Other theologians present a different and, in my opinion, a more convincing position.[37] Their basic argument is that the only subject

---

34. "I sinodi dei vescovi del 1969 e del 1974: Funzionamento insoddisfacente e risultati significativi," in *L'ecclesiologia del Vaticano II*, p. 271.

35. Bishop Zinelli at Vatican I made a similar statement even though he did not use the language of collegiality. Mansi 52:1109 C D.

36. See Edward Schillebeeckx, "The Synod of Bishops: One Form of Strict but Non-Conciliar Collegiality," *IDO-C Dossier* 67-9 (March 12, 1967), and Angel Antón, "Episcoporum synodus: 'Partes agens totius catholici episcopatus,'" *Periodica de re morali, canonica, liturgica* 57 (1968):495-527, and "Verso una collegialità più effettiva nel sinodo dei vescovi," *La revista del clero italiano* 64 (1983):290-302, 482-498, 562-576.

37. Henri de Lubac, *The Motherhood of the Church followed by Particular Churches in the Universal Church* (San Francisco: Ignatius, 1982), pp. 233-304; Jérôme Hamer, "La responsabilité collégiale de chaque évêque," *Nouvelle revue théologique* 105 (1983):641-654; Bonaventure Kloppenburg, *The Ecclesiology of Vatican II* (Chicago: Franciscan Herald, 1974), pp. 205-217; and Marian Zurowski,

of a true collegial act is the entire *ordo episcoporum* and not a part of it. Thus, the synod cannot perform a strict collegial act, because individual bishops cannot delegate the supreme and full authority of the College of Bishops to those few bishops who are selected as representatives to the synod.

The Code of Canon Law seems to support this second opinion. The synod, as the Code indicates, is clearly dependent on the Pope in all its stages. It is the Pope who convokes it, ratifies the election of its members, determines its agenda, and decides whether to act on its recommendations. It is a consultative body whose primary function is to advise the Pope rather than to be a decision-making instrument of the world-wide episcopate. According to canon 344, "a synod of bishops is directly under the authority of the Roman Pontiff." This canon obviously affirms the primatial role, but it may just mean that there should be no intermediary body, such as the Roman Curia, between the Pope and the synod.

The 1985 Synod of Bishops followed the Code. It taught that only effective collegiality could produce a true collegial act and that it involves the activity of the whole College of Bishops as in an ecumenical council. Affective collegiality, or the spirit of cooperation among the bishops, is only a partial realization of collegiality. The Synod of Bishops and the episcopal conference are "sign and instrument of the collegial spirit."[38]

An episcopal synod is not a mini-ecumenical council, which, by meeting a few weeks in Rome, can make decisions with the Pope that commit the entire episcopate on serious issues affecting the whole Church. The synod, therefore, is a most important and useful collective action of the bishops, but it is not strictly collegial. At the same time, the synod may by its actions help prepare the way for future actions of the entire episcopate.

Suggested Changes

The Synod of Bishops, even if it is an advisory body and not an expression of the full episcopate, still has unrealized potential. It is, as the *motu proprio* reminds us, a human institution and "will admit

---

"Synodus episcoporum in quantum 'partes agens totius catholici episcopatus,'" *Periodica de re morali, canonica, liturgica* 62 (1973):375–391.

38. *Extraordinary Synod*, p.19.

of improvement in its form in the course of time" (*Proemium*). I offer four suggestions.

First, the process of consultation needs improvement. The present procedures used by Rome, not only in preparation for the synods but also in its other teaching functions, appear to be too narrow and not adequately representative of the wide range of acceptable theological opinion. More than one school of thought should be consulted. A restricted presentation of the truth fails to take into account the pluralistic dimension of contemporary theology, the variety of cultural matrices, and the many legitimate expressions of the same faith. This diversity becomes more evident with each succeeding synod. It is encouraging that there was extensive consultation for the 1987 synod on the laity.

Second, the rule of secrecy should be relaxed. Excessive secrecy can easily give the wrong impression that genuine dialogue is discouraged in the synodal deliberations and that the bishops can function without accountability to the wider Church. The perennial Roman passion for secrecy—often used as an instrument of power—seems unnecessary and cumbersome. At the 1985 synod, where the number of journalists outnumbered the participants, efforts were made to accommodate the press, radio, and television media by briefings and news releases. The journalists, however, received summaries and not the full texts of the speeches and only sketchy outlines of the discussions. This situation made reporting difficult and encouraged unfounded rumors and speculations. Since a synod is a media event, more open and complete disclosure of its proceedings would benefit all parties concerned.

Secrecy was also evident in the preparation for the 1985 synod. The presynodal reports of the Dutch, English, and United States episcopal conferences were published before Rome instructed the other conferences not to make their reports public.[39] The Vatican has announced that this rule will also apply to the synod on the laity in 1987.

---

39. Fifteen of the reports from the national and regional conferences along with other documents were subsequently published in *Synode extraordinaire: Célébration de Vatican II*, introduction by Joseph A. Komonchak (Paris: Cerf, 1986). For an analysis of the 1985 synod see Giuseppe Alberigo and James Provost, eds., *Synod 1985—An Evaluation, Concilium* no. 188 (Edinburgh: T. & T. Clark, 1986).

Archbishop John P. Foley, president of the Pontifical Commission for Social Communications, explained the reason for this prohibition.[40] The publication of reports puts undue pressure on bishops in countries where the Church is oppressed; they would be impeded in what they could say because of their delicate political situation. Some conferences, he added, requested that the reports be kept secret in order to give the bishops complete freedom in their communications with Rome.

These arguments are not without merit; yet the benefits of full disclosure of the reports seem to outweigh the objections. If the laity have been consulted beforehand, it seems that they should know how the bishops have responded to their views in their official reports. Could not the decision rest with the individual conferences? Some may wish to publish their reports and others, because of their particular situation, may prefer not to make them public or to issue only partial reports to the press.

Third, the membership of the synod should be expanded. At three assemblies—1971, 1980, and 1985—clerical and lay auditors were invited. Although the law makes no provision for this, it is hoped that further synods will continue the practice. Formal membership, however, is limited to bishops and to a determined number of representatives—who are not bishops—from male religious congregations. Since nonepiscopal individuals, the religious superiors, have attended the synods as voting members, there is no intrinsic reason why future synodal membership should not include at least a small number of diocesan priests, female religious, and lay representatives, both men and women.

Can we still justify the total exclusion of religious women and lay persons from the synod or restrict them to the status of nonvoting auditors or observers? Must ordination be a requirement for the exercise of authority in the Church? A wider synodal membership, even though the majority would be bishops, would better express the universal communion of the Church and encourage a fuller presentation of various views. It would help make the synod a more effective institution for dialogue within the Church. What more appropriate time to have inaugurated the practice of lay involvement than in the 1987 synod, which had for its theme the vocation and the mission of the laity in the Church and in the world?

---

40. *The Tablet* (London), May 17, 1986, p. 521.

Fourth, serious consideration should be given to the conferral of a deliberative vote to the participants of the synod.[41] The Pope can confer such a right, but it has not yet been done.[42] A consultative vote allows the participants to be heard and to provide advice, but in a nonbinding manner. A deliberative vote allows, in addition, the members to determine the final position taken by the body whose decrees would become binding upon confirmation and promulgation by the Pope. Thus, the documents of Vatican II are not simply papal statements but the products of the entire episcopate.

If the synod functioned as a deliberative body, it would strengthen the collegial nature of the assembly and contribute to its effectiveness and credibility. Even if the synod were granted a deliberative vote, it would still juridically represent only the authority of the synod and, as Charles M. Murphy notes, it would be "qualitatively different from that of the entire college as such."[43]

Archbishop Maxim Hermaniuk of Winnipeg, Manitoba, leader of Canada's Ukrainian Catholics, made a radical proposal at the 1985 synod.[44] Characterizing the synods until now as "international study days of the Catholic bishops," he said that unless the synod has legislative and not merely consultative power, one may not speak of real collegial governance in the Church. He suggested the creation of a permanent Synod of Bishops of twenty-five members, in addition to the present synodal structure, which would be empowered to act "in the name of the whole College of Bishops." The elected members would have a six-year term. This group would be given legislative power to decide with the Pope and under his authority "all the questions in the life of the Church which are today decided by the Holy Father with the Roman Curia."[45] Hermaniuk argued

---

41. On this point see Kloppenburg, *Ecclesiology*, p. 216; Alexander Ganoczy, "How Can We Evaluate Collegiality vis-à-vis Papal Primacy?" in Hans Küng, ed., *Papal Ministry in the Church*, Concilium no. 64 (New York: Herder and Herder, 1971): 93; and Groupe des Dombes, *Le ministère de communion dans l'Eglise universelle* (Paris: Centurion, 1986), p. 96.

42. Canon 343: "It is the role of the Synod of Bishops to discuss the questions on their agenda and to express their desires about them but not to resolve them or to issue decrees about them, unless the Roman Pontiff in certain cases has endowed the synod with deliberative power, and, in this event, it is his role to ratify its decisions."

43. Murphy, "Collegiality," 42.

44. *Origins*, December 12, 1985, vol. 15, no. 26:432.

45. Idem.

that this new structure would permit the real participation of the bishops in the life of the universal Church and would help solve some very important ecumenical problems.

Hermaniuk's suggestion indicates the frank atmosphere of the 1985 synodal discussions. It has both advantages and disadvantages. Positively, by broadening the base of decision making, it might lead to a more collegial and open approach to Church leadership. In addition, it might contribute to the reform of the Curia, by making it more a servant than a master of the bishops. A permanent synod could review curial decisions and introduce a system of greater accountability. Negatively, it could slow down the administrative process by establishing an intermediary body between the Pope and the Curia. A careful selection process of the members of the permanent synod would be imperative to ensure its representative quality and to avoid creating another Curia. The major theological problem is whether twenty-five bishops—some elected and others appointed by the Pope—could legitimately represent the entire episcopate and exercise legislative power in its name.

Other suggestions have been made about the synodal structure. The Brazilian bishops, for example, suggested that the synods be held each time in a different continent.[46] The president of the Canadian Conference of Catholic Bishops, Bishop Bernard Hubert of St. Jean Longueil, Quebec, suggested that since it was impossible for the synod to deal with all the issues raised, it should rather spend the time in identifying the major problems. The bishops then could return home to discuss these matters with other bishops in the conference and to consult with the laity. In a year or two the bishops would reconvene. This process, he felt, would encourage widespread consultation and genuine participation among the bishops and the laity.[47]

How does the Synod of Bishops relate to our concern over the limits of the papacy? The synod is not a parliament; it cannot be equated with similar institutions in civil politics. It is unique because it is a gathering of the successors of the Apostles and hence a charismatic and spiritual entity. Despite some areas that need improvement, the synod has been a significant element in the implementation of the

---

46. *Synode extraordinaire*, p. 127.
47. *Origins*, December 12, 1985, vol. 15, no. 26:429–430.

doctrine of collegiality. It has sought to respond to its threefold purpose ennunciated by Paul VI when he established it in 1965: to bring the bishops closer together, to provide information concerning Church problems, and to seek consensus in doctrinal and procedural matters.

As an advisory or consultative body, the synod does not directly limit the authority of the Pope. He is free to accept or reject its advice. Morally, however, the Pope is obliged to give the deliberations of the synod serious consideration. Indirectly, it can influence the Pope and determine what actions he will or will not take. It can be an important factor that helps shape the direction the Church will take under papal leadership. The contact between bishops representing local Churches throughout the world brings to the synod a spectrum of views that reflects the pluralism in the universal Church. If most of the bishops at a synod, for example, suggested a particular course of action, it is unlikely that the Pope would act contrary to it, unless he had convincing and overriding reasons. Episcopal synods may act as a restraint on an authoritarian Pope. The synod, then, assuming that the bishops are candid and courageous, can be most influential in determining the style and the substance of the papacy.

The Episcopal Conference

The episcopal conference is another expression of collegiality, one limiting the papacy but even more indirectly. Its origins date back to the early Church where, in both the East and the West, synodal structures of bishops played a major role. *Lumen gentium*, in article 23, compared the role of episcopal conferences with that of the ancient patriarchates. Although bishops of many countries in the century before Vatican II met regularly to discuss common concerns, the 1917 Code of Canon Law did not provide any laws for such assemblies. They were given formal status at Vatican II in its *Decree on the Bishops' Pastoral Office in the Church* (*Christus Dominus*). In 1966, Paul VI in his *motu proprio Ecclesiae sanctae* mandated that each nation or territory establish a permanent conference of bishops, if one did not already exist, and he set forth norms governing their activity. The 1983 Code of Canon Law has a separate section

tion on episcopal conferences (cans. 447–459). Questions emerge: What is the theological status of the conferences of bishops? Do they have teaching authority? How do they relate to papal authority?[48]

Theological Basis

At Vatican II some of the Fathers were opposed to granting episcopal conferences formal status. Others, affirming that only the papacy and the College of Bishops have authority by divine law, insisted that episcopal conferences have a basis only in ecclesiastical law.[49] *Lumen gentium*, however, spoke of the collegial spirit operating concretely in groups of bishops (art. 23); *Christus Dominus* recalled the first centuries of the Church when synods and councils taught the truths of the faith and ordered ecclesiastical discipline (art. 36). Furthermore the Council decreed:

> This most sacred Council considers it supremely opportune everywhere that bishops belonging to the same nation or region form an association and meet together at fixed times. Thus, when the insights of prudence and experience have been shared and views exchanged, there will emerge a holy union of energies in the service of the common good of the churches (*Christus Dominus*, art. 37).

Theologians after the Council strongly affirmed the theological foundation of bishops' conferences. Jérôme Hamer, for example, maintained that the episcopal conference is "an appropriate expression of the solidarity of the body of bishops, which is a reality of divine right in the Church of Christ."[50] Joseph Ratzinger labeled as "one-sided and unhistorical" the view that bishops' conferences lack

---

48. For this section I have found most useful the article by Avery Dulles, "Bishops' Conference Documents: What Doctrinal Authority?," *Origins*, January 24, 1985, vol. 14, no. 32:528–534. Also see Bernard Franck, "La conférence épiscopale et les autres institutions de collegialité intermédiaire," *L'année canonique* 27 (1983):67–120.

49. Bishop Luigi Carli made this latter point both at Vatican II and at the 1969 Synod of Bishops. See *Acta synodalia concilii Vaticani Secundi* (Vatican City: Typis Polyglottis Vaticanis, 1960-61), vol. II, part 5, 72–75, and Giovanni Caprile, *Il sinodo dei vescovi* (Rome: La civiltà cattolica, 1970), p. 77.

50. "Les conférences épiscopales, exercise de la collégialité," *Nouvelle revue théologique* 85 (1963):969.

all theological basis. He argued that they offer today "the best means of concrete plurality in unity" and that they are "one of the possible forms of collegiality that is here partially realized but with a view to the totality."[51]

A different view of episcopal conferences has recently appeared in several Roman statements. Ratzinger, for example, now holds that "episcopal conferences have no theological basis; they do not belong to the structure of the Church, as willed by Christ, that cannot be eliminated; they have only a practical, concrete function."[52] The International Theological Commission (ITC), which is under the chairmanship of Cardinal Ratzinger, distinguished between the Church's "essential structure," which is of divine law, and its "concrete and evolving shape," which is of ecclesiastical law. The ITC also stated that episcopal conferences are concrete developments that belong to ecclesiastical law and concluded that "such terms as 'college,' 'collegiality,' and 'collegial' can have no more than an analogical and theologically improper sense," when used in reference to episcopal conferences.[53] The 1985 Synod of Bishops taught that Synods of Bishops and episcopal conferences are only partial realizations of collegiality: "All of these actualizations cannot be directly deduced from the theological principles of collegiality, but they are regulated by ecclesiastical law."[54]

Do episcopal conferences have a theological basis? It depends on what theological means. The later Ratzinger, the ITC, and the 1985 synod spoke of theological as something directly connected with divine law. That narrow interpretation tends to diminish the importance of episcopal conferences and the vital role they have played in postconciliar Catholicism.

---

51. "Pastoral Implications," 63-64.

52. Joseph Cardinal Ratzinger with Vittorio Messori, *The Ratzinger Report: An Exclusive Interview on the State of the Church* (San Francisco: Ignatius, 1985), p. 59.

53. *Themata selecta de ecclesiologia* (Vatican City: Libreria editrice Vaticana, 1985), p. 34. French translation in *Documentation catholique*, January 5, 1986, p. 65.

54. *Extraordinary Synod*, p. 19. Unfortunately, the 1985 synod did not discuss the practical aspects of collegiality and the role of episcopal conferences. See Joseph A. Komonchak, "The Theological Debate," in Alberigo and Provost, *Synod 1985 —An Evaluation*, 53-63.

I find more convincing the argument in favor of the theological basis of episcopal conferences as proposed by Avery Dulles. He holds that although bishops' conferences are not formally authorized by divine law, "divine law does give the hierarchy the right and duty to establish the structures that are found helpful for the exercise of their divinely given mission as individuals and in groups."[55] Ecclesiastical structures such as parishes, dioceses, the Roman Curia, and episcopal conferences are not essential to the Church, "but they have real authority based on the divinely established order of the Church."[56]

Episcopal conferences, then, are legitimate theological expressions of the ministry of bishops and valid applications of the spirit of collegiality. They have made significant contributions in this critical period of institutional development. Bishop James W. Malone, the former president of the National Conference of Catholic Bishops, considers the episcopal conference a valid instrument of collaboration among the bishops in their role of pastoral service.[57] Speaking at the 1985 Synod of Bishops, he said: "The expressions of collegiality in the episcopal conference of the United States are not just instances of those gimmicks and pragmatic contrivances for which Americans are thought to have a penchant. We see collegiality as embodied in our conference as an important service of evangelization."[58]

Teaching Authority

Episcopal conferences throughout the world have been involved in extensive teaching activity since Vatican II. American bishops too have recognized the value of the national conference in teaching. "We have to admit," wrote Archbishop James Hickey of Washington, "that the conference offers the most effective vehicle nationally for our teaching office. Our collective exercise of the teaching office is necessary to answer specific challenges that arise for us from the collective life of the nation."[59]

---

55. "Bishops' Conference," 530.

56. Idem.

57. See his address to U. S. bishops, *Origins,* July 4, 1985, vol. 15, no. 7:101, and his presynodal report to Rome, *Origins,* September 26, 1985, vol. 15, no. 15:229.

58. *Origins,* December 12, 1985, vol. 15, no. 26:431.

59. *Origins,* July 29, 1982, vol. 12, no. 9:142.

The United States bishops' conference has issued many important pastoral documents with an explicit doctrinal component. They include the following: "The Church in Our Day" (1967), "Human Life in Our Day" (1968), "Basic Teachings for Religious Education" (1972), "Behold Your Mother" (1974), "Brothers and Sisters to Us" (1979) on racism, "To Live in Christ Jesus" (1976) on the moral life, "The Challenge of Peace" (1983), and "Economic Justice for All" (1986). Other documents have treated such various topics as abortion, communism, ecumenism, the parish, catechetics, the laity, and priestly formation.

Granting the fact that episcopal conferences do teach, theologians ask if they have the *formal authority to teach*—the so-called *mandatum docendi*. Here again we have a lively theological debate. Cardinal Ratzinger's position is unambiguous: "No episcopal conference, as such, has a teaching mission; its documents have no weight of their own save that of the consent given to them by the individual bishops."[60] He referred to canon 455, 4, which states that, unless the Apostolic See gives a special mandate, "neither the conference nor its president may act in the name of all the bishops unless each and every bishop has given his consent."

Although Vatican II did not explicitly state that bishops' conferences have the authority to teach, there is evidence in the conciliar documents for such authority. *Christus Dominus*, article 11, described the pastoral office of the bishops as including teaching, sanctifying, and governing functions. In addition, article 38 declared: "An episcopal conference is a kind of council in which the bishops of a given nation or territory jointly exercise their pastoral office by way of promoting that greater good which the Church offers mankind." Furthermore, canon 753 states that bishops both individually and gathered in conferences of bishops or in particular councils are authentic teachers of the faith, and that believers are obliged to adhere to their teaching. A legitimate conclusion from these texts would seem to be that bishops performing their pastoral ministry in a group can teach collectively. Episcopal conferences, then, have a teaching authority.[61]

---

60. *The Ratzinger Report*, p. 60.
61. This argument is substantially present in A. Dulles, "Bishops' Conference," 530, and Ladislas Orsy, "Episcopal Conferences: Their Theological Standing and Their Doctrinal Authority," *America*, November 8, 1986, pp. 282-285.

Cardinal Ratzinger is correct, of course, in insisting that the episcopal conference should not interfere with the authority of an individual bishop in his own diocese. The 1985 synod said that the episcopal conference should recognize "the inalienable responsibility of each bishop in relation to the universal Church and the particular Church."[62] The conference, however, can assist the local bishop in his own ministry by providing information, support, and direction. The observation of Bishop Malone is pertinent: "The conference does not substitute for the voice of individual bishops, but it provides a framework within which a coherent theological, moral, and social vision can be articulated and a sense of direction for the Church can be determined."[63]

A more difficult aspect of this question, which is beyond the scope of this book, concerns the obligation to assent to the teachings of episcopal conferences. Are the dissenting minority bishops in an episcopal conference bound by the decision of the majority, or can they teach a different opinion in their own dioceses? Can the faithful choose the teaching of the conference over their own dissenting bishop, or can they refuse to assent to the teaching of their own conference and bishop and assent rather to the different teaching of another conference?

These theoretical choices are perhaps more probable in regard to statements that deal with concrete political issues and strategies. The two most recent pastorals from the U.S. bishops briefly discussed assent. In "The Challenge of Peace" (1983) the bishops said that not everything in the letter has the same moral authority. They referred to universally binding moral principles and the teachings of recent Popes and Vatican II; they also applied moral principles to specific cases. Noting that such application involves prudential judgments that may be interpreted differently by people of good will, the bishops concluded: "The moral judgments we make in specific cases, while not binding in conscience, are to be given serious attention and consideration by Catholics, as they determine whether their moral judgments are consistent with the Gospel."[64] The pastoral "Economic Justice for All" (1986) made a similar distinction.[65]

---

62. *Extraordinary Synod*, p. 19.
63. *Origins*, November 29, 1984, vol. 14, no. 24:388.
64. *Origins*, May 19, 1983, vol. 13, no. 1:3.
65. *Origins*, November 27, 1986, vol. 16, no. 24:411–412.

Relationship to Rome

A final question, one that looks explicitly to the issue of limiting papal power, concerns the relationship between episcopal conferences and Rome. Conferences with excessive nationalistic preoccupations would seriously affect the bond of communion between the local Churches and their connection with the Bishop of Rome. There would also be a danger of destructive fragmentation if conferences issued contradictory statements on the same topic and thus generated confusion among the Catholic faithful. Initiatives and creative actions should be welcomed from various parts of the Church as different expressions of unity, but they should be in harmony and not in competition with the teaching of the Pope.

Rome, at times, may be justified in coordinating the efforts of episcopal conferences. It has the right to reconcile differences between conferences and encourage mutual cooperation and support. Several national conferences of bishops have collaborated with Rome in the last decade. In June 1981, the bishops of Central America met for a consultation in Rome, and in October 1984 the Peruvian bishops met. In January 1983, representatives from the U.S. bishops' conference assembled in Rome with representatives of European bishops' conferences and Vatican officials to discuss the second draft of the American bishops' pastoral on war and peace. The participants found these exchanges helpful.[66]

Perhaps the most unusual and significant episcopal meeting was the three-day conference in Rome (March 13-15, 1986) with the Pope, twenty-one bishops from the Brazilian hierarchy, and ten officials from key curial offices. This meeting expressed collegiality in a new form, yet it differed in many ways from the consultations mentioned above. It was the culmination of the Brazilian *ad limina* visits that involved a year-long process of contact between the Brazilian bishops and curial offices; it was suggested by the Brazilian episcopal conference itself; and it dealt with broad issues rather than specific ones. Most importantly, John Paul II was present throughout the morning and afternoon sessions. The purpose of the meeting was to renew, deepen, and improve dialogue, which was recognized as a way to achieve communion. From all accounts it was successful.

---

66. *Origins*, April 7, 1983, vol. 12, no. 43:690-696.

This informal meeting encouraged open exchange between the curial officials and the bishops in the presence of the Pope.[67]

Although such consultations do not presently have formal canonical status, they may set a precedent for the future. They have intriguing implications for episcopal collegiality and the development of dialogue within the Church. The Pope, his advisors in the Curia, and the bishops meeting together could share their common concerns in an atmosphere of genuine dialogue. Other national conferences might welcome such a meeting as a positive step in linking the local Churches more closely with the Church of Rome.

In juridical terms the episcopal conference may not be an example of collegiality in the fullest sense. But the life of the Church overflows juridical categories, and it is clear that episcopal conferences have made valuable contributions to the Church since the Council. The 1985 synod called the episcopal conferences "useful, indeed necessary in the present-day pastoral work of the Church."[68] Yet, as our analysis indicates, there is much uncertainty and disagreement over some of the practical implementations of collegiality in the form of bishops' conferences. To help clarify the situation, the 1985 synod recommended that further study be made of the theological status and the doctrinal authority of episcopal conferences, especially in the light of *Christus Dominus*, article 38, and canons 447 and 753.

Conclusion

Collegiality limits papal authoritarianism but fosters the optimal use of papal authority. The Synod of Bishops and episcopal conferences, which have been approved and encouraged by recent Popes, also limit but indirectly any disproportionate exercise of papal power. In the decision-making process the collegial interaction among bishops is a balancing factor that protects the Church from unilateral and isolated leadership.

---

67. For an analysis of this meeting see Peter Coughlan, "Quiet Breakthrough in Rome," *The Tablet* (London), 29 March/5 April, 1986, pp. 356–357. The Pope's letter to the Brazilian bishops is in *Origins*, May 22, 1986, vol. 16, no. 1:12–15.

68. *Extraordinary Synod*, p. 21.

Understood in the broader context of communion, collegiality seeks to promote greater collaboration between the Pope and the bishops in their governance of the entire Church. The College of Bishops has a sacramental relationship to the Bishop of Rome, who is a fellow member and head of the college. If the collegial principle operated effectively in Church governance, the Pope's power would not be diminished, but it would be exercised differently and ultimately enhanced. It would encourage greater communication between the Pope and the bishops and preserve the rights of both offices.

Has collegiality, which Edward Schillebeeckx called in 1967 a "mysterious reality which lies dormant in the lap of the Church,"[69] realized its potential? Has it been adequately received? Yes and no.

On the positive side, collegiality—the sharing of authority by Pope and bishops—has accomplished much. First, it has restored at least a theoretical balance to ecclesiology by countering the one-sided papalism of the past. Second, it has fostered a greater recognition of the local Church and its role in the larger world Church. Third, it has led to the establishment of ecclesial institutions, like the Synod of Bishops and the episcopal conference, to foster dialogue and accountability. Fourth, it has encouraged ecumenical relations by making the papacy more acceptable to other Christians.

On the negative side, collegiality proves to be a promise as yet unfulfilled. First, the Church has neither sufficiently communicated this insight of Vatican II nor overcome widespread objections to it. The various bearers of authority in the Church must engage in more active fraternal interaction. Second, the Church, in its official capacity as teacher and pastor, continues to manifest a centralist tendency to view itself as one large diocese. Rome still considers subsidiarity and legitimate diversity as threatening. Collegiality cannot function at the diocesan level if it is not operative at the curial level. Thus, the Dutch bishops asked: "Has the Holy See sufficiently accepted that collegiality which it demands of others?"[70] Third, the Church needs more effective structures and procedures for the exercise of collegiality on all levels, if it is to be a living reality. We have

---

69. *The Real Achievement of Vatican II* (New York: Herder and Herder, 1967), p. 15.

70. *Synode extraordinaire*, p. 255.

only begun the process. Fourth, the Church is still perceived, by Catholics and others, as a public institution that all too often acts in a monarchical way.

In conclusion, collegiality, if it is to be more than a great but abstract idea, must be freely appropriated and selflessly carried out by popes and bishops. With the Trinity as its role model, the College of Bishops, head and members, can then witness by their dialogic fruitfulness to "the faith which operates through charity" (Gal. 5:6). An effective collegial Church would help make the *Koinonia* a more visible and credible witness to the abiding presence of the Spirit in the world. Through its relationship with Christ, the Church can become, in the words of *Lumen gentium*, what it truly is, namely, "a sacrament or sign of intimate union with God and of the unity of the human race" (art. 10).

·V·

The Church of Rome
and the Local Church

*The Pope alone is the universal bishop
of all the Churches.*

—*St. Peter Damian**

*The Pope is the Bishop of Rome, not the
bishop of the world as though the world
were all one diocese.*

—*Bishop Kenneth E. Untener*†

The limitations of the papacy in relation to the local Church continues to reflect an ongoing dialectical tension. Any discussion of the limits of the papacy has to take into account the unique relationship between the local Churches throughout the world and the local Church of Rome—the Church of Peter and Paul. How we understand this relationship shapes our view of Church, papacy, and episcopacy. In turn it throws new light on the Pope's role as universal pastor.

The term "Church" can be understood in many different ways. From all the possible connotations, three obvious meanings emerge. First, Church may mean the entire body of believers who confess the Lordship of Jesus. Christians throughout the world, whatever their particular denomination, belong to the Church of Christ. This universality applies both to the association of all Christians living today and to their kinship with all Christians from the time of Christ.

Second, Church may mean the hierarchy, the central authority figures—the Pope and the bishops. We often speak of the teaching of the Church on a particular point as the official position of the Pope and the bishops on a doctrinal or moral issue. Medieval proponents

---

* Opusc. 23, cap. 1, *Patrologia latina* 145:474.
† "Local Church and Universal Church," *America*, October 13, 1984, p. 201.

of this usage, as Congar points out, never denied that the community called Church is made up of all the faithful, but they did have a diminished view of the full reality of the Church.[1] To equate the Church with the hierarchy is to make a part identical with the whole. If taken to an extreme, this idea can lead to an ecclesiology that promotes clerical triumphalism, disregards the gifts of the entire community, and discourages broad participation in Church life.

Third, Church may mean the local Church—the concrete realization of the Church in a particular geographical place: the Church in Corinth, Carthage, Rome, New York, or Paris. A diocese or several dioceses, a parish, a religious community, or smaller Christian assemblies may all be called local Churches. The cultural dimensions of the local Church contribute to its uniqueness and determine its role in the universal Church. Vatican II recognized the legitimacy and importance of the local Church and gave us a rich source of theological insights. One of the achievements of the Council, according to Alois Grillmeier, was a twofold rediscovery: "the rediscovery of the universal Church as the sum and communion of the local Churches, understood fully as themselves, and the rediscovery of the universal Church in the local Church."[2] In a similar vein, Emmanuel Lanne speaks of the Council's theology of the local Church as a Copernican revolution: the local Church does not revolve around the universal Church; rather the Church of God exists in every celebration of the eucharist.[3]

The three ways of speaking of the Church are, of course, interrelated. This chapter will reflect on the relation between particularity and universality and the unique position of the Church of Rome. I shall present first the broad principles undergirding the meaning of the local and universal Church, second the relative autonomy of the local Church vis-à-vis the primatial role of the Church of Rome, and finally the meaning of the principle of subsidiarity. Our goal here, as elsewhere, is to discern a further aspect of the limits of the papacy.

---

1. Yves Congar gives several examples of this usage from the twelfth to the sixteenth century in *Lay People in the Church* (Westminster, Md.: Newman, 1957), p. 42. note 22.

2. In Herbert Vorgrimler, ed., *Commentary on the Documents of Vatican II* (New York: Herder and Herder, 1967), I:167.

3. "L'Eglise locale et l'Eglise universelle," *Irénikon* 43 (1970):490.

The Local Church and the Universal Church

The contemporary theology of the local Church, a retrieval of an ancient tradition, represents a major shift in our understanding of Church. Theologians in the two centuries before Vatican II tended to view the Church as a perfect society; that is, a society that is complete and independent in itself and posesses all the means necessary to attain its proposed end.[4] "Perfect" does not refer to holiness or excellence but to autonomy and self-sufficiency. First used by canonists, the perfect-society ecclesiology, a product of the eighteenth and nineteenth centuries, was gradually adopted by the magisterium and theologians. They argued that both the Church and the state are perfect societies, and each should operate without interference from the other. This conceptual argument was used to protect the Church from any external interference from the state that sought to control it. What began, however, as a political expedient ended up as a description of the essence of the Church.

Perfect-society ecclesiology encouraged the development of a juridical view of the Church and a preoccupation with external and hierarchical elements. Furthermore, it discouraged ecumenical dialogue, since it equated the true Church of Christ and the perfect society. The Roman Catholic Church was considered to be the only true Church, so all other Christian Churches were in effect non-Churches. Finally, perfect-society ecclesiology fostered a universalist ecclesiology that left little room for a theology of the local Church, stressing as it did papal power and the privileged role of the universal Church. Dioceses are not perfect societies because they do not possess the fullness of legislative, judicial, and coercive power. This universalism resulted in other ecclesiological formulations: the universal Church is the source of the local Churches; bishops receive their authority from the Pope; uniformity is the ideal and diversity the exception. Centralization and monarchical governance became

---

4. See P. Granfield, "The Rise and Fall of *Societas Perfecta*," in Peter Huizing and Knut Walf, eds., *May Church Ministers Be Politicians? Concilium* no. 157 (New York: Seabury, 1982), 3–8, and "The Church as *Societas Perfecta* in the Schemata of Vatican I," *Church History* 48 (1979):431–446.

normative, and the entire Church was looked upon as one large diocese with the Pope as bishop.[5]

Vatican II took a different approach by reaffirming the presence of the universal Church in the local Church. The documents of Vatican II, their translations and commentaries, and the theological literature used various terms to designate the local Christian community in contradistinction to the universal Church. The two most common terms are "particular" and "local." At times they are used interchangeably. The Council and the Code of Canon Law (can. 368) use the term "particular Church" to refer to a diocese, a patriarchal Church, or Churches of the same rite, region, or culture. Yet the term "local Church" is also used in the Council documents and by theologians.[6]

The local Church may be defined in two ways that reflect the meaning or intention of Vatican II. In the *strict* sense the local Church is that community of Christians called together by the Holy Spirit; under the leadership of the bishop, priests, and other ministers, it preaches the Word, celebrates the eucharist and other sacraments, and manifests the redemptive work of Christ in the world. The local Church, then, is primarily the diocese, but it may refer to several dioceses in the same nation or region (the Church in the United States) or to Churches in the same rite (the Maronite Church).

The two essential features of this definition are the bishop and the eucharist. The earliest local Churches were established along the great trade routes of the Roman Empire and were centered around the bishop as successor of the Apostles. He presided over his congregation, preached the Word, celebrated the Lord's Supper, and sought to create an atmosphere of joy and peace in the living Spirit

---

5. For historical sources related to this idea see Yves Congar, "De la communion des Eglises à une ecclésiologie de l'Eglise universelle," in Yves Congar and Bernard-Dominique Dupuy, eds., *L'épiscopat et l'Eglise universelle* (Paris: Cerf, 1962), pp. 238–239.

6. A major topic in the drafting of the 1983 Code of Canon Law concerned the status of personal prelatures and their relationship to local or particular Churches. The establishment of Opus Dei in 1982 — the first and so far the only such prelature — generated further interest. The Code (cans. 294–297) made it clear that personal prelatures are theologically and canonically distinct from particular Churches. For a detailed analysis of this question see Pedro Rodríguez, *Particular Churches and Personal Prelatures* (Dublin: Four Courts, 1986).

of Christ. The Council calls the bishops the "visible principle and foundation of unity in their own particular Churches" (*Lumen gentium*, art. 23). The bishop, assisted by priests and other ministers, is a shepherd of his flock, servant of Christ, and steward of the mysteries of God (1 Cor. 4:1). The preaching of the Gospel has pride of place in the episcopal ministry. As successors of the Apostles, bishops receive the mission to preach the Gospel to all creatures and to promote and safeguard the unity of faith and discipline common to the whole Church.

The eucharist, "the source and summit of the Christian life" (*Lumen gentium*, art. 11), is also essential to the meaning of the local Church in the strict sense. The eucharist is the *sacramentum ecclesiae*, the center of its life. The theology of the Church must be related to the doctrine of the eucharist, since the full mystery of the Church is actualized in the eucharistic celebration. "No other action of the Church," according to Vatican II, "can match its claim to efficacy, nor equal the degree of it" (*Sacrosanctum concilium*, art. 7). At the eucharist, the faithful are united with Christ and with one another. If it is true to say that the Church makes the eucharist, it is equally true that the eucharist makes the Church by establishing a covenant community. "The celebration of the eucharist," writes Karl Rahner, "is the most intensive event for the Church."[7]

In the *broad* sense, the local Church designates the parish (*Sacrosanctum concilium*, art. 42), the domestic Church or family (*Lumen gentium*, art. 11 and *Gaudium et spes,* art. 48), and other Christian assemblies (e.g., religious communities, basic Christian communities, etc.) Emmanuel Lanne presents the outer limits of the local Church in what he calls "an extreme case": "In the meeting of two or three Christians to pray for unity, there is a certain manifestation of communion, a kind of local Church—embryonic and unstable, if you will, but real."[8] These smaller groups are not complete in themselves but are related and ordered to the local Church in the strict sense and in communion with it.

Small-group Churches are increasing in the contemporary Roman

---

7. *The Episcopate and the Primacy* (New York: Herder and Herder, 1962), p. 25.

8. "The Local Church: Its Catholicity and Apostolicity," *One in Christ* 6 (1970):311.

Catholic world. In Latin America, for example, there are hundreds of thousands of basic ecclesial communities, Christian grass-roots communities called *comunidades eclesiales de base*. Brazil alone has some ninety thousand.[9]

In parts of Western Europe and in the United States the shortage of priests has meant that many parishes have only a weekly or even monthly eucharist; in these places the liturgy of the Word or paraliturgical services are becoming more common than the eucharistic celebration. The pastoral challenges inherent in this new phenomenon are obvious. The traditional priest-people relationship is changing in many places where lay or religious pastoral administrators deal with everything but the formal sacramental aspects of parish life.

In both the strict and the broad sense, these faith assemblies are not simply administrative units of the universal Church, but are concrete realizations, admittedly in varying degrees, of the entire mystery of the Body of Christ which is one. The local Church is the Church, because it possesses the entire promise of the Gospel, the full reality of the faith, and the grace of the Triune God. The local Church is the Church, because in it Christ is wholly present. In the words of Vatican II, "This Church of Christ is truly present [*vere adest*] in all legitimate local congregations of the faithful" (*Lumen gentium*, art. 26). The Church of Christ, then, develops from the local communities and has no existence apart from them.

The word *"ecclesia"* in the New Testament Church—at least in Corinthians, Romans, and Luke/Acts—meant first of all the local community that contained the full mystery of the Body of Christ and was related to other local Churches. The universal Church is not an abstraction; it does not exist without local Churches. One enters the Church only through a local Church; every Christian, including the Pope, belongs to some local Church. The Pope is the Bishop of Rome and head of the universal Church, but he is also a member of the local Church of Rome.

What then is the universal Church? It is not a mere collection or external union of many local Churches, but the communion of local

---

9. Leonardo Boff makes a strong argument for basic Christian communities as local Churches in *Ecclesiogenesis: The Basic Communities Reinvent the Church* (Maryknoll, N.Y.: Orbis, 1986).

Churches. The universal Church comes to be out of the mutual reception and communion of the local Churches united in faith and the Holy Spirit. The universal Church is the communion of local Churches. "In and from such particular Churches there comes into being the one and only Catholic Church" (*Lumen gentium*, art. 23). The local Church manifests the one, holy, catholic and apostolic Church, but it does not exhaust that reality. "The local Church is wholly the Church, but it is not the whole Church," wrote J. J. Von Allmen.[10]

Concretely, the universal Church realizes itself only in the local Churches that are united by the bond of communion. The local Churches throughout the world recognize one another and acknowledge their communal bonds. By enriching other local Churches, each Church contributes to the universal Church. The sharing of responsibilities and resources among local Churches fosters the wider mission of the Church.

The local and universal Church are not opposed but mutually dependent. The Church is universal because it is incarnate in a particular locality. Dialogue must exist between all the local Churches, because if there is communion there must also be communication. "Where there is one communion," writes St. Ambrose, "there should also be common judgment and harmonious consent."[11] Local Churches are not self-sufficient nor isolated; they do not stand alone but always in communion with other local Churches. Otherwise the unity of both the universal Church and the local Church is endangered. "The perfect identity of the local Churches," according to John Paul II, "is to be found in complete openness to the universal Church."[12]

The universal and the local Church are interrelated, but some tension is almost inevitable. The Indonesian hierarchy, for example, in their report to the 1985 Synod of Bishops asked that if the local Church has esteem for the universal Church, does the universal Church sufficiently esteem the local Church?[13] The Dutch bishops spoke of a certain lack of confidence by Rome and observed that at

---

10. "L'Eglise locale parmi les autres Eglises locales," *Irénikon* 43 (1970):512.

11. Epist. 13, 8. *Patrologia latina* 16:953.

12. Address to Bishops of Paupua, New Guinea and the Solomon Islands, *Osservatore Romano*, English edition, November 5, 1979, p. 13.

13. *Synode extraordinaire: Célébration de Vatican II* (Paris: Cerf, 1986), p. 229.

times universality is presented as essentially valid and particularity "as a deviation, as a concession to local conditions and not as an enrichment."[14] It is necessary, they continued, to recognize the concept of the local Church and legitimate pluralism in relationship to the universal Church, the Holy See, and the Curia. These observations lead us to our next section: the nature of the independence enjoyed by the local Churches in view of their link to the Church of Rome.

The Relative Autonomy of the Local Church

In the communion of Churches, the Church of Rome under the leadership of its bishop is considered by Roman Catholics to be the *prima sedes*—the First See, the Church with special authority in the universal Church. The concept of the local Church, then, is relational; its proper understanding and validity depend on its connection with other local Churches and with the *prima sedes*. The full catholicity of the Church is possible only when there is mutual communion between the local Churches and the Church of Peter and Paul.

The local Church is to some extent self-regulating. As a specific concretization of the Body of Christ, it controls its own destiny to a large degree. But the local Church remains a relational reality, only partially autonomous and always in contact with the shared faith of the universal Church and with the Church of Rome. The concept of limitation is involved here, because the Pope cannot act as if he were the only bishop in the world.

The Pope and the Diocesan Bishop

A delicate balance exists between the respective rights of the Pope and the diocesan bishops. Granted that the scope of power is different, the Pope and the bishops have many similar prerogatives. The following description makes this clear.

---

14. Ibid., p. 254.

Pope	Bishop
Papacy is of divine right. (Vatican I–DS 3058)	Episcopate is of divine right. (Vatican II–LG 20)
Pope is Vicar of Christ. (Vatican I–DS 3068)	Bishop is Vicar of Christ. (Vatican II–LG 27)
Pope has ordinary, immediate, and truly episcopal jurisdiction over the entire Church. He has full, supreme, and universal power. (Vatican I–DS 3060, 3064)	Bishop has proper, ordinary, and immediate power in his diocese. (Vatican II–LG 27)
Pope is the permanent and visible foundation of the unity of the bishops and the faithful. (Vatican II–LG 23)	Bishop is the visible principle and foundation of unity in his particular Church. (Vatican II–LG 23)

It would seem at first glance that there are two concurrent authorities or powers in the same place, and both are of divine institution. Although the purpose of the Pope's universal power is directed to the unity of the entire Church and not the daily administration of any one particular diocese, the potential for conflict is real.[15]

This problem, as we saw earlier in Chapter Two, has concerned the Church from the earliest days of the papacy. The Fathers of Vatican I spent much time debating whether the supreme power of the Pope over each diocese would interfere with the authority of the individual bishop. Some of the Fathers objected to the first draft of the constitution on the Church because it gave the impression that bishops are only vicars of the Supreme Pontiff.[16] Thus Bishop Connolly of Halifax, Nova Scotia, said that according to the schema "all the bishops of the Catholic Church equal zero, which is mathematically absurd."[17] Bishop Zinelli of the Deputation on the Faith explained that the Pope has the power to perform genuine episcopal acts in any diocese, but not indiscriminately. "If he [the Pope]

---

15. J. M. R. Tillard treats this issue in *The Bishop of Rome* (Wilmington, Del.: M. Glazier, 1983).

16. Mansi 51:957 B, 969 B.

17. Ibid., 52:817 C.

should as it were multiply his presence and should day after day and without regard for the local bishop tear down what the latter has prudently ordained, then he would be using his power to tear down and not to build up."[18] Calling such a possibility an "absurd supposition," which would subvert true spiritual administration, he advocated trust in the moderation of the Holy See "which will use its authority to protect, not to harm, the power of the bishops."[19]

In a more formal statement, the Council itself declared that there is no conflict between the Pope and the bishops. In a concise summary of the theology of the episcopate, the Council taught:

> This power of the Supreme Pontiff is far from standing in the way of the power of ordinary and immediate episcopal jurisdiction by which the bishops who, under the appointment of the Holy Spirit, succeeded in the place of the Apostles, feed and rule individually, as true shepherds, the particular flock assigned to them. Rather their episcopal power is asserted, confirmed, and vindicated by this same supreme and universal shepherd.[20]

This same issue appeared again shortly after Vatican I when, in 1874, the Imperial Chancellor Bismarck of Germany published a circular severely critical of the Council's teaching on papal primacy and infallibility. For him, Vatican I meant that the Pope is an absolute monarch who takes the place of each bishop in his diocese, making them his agents. The German bishops rejected Bismarck's assertions in their 1875 response. The Pope, they stated, is the Bishop of Rome, not the bishop of any other diocese—Cologne, Breslau, or anywhere else. Yet the Pope is the shepherd of the entire Church and has the duty to see that each bishop properly carries out the duties of his office.

The German bishops made seven assertions that directly contradicted Bismarck. Pius IX praised them for presenting "the true meaning of the Vatican decrees."[21]

---

18. Ibid., 52:1105 C D.

19. Idem.

20. DS 3061. The essence of this passage is repeated in *Lumen gentium*, article 27, and canon 333, 1.

21. The text of the German bishops' response and the letter of Pius IX is in DS 3112-17, and the English translation in TCC 388 a. Also see texts and commentary

1) The Pope cannot claim the rights of the bishops or substitute his authority for theirs.

2) Episcopal jurisdiction is not absorbed into papal jurisdiction.

3) The Pope does not possess the fullness of episcopal authority in such a way as to replace the power of the bishops.

4) The Pope does not in principle replace each individual bishop.

5) The Pope cannot in dealing with the government take the place of the bishop at any given moment.

6) The bishops are not tools of the Pope with no proper responsibility.

7) The bishops are not agents of a foreign sovereign in their relation with a government.

Diocesan bishops are not mere functionaries of the Pope; they possess proper, ordinary, and immediate power that they exercise in the name of Christ. Yet episcopal authority is not unlimited; bishops are still subject to the Pope. The Pope does not exercise daily and continual power in a diocese and should not intervene arbitrarily. Leo XIII argued that there is no conflict between papal and episcopal authority, since they are not of equal rank. "The power of the Roman Pontiff is supreme, universal, and absolutely independent, whereas the power of the bishops is fixed within definite limits and is not absolutely independent."[22]

Vatican II's doctrine of collegiality helped clarify the relationship between the Pope and the bishops. But concern was occasionally raised. Paul VI, in his apostolic letter *Pastorale Munus* (November 30, 1963), conceded forty faculties and eight privileges to the bishops.[23] Some of the faculties were minor—the right to dispense blind priests from the Breviary or to authorize nuns to wash altar linens the first time—but others were significant—the power to dispense from certain marriage impediments and to absolve most reserved censures. Patriarch Maximos IV of Antioch, apropos of the discussion of this issue at the Council, made the following observation:

Some of the "faculties" which it is proposed to "delegate" to bishops make one wonder: the "faculty" to allow the bishop to keep the Blessed

---

by Olivier Rousseau, "Le vrai valeur de l'épiscopat dans l'Eglise d'après d'importants documents," *Irénikon* 29 (1956):131–150.

22. DS 1961.

23. *Acta apostolicae sedis*, 56 (1964):5–12.

Sacrament in his chapel . . . to permit priests to offer two or three Masses a day, to allow nuns to wash corporal, purificators, and palls *prima quoque ablutione*. Really, if a successor of the Apostles cannot on his authority allow nuns to wash purificators, what can he do? The length to which the theory of the Pope as the source of all authority has gone shows how much it needs drastic revision if we are ever to get a sound ecclesiology.[24]

The same concern, though less colorfully phrased, was expressed in some of the reports from the episcopal conferences to the 1985 Synod of Bishops. In words reminiscent of some of the interventions at Vatican I, the bishops of Scandinavia and Finland said that it was their impression that "in the Church, the proper power of jurisdiction of the bishops is more understood as a delegated power and the bishop, in this view, is simply the representative of the Pope."[25] The Indonesian bishops also noted that some of their colleagues think that Rome is trying to limit the liberty of the bishops.[26]

In the United States, the Vatican's treatment of Archbishop Raymond G. Hunthausen of Seattle, which we mentioned in Chapter One, is a striking example of conflict. In an unusual move, Rome ordered the archbishop to hand over to his auxiliary bishop Donald Wuerl five major areas of diocesan governance with final decision-making power. Several bishops reacted immediately. Bishop Thomas J. Gumbleton, Auxiliary Bishop of Detroit, called the action "cruel" and "demeaning" and felt it would intimidate other American bishops: "They'll always be looking over their shoulder to see who's watching and afraid to speak out."[27] Bishop Leroy T. Mattheisen of Amarillo, Texas, saw it as "being part of the effort to centralize, to control."[28] However, Cardinal Bernard F. Law of Boston said that the Vatican had acted correctly. "It appears that certain erroneous practices were so widespread that concern was manifested by priests, laity, and neighboring bishops, leading to the

---

24. Quoted in Hervé Legrand, "Nature de l'Eglise particulière et rôle de l'évêque dans l'Eglise," in P. Veuillot, ed., *Décret sur la charge pastorale des évêques dans l'Eglise* (Paris: Cerf, 1969), p. 122.

25. *Synode extraordinaire*, p. 274.

26. Ibid., 229.

27. *New York Times*, September 18, 1986, p. B15.

28. Ibid.

intervention of the Holy See. Not to have acted would have been irresponsible."[29]

The Hunthausen case raises several problems. On the basis of what has been published, it would seem that Rome did have sufficient grounds at least for being concerned with certain pastoral practices in the Archdiocese of Seattle. One may disagree with the final outcome, but Rome had the right and duty to settle the conflict in some manner. Communication between the Holy See and Archbishop Hunthausen began in 1978. The resolution, however, was unsatisfying for all parties concerned: Hunthausen, Wuerl, the Vatican and, especially, the people of Seattle. The procedure employed raises problems in three particular areas.

First, the facts of the case are not clear to us. The chronologies released by Hunthausen and the Vatican were not in complete agreement. This discrepancy, for whatever reason, only added to the confusion. The documents indicate that Rome and Hunthausen had different understandings about the "special faculties" that would be given to the auxiliary bishop. A failure of communication was obvious.

Second, the secrecy surrounding the investigation also created difficulties. Because of the seriousness of the matter, Rome was justified in acting discretely. But Hunthausen said that he never received the full report sent to Rome by Archbishop Hickey. It has been argued that confidentiality was rightly preserved and that it was proper not to identify those who were critical of Hunthausen during the formal visitation by Archbishop Hickey. On the other hand. basic fairness would seem to dictate that the charges and the names of those who made them should have been given to Hunthausen. The Vatican's refusal to do this put him at a disadvantage and severely limited his ability to respond adequately to the objections.

Third, the episcopal conference was not directly involved. Even though the conference did not have juridical authority, it would seem, on the basis of collegiality, that the first level of recourse should have been the episcopal conference; Rome should have been appealed to only as the last step. Hunthausen's observation in his address to his fellow bishops has merit:

---

29. *The Pilot* (Boston), October 31, 1986.

> I believe, too, it is the proper role of a conference such as this to address the issue of legitimacy as well as the limits of adaptation which are truly reflective of a particular Church, its history, traditions, and life-style, not to mention its special characteristics and problems.[30]

The action of the National Conference of Catholic Bishops at their meeting in November 1986 was predictable. The bishops expressed concern for the parties involved, said that they had no legal competence to judge the case, and affirmed their loyalty to the Holy See. Given the delicacy of the situation, the confusion over the facts, the media attention devoted to it, and the diversity of opinion within the conference itself, the final statement was reasonable.

The conference's response was not, as some have suggested, a failure in collegiality or a sign of the weakness of the American hierarchy. A public confrontational statement rebuking the action of the Vatican—assuming that it would have been possible given the mixed feelings in the membership of the conference—would have accomplished little. It would have divided the bishops, polarized the faithful, and harmed the Church in Seattle. Other more private channels, however, exist whereby individual bishops can communicate their opinion in person or through correspondence to the Pope and to the Curia. Behind-the-scenes negotiations with Rome had been underway for several months before the Vatican appointed the three-member episcopal commission in January 1987 to assess the situation in Seattle.*

The Pope as Center of Unity

The Catholic understanding of the theology of the local Church means that in the family of Churches, the *communio ecclesiarum*, the See of Rome has a unique function to preserve the unity of faith in the other Churches. The purpose of the Pope's universal authority is not to absorb the apostolic responsibility of the local bishop. The Pope as Bishop of the Church of Peter and Paul manifests solicitude for all the Churches; he is at the service of the universal communion. Exercising his particular charism of leadership, the Pope acts as the center or guardian of the faith. This theme was stated by Paul VI at

---

30. *Origins*, November 20, 1986, vol. 16, no. 23:404.

* For the most recent developments in the Hunthausen case, see the addendum on page 196.

the beginning of the third session of Vatican II, when he declared that the Apostolic See needed the bishops in order that the catholicity of the Church would have consistency and shape: "You need a center, a principle of unity in faith and communion, and you will find it in the See of Peter."[31]

The Bishop of Rome, then, protects and encourages the ecclesiality of the Churches. As a unifier, he deals with those doctrinal and disciplinary realities that are essential to the unity of the Churches. He takes responsibility for sound teaching, fosters mutual cooperation between the Churches, and arbitrates differences. But the Pope is also limited; he cannot impose uniformity as if the whole world were the Diocese of Rome.

Vatican II called the Pope "the perpetual and visible principle and foundation of the unity of the bishops and of the multitude of the faithful" (*Lumen gentium*, art. 23). The term "principle" (*principium*) is translated as "source" in some of the English versions of the Council documents.[32] That interpretation can lead to confusion. Theologically it is more precise to call the Pope the principle, center, or foundation of unity rather than the source. Yves Congar has observed that Rome is the center of ecclesial communion without being its source.[33]

Jesus through his Spirit is the ultimate principle and source of unity in the Church. The Patriarch Maximos IV insisted on this point at the Council: "It should be clear that the only head of the Church, the only head of the Body of Christ which is the Church, is our Savior Jesus Christ, and him alone. It is not fitting to say of the Roman Pontiff, what one says of Christ, that he is the head of the Church."[34]

---

31. *Acta apostolicae sedis* (1964):813.

32. In both the Abbott-Gallagher and the Flannery editions. The Holy Office under Pius IX referred to the papacy as "the principle, root, and indefectible source [*origo*]" of unity (DS 2888).

33. "Autonomie et pouvoir central dans l'Eglise vus par la théologie catholique," *Irénikon* 43 (1980):291–313, esp. 302 and 312.

34. *Acta synodalia sacrosancti concilii oecumenici Vaticani II* (Vatican City: Typis Polyglottis Vaticanis, 1972), vol. II, part 2, 239. *Lumen gentium* used the term "*caput*" (head) twenty-eight times to refer to Christ and the Pope. Christ is called the head of the Body which is the Church seventeen times (arts. 7, 9, 13, 17, 28, 30, 33, 50, 52). The Pope is called "head" eleven times: "the visible head of the whole Church" (art. 18) and, more frequently, "the head of the College of Bishops" (arts. 21, 22, 25, and several times in the *Nota praevia*).

The See of Rome, then, is the center of unity in the universal Church. The 1985 Synod of Bishops spoke of "the center of unity given to us by Christ in the service of Peter."[35] Diversity, however, has coexisted with unity from the earliest days of the Church. A plurality of cultures, religious expressions, theologies, and traditions need not undermine the unity of faith. Within the one communion of the Catholic Church, for example, we have several rites, two Codes of Canon Law, celibate and married priests, leavened and unleavened bread, and a wide variety of liturgical rituals. God's revelation and its theological expression are always incarnate in particular cultural and historical situations. Pluralism exists among the local Churches within the framework of essential unity.[36]

Throughout the history of the Church diverse customs and theologies flourished without breaking the bond of communion.[37] Augustine formulated the operative principle: "It is legitimate to think differently as long as communion is preserved."[38] Different liturgical expressions were common for centuries, but there was also a definite policy of many Popes to promote uniformity in accord with the liturgy celebrated in Rome.[39]

The Pope has the responsibility to protect both unity and diversity. The ideal is the complementarity of diversities and not simply uniformity, which may impede the work of the Spirit in diverse cultures and historical situations. The papal charism is to evaluate valid diversity and to allow it to enrich the unity of the entire Church. It is the role of the local Churches to embody the Church in their various

---

35. *Extraordinary Synod of Bishops, Rome 1985: A Message to the People of God and the Final Report* (Washington: NCCB, 1986), p. 18.

36. The 1985 synod made the unusual distinction between pluraformity and pluralism. Pluraformity is richness, fullness, and hence, true catholicity. On the other hand, "the pluralism of fundamentally opposed positions instead leads to dissolution, destruction, and the loss of identity" (p. 18).

37. The history of this development is given by Yves Congar in "Autonomie central," and by Emmanuel Lanne, "Les différences campatibles avec l'unité dans la tradition de l'Eglise ancienne," *Istina* 8 (1961–62):227:253.

38. *De Baptismo*, II, 3, 5, *Patrologia latina* 43:141.

39. See Pierre-Marie Gy, "L'unification liturgique de l'occident et la liturgie de la curie romaine," in Conférences Saint-Serge, XXIIe semaine d'études liturgiques (1975), *Liturgie de l'Eglise particulière et liturgie de l'Eglise universelle* (Rome: Edizioni liturgiche, 1976), pp. 155–167, and S. J. P. Van Dijk and J. Hazelden Walker, *The Origins of the Modern Roman Liturgy* (Westminster, Md.: Newman, 1960).

locales in accordance with their diverse situations and cultures. The papal role is to watch over this development and to see that the bonds of unity are preserved.

This task, as the bishops of England and Wales noted, is not easy: "Deciding where there must be unity and where there can be diversity is a difficulty which constantly faces the Church. It is a difficulty which cannot be resolved easily or quickly."[40] A sound pluralism can contribute to the vitality of the local Churches and the universal Church. It is a sign of strength and not a sign of weakness. "Each of these churches," says John Paul II, "brings its own 'gifts' to the whole. True pluralism is never a divisive force but an element which contributes to the building up of unity in the universal communion of the Church."[41] *Lumen gentium* makes this same point in article 13.

The Principle of Subsidiarity

Another dimension of the limits of the papacy focuses on the division of authority between the Pope and the local Churches. Is centralization a necessary characteristic of primacy or is decentralization possible and even desirable? The issue here concerns the principle of subsidiarity, a basic element in human societies that also has significant ramifications for the ecclesial community. Subsidiarity also raises the question of limitation: the Pope should not do for all other local Churches what they can well do for themselves.

This section presents, first, the meaning of the principle of subsidiarity; second, the call from the local Churches for its implementation; third, some criteria that determine papal intervention in the life of the local Church; and fourth, a response to objections raised against subsidiarity.

The Meaning of Subsidiarity

The principle of subsidiarity is part of the Church's social teaching. Pius XI in *Quadragesimo anno* (1931) called it a "fundamental prin-

---

40. *Origins*, September 5, 1985, vol. 15, no. 12:181.
41. Ibid., January 10, 1985, vol. 14, no. 13:499–500.

ciple of social philosophy" that is "fixed and unchangeable." He described it as follows:

> One should not withdraw from individuals and commit to the community what they can accomplish by their own enterprise and industry. So too it is an injustice and at the same time a grave evil and a disturbance of right order, to transfer to the larger and higher collectivity functions which can be performed and provided for by lesser and subordinate bodies.[42]

John XXIII elaborated these ideas and expanded their application in *Mater et magistra* (1961) and *Pacem in terris* (1963). The principle of subsidiarity rests on the idea that society exists for the person and not the reverse. In the words of *Gaudium et spes* (art. 63): "Man is the source, the center and the purpose of all socioeconomic life." Society provides for its citizens what is necessary in view of their limitations. It assists individuals and small groups that make up the social body; it does not substitute for them.

The purpose of societal action is restricted to those areas that are necessary. The state must recognize the rights of the intermediate communities, determine how individuals and communities interact, and promote the dignity of the human person. What individuals and small groups can do for themselves, using their own resources and energies, should not be absorbed or destroyed by larger social bodies. The principle of subsidiarity, a principle of acting, implies a division of competencies and cooperation, and seeks to prevent the excessive power of larger communities.

Does the principle of subsidiarity apply to the Church? Yes, according to Pius XII. He declared that the subsidiary function "is valid for social life in all its organizations and also for the life of the Church, without prejudice to its hierarchical structure."[43] This principle is found in *Lumen gentium*, even though the word itself does not appear.[44] The Council developed this theme in light of its teaching on the radical sacramental equality of all Christians and the full

---

42. *Acta apostolicae sedis* 23 (1931):203.

43. *Acta apostolicae sedis* 38 (1946):145.

44. See Otto Karrer, "Le principe de subsidiarité dans l'Eglise," in Guilherme Baraúna, ed., *L'Eglise de Vatican II* (Paris: Cerf, 1967), pp. 575–606.

ecclesial reality of the local Church. The doctrines of collegiality and lay participation encouraged the members of the Church to act rightly, freely, and responsibly.

Good pastoral authority, then, does not rule by fear or threats, but realizes that the People of God incarnate in the local Church possess freedom because the Spirit is within them (2 Cor. 3:17). Wilhelm Bertrams has argued that "the principle of subsidiarity can and must be applied to the Church, to the extent that the Church is an authentically human society and carries on its life through organized social activity."[45] The supernatural character of the Church does not render this principle useless.

At the practical level of Church life, the principle of subsidiarity respects different functions, charisms, and responsibilities. By affirming that problems should, when possible, be resolved at the local level, it encourages individual and small-group participation. The central authority of the Church should acknowledge the competence of the local Church and of episcopal conferences and only rarely intervene in their activities.[46] Subsidiarity is a mandate for legitimate diversity in opposition to uniformity and is a call for decentralization. Concretely it means that Rome should not interfere when smaller groups in the Church can manage their own affairs. Rome should encourage the participatory decision-making of episcopal conferences, diocesan pastoral councils, and parish councils.

The Call for Subsidiarity

To illustrate the demand for more effective subsidiarity in the universal Church, an examination of the presynodal reports of the episcopal conferences offers compelling evidence. These reports, sent to Rome in preparation for the 1985 synod, contain specific recommendations. A recurring theme was the need to clarity the relationship between the local and universal Church.

The Swiss bishops, for example, lamented the climate of distrust

---

45. "De principio subsidiaritatis in iure canonico," *Periodica de re morali, canonica, liturgica* 46 (1946):63. Also see his "Das Subsidiaritätsprinzip in der Kirche," *Stimmen der Zeit* 169 (1957):262-267.

46. Cardinal Daniélou spoke of the richness of the principle of subsidiarity as a way of organizing the Church and called it "extrêmement valable" (*Osservatore Romano*, French edition, March 13, 1970, p. 7).

between the local and universal Church and urged the reestablish-
ment of mutual trust.[47] The bishops of England and Wales said that
it is important that papal and episcopal authority allow the lower
levels of the Church to assume sufficient responsibility to achieve
their purpose and to become genuine expressions of the Church of
Christ.[48] Both the Swiss and English bishops also argued for greater
episcopal collegiality and freedom to exercise true responsibility.
The Dutch bishops pointed out that consultation and advice must
operate at both the diocesan and the Roman levels of authority.
Other important observations also emerge from these reports.

First, several of the episcopal conferences referred explicitly to the
principle of subsidiarity: Brazil, Canada, England, Indonesia,
North Africa, and Scandinavia. Almost all the others equivalently
expressed similar ideas in their requests for greater autonomy. The
English bishops stated that the principle of subsidiarity "must give
shape to the exercise of authority in the Church."[49] For the Canadian bishops, subsidiarity is the hinge of the Church's social
teaching and must be applied more effectively to the Church itself.[50]
The North Africans saw subsidiarity as a guarantee of the dynamism
of the Spirit,[51] and the Scandinavians pleaded for its more consistent
use in the Church.[52] The latter further insisted that the life of the
local Church must be allowed to develop without external interference by papal representatives.

Second, many of the reports criticized the growing centralization
in the Church. This objection took various forms. Some of the bishops (England, Netherlands, Indonesia, Brazil, and Scandinavia)
argued that in the nomination of bishops greater attention should
be paid to the advice of the diocesan bishop or the episcopal conference; they also suggested more consultation with the local Churches.
The list of episcopal candidates mentioned by the conferences should
not be rejected without further questions being asked (Scandinavia).
The Canadian bishops spoke of a tendency toward centralization
and uniformity, and the Scandinavians of an overemphasis on the

---

47. *Synod extraordinaire*, pp. 293-294.
48. *Origins*, September 5, 1985, vol. 15, no. 12:180.
49. Idem.
50. *Synode extraordinaire*, p. 176.
51. Ibid., p. 71.
52. Ibid., p. 274.

papacy, the Curia, and the papal nuncio. The latter also urged better communication between the Vatican and the local Churches, especially when important documents are issued. At times, they said, the text arrives after it has already been announced publicly, making it difficult for diocesan authorities to respond to the media.

Third, there was clear dissatisfaction with the Roman Curia. The Swiss reported that the faithful, priests, and bishops were still waiting impatiently for the reform of the Curia announced by recent Popes. The Indonesians called for decentralization of the Curia and said that some feel "that the attitude of the Roman Curia seems at times to be insufficiently 'dialogic' and collegial, and very demanding."[53] In order to improve the relations between the Curia and the bishops, they made several suggestions: that the Curia encourage subsidiarity and dialogue; that the local Churches have greater freedom to decide liturgical and marriage questions; and that local Churches receive greater encouragement to develop the spirit of Vatican II in accord with their own special situations. The Brazilian bishops listed among the postconciliar difficulties the centralism of the Curia which does not always respect the particularities of the local Churches and increases tensions.

Several conferences (England, North Africa, Belgium, and Indonesia) said that the too frequent interventions of the curial congregations did not correspond with the theology of Vatican II. The English observed that "a difficulty arises when decisions which could be made locally have to be referred to Rome, e.g., permissions for liturgical practices such as communion under both species and the *recognitio* of particular laws."[54] They also pointed out that collegiality is weakened when there is a lessening of the bishops' participation in Curia meetings. They recommended that all episcopal consultors to Roman congregations should be free to attend all the regular plenary sessions.

The Criteria for Papal Intervention

The above section makes it clear that many bishops throughout the world are disenchanted with the present centralization of authority

---

53. Ibid., p. 226.
54. *Origins*, September 5, 1985, vol. 15, no. 12:179.

in the Church. Appealing to the principle of subsidiarity, they plead for greater autonomy of the local Church and less interference from Rome. Their objections and requests are not against the supreme and universal shepherding role of the Pope, which they obviously accept, but against the exercise of this ministry in ways that neglect or diminish collegiality and the true responsibilities of the local Church under episcopal leadership. The ultimate question is: are there any criteria that would validate — and in some sense limit — interventions by Rome?

The First Vatican Council debated this very question during its discussions on the episcopal power of the Pope (*potestas vere episcopalis*) and his relationship to the bishop of the local Church. Some of the Fathers felt that the juxtaposition of two episcopal powers could easily lead to the Pope's taking over the authority of the diocesan bishop. Many Fathers, most of them of the conciliar minority group, suggested ways to clarify this issue. Archbishop Haynald of Hungary, for example, objected to the word "episcopal," since the Pope could not exercise episcopal jurisdiction in all dioceses. For him the norm governing papal intervention in a particular diocese was linked to the purpose of the papacy: the unity of the Church. The purpose of the primacy, he said, is to preserve unity, to promote peace, to make up for deficiencies, to root out abuses, and to avoid calamities. Therefore, "the power of the primacy enables it to accomplish all that a bishop does, if the purpose of the primacy requires it."[55]

Other criteria for intervention were suggested. Bishops Krementz,[56] Dupanloup,[57] and Ketteler[58] said that the Pope should intervene only when it is necessary or when the utility to a diocese or of the universal Church requires it. Bishop David of Saint-Brieuc, France, asked the question on the minds of many:

> Is the power of the sovereign pontiff ordinary in the sense that the Pope could habitually — without necessity or evident utility to the Church and simply at his own pleasure — perform in every diocese, by himself or his collaborators, the functions of the bishops in the way that the Ordinary of the diocese performs them? Who is there that

---

55. Mansi 52:668 D.
56. Ibid., 51:948 D.
57. Ibid., 51:956 C.
58. Ibid., 51:934 C.

could not see the awkwardness and friction which would arise from such confusion?[59]

The First Vatican Council, however, did not include any criteria for papal intervention in the final version of *Pastor aeternus,* for fear that it would restrict the universal and supreme power of the Pope.

The problem, however, appeared again in the discussion of the Pope as the supreme judge and the right of all the faithful to have recourse to his judgment in all cases pertaining to ecclesiastical jurisdiction. Bishop Dupanloup objected to that phrasing because it was vague, unconditional, and universal. He asserted that in any well-ordered society the right of immediate appeal is not in favor of the supreme authority, save in exceptional cases. Intermediate jurisdiction, he insisted, must be respected.[60] Therefore, he proposed that the phrase, "without passing over intermediate jurisdiction," be added to the text dealing with the right of appeal to the Pope.[61] Bishop Zinelli, in the name of the Deputation on the Faith, rejected the amendment, claiming it would be injurious to the divine rights of the primacy.[62]

Criteria for papal interventions have a long canonical history. The traditional criteria included the unity of the Church, necessity, and the good (*utilitas*) of the Church.[63] Medieval Popes regularly justified their intervention in metropolitan and episcopal sees by appealing to these objective criteria.[64] Even the *Dictatus papae* of Gregory VII (1073–85) declared in number 13 that the Pope may transfer bishops from one see to another, if necessary (*necessitate cogente*). Admittedly, the appeal to criteria was often a formality, but it did indicate that the Pope's actions were based on objective reasons and were not arbitrary, inopportune, or habitual.

The Pope intervenes in the affairs of a diocese only for the most

---

59. Ibid., 52:593 D–594 A.

60. Ibid., 52:574 D–575 A.

61. Ibid., 52:1096 A, emendatio 58.

62. Ibid., 52:1114 C, emendatio 58.

63. See Yves Congar, "Quelques expressions traditionnelles du service chrétien," in Yves Congar and Bernard-Dominique Dupuy, eds., *L'épiscopat et l'Eglise universelle* (Paris: Cerf, 1962), pp. 106–123.

64. On this point see Gustave Thils, *La primauté pontificale. La doctrine de Vatican I. Les voies d'une révision* (Gembloux: J. Duculot, 1972), pp. 219–225.

serious reasons: when grave conflicts are unresolved, when other solutions have failed, or when a bishop is unwilling or unable to settle
a matter. The ultimate reason is the unity and good of the Church.
Even when the criteria are not expressed, the Pope is morally obliged
to have adequate reasons. But he alone is the final judge of their
adequacy. It is presumed that he acts for the benefit of the Church.

Criteria determining the intervention of the Pope in a diocese limit
papal authority. They are rooted in the very nature of the purpose of
the papacy: the ministry of unity for the good of the entire Church.
When they are expressed, they manifest clearly that the Pope is not
acting carelessly or at his own pleasure, but for serious reasons concerning faith and communion. Vatican II indicated this in two
texts. *Lumen gentium*, article 27, stated that episcopal authority,
which is proper, ordinary, and immediate, "is ultimately regulated
by the supreme authority of the Church, and can be circumscribed
by certain limits, for the advantage of the Church [*intuitu utilitatis
ecclesiae*] or of the faithful." Likewise, *Nota praevia*, number 3, affirmed that the Pope "proceeds according to his own discretion and
in view of the welfare of the Church [*intuitu boni ecclesiae*] in struc-
turing, promoting, and endorsing any exercise of collegiality."

The Objections Against Subsidiarity

The 1985 Extraordinary Synod of Bishops referred to the principle
of subsidiarity only once. It made the following suggestion: "It is
recommended that a study be made to examine whether the principle of subsidiarity in use in human society can be applied to the
Church and to what degree and in what sense such an application
can and should be made" (cf. Pius XII, *AAS* 38 [1946]:144).[65] The
reference is to Pius XII's application of subsidiarity to the Church.
The synod's statement is peculiar, since the presynodal reports of the
episcopal conferences that we examined above emphasized the importance of the principle of subsidiarity in the life of the Church. No
one raised the question *whether* subsidiarity was applicable to the
Church but only *how* it could be best applied.

The first sign of a different view of subsidiarity appeared in the
second report of Cardinal Danneels at the synod. He noted that the

---

65. *Extraordinary Synod of Bishops*, p. 21.

principle of subsidiarity is important in human social life, but asked if this principle can be used for the Church inasmuch as the Church is a human reality. "The ecclesial communion," he observed, "in the strict sense and in the theological sense has a sacramental foundation."[66] How to explain this shift? I concur with Joseph A. Komonchak that one must look at the address of Cardinal Jérôme Hamer given at the plenary session of cardinals that was held immediately before the synod.[67]

Cardinal Hamer pointed out that Vatican II referred to the principle of subsidiarity only three times—all of them in a social sense: twice in the *Declaration on Christian Education* (arts. 3 and 6) and once in the *Pastoral Constitution on the Church in the Modern World* (art. 86). Since it is not found at all in reference to the doctrine of the Church, Hamer asked if it is pertinent and relevant to the Church. He answered negatively for two reasons. First, the principle of subsidiarity has too much of a sociopolitical connotation. There is no reason to appeal to a principle of social philosophy when the teaching of Vatican II on the Church is sufficient. *Lumen gentium* (arts. 23 and 27) and *Christus Dominus* (art. 11) respect the proper competence of the local Church and the authority of the diocesan bishop. Second, "it attributes to the universal Church a subsidiary role in relationship to the local Church. This does not correspond to the real relationship that exists between them."[68] Archbishop Schotte was sympathetic to this view when, at the final press conference of the synod, he stated flatly that "the principle of subsidiarity is not a theological principle."[69]

A few observations are in order. First, the principle of subsidiarity is applied only analogically to the Church because of its uniqueness. The relationship between the Pope and the local Churches is not the same as that between the central power in the state and smaller administrative units. Nevertheless, the essence of subsidiarity—the protection of the rights, functions, and responsibilities of small groups vis-à-vis larger social units—can apply to the Church. It does not attribute a subsidiary role to the universal Church; it views the

---

66. *Synode extraordinaire*, p. 466.
67. Ibid., pp. 32–33.
68. Ibid., p. 604.
69. Ibid., p. 31.

universal Church not as an abstraction but as the communion of local Churches that can profit from legitimate diversity as long as the bond of faith is preserved.

Second, primatial authority can exist in a decentralized Church, since centralism is a later development and not an absolutely essential element in papal primacy. For centuries local bishops freely granted dispensations, faculties, and rights. Pluralism is not opposed to unity; relatively autonomous Churches with their own traditions, rites, and customs can contribute to the richness of the universal communion.

Third, Roman acceptance of subsidiarity, which encourages local resolution of problems, would help avoid the unwelcome practice of those who bypass the local bishop and the episcopal conference and go directly to Rome with their complaints.

Bishop Kenneth E. Untener of Saginaw, Michigan, has written of the carefully organized campaigns and horror stories sent to Rome that convey a distorted picture of what was taking place in many local Churches—all without the knowledge of the local bishop. Such behavior, he concluded, "is not only contrary to proper ecclesiology, it is contrary to the Gospel."[70]

A similar sentiment was expressed at the 1985 synod by Bishop John W. Gran, retired Bishop of Oslo. Granting the right of appeal to Rome, he said that "it should not be possible for a member of the local clergy to appeal to Rome only for the sake of harming his bishop by going behind his back to a superior authority. An accused person must always have the right to defend himself. That applies also to bishops."[71]

Conclusion

The dialectical tension between the authority of the Pope and the bishops of the local Churches relates to the question of limitation. It should be noted that unlike the dichotomy between two opposites— truth and error, virtue and vice—this relationship is between two authentic and legitimate realities. The papacy and the episcopate

---

70. "Local Church and Universal Church," p. 205.
71. *Synode extraordinaire*, pp. 388–389.

are both of divine origin and both share the same communion of faith. The tension between them can perhaps never be fully and finally resolved to the satisfaction of both parties. The most reasonable approach, then, is to seek ongoing balance by the avoidance of domination.

On the one hand, the Pope should not dominate the local Church by failing to acknowledge its genuine reality as Church. Not all ideas and decisions in the Church must come from the top. Rome should encourage legitimate pluralism, subsidiarity, and broad participation in decision making by recognizing the proper responsibilities of the local Churches. Although the Pope can always intervene in the life of the dioceses, this intervention should be limited to those instances where the local Church cannot fulfill its mission or fulfills it badly with harm to God's People. The entire Church benefits when ample opportunity is allowed for initiatives and adaptations by dioceses, parishes, and religious communities. Rome should also grant greater decision-making authority to the national episcopal conferences.

On the other hand, the local Church should not disregard the universal Church by claiming an unfounded independence and autonomy. It must acknowledge, as Paul VI reminded us, that subsidiarity does not mean that the local Church is "free, detached, and self-sufficient."[72] Subsidiarity is valid in the Church but "the nature of the primacy of the Roman Pontiff must not be compromised."[73] The local Church must always be in communion with other local Churches and recognize the unique competence of the universal ministry of the Church of Rome.

The key, then, to the relationship between the Church of Rome and the local Churches is the avoidance of domination by either party. Otherwise, the necessary and fruitful tension will be replaced by authoritarianism or anarchic rigidity. This tension should not and cannot be resolved once and for all; indeed it must be cherished as a sign of ecclesial health evidencing mutual respect of the Church of Rome and the local Churches in their continuing attempt to attune their relationship to the manifold gifts of the Spirit.

---

72. *Acta apostolicae sedis* 64 (1972):498–499.
73. John Paul II, *Origins*, August 14, 1986, vol. 16, no. 10:195.

·VI·

The Pope and the Catholic Faithful

Lay persons have always been enemies of the clergy.

—Boniface VIII*

The lay apostolate is a participation in the saving mission of the Church itself.

—Vatican II†

I n the Catholic communion there are 855 million members with one Pope and some thirty-five hundred bishops. The Church is not the hierarchy alone; it includes all believers who have answered the call of Christ and form one body animated by the Holy Spirit. The relationship between the Pope and the Catholic faithful is an important dimension of our analysis of the limits of the papacy. Since the laity constitute the majority in the Church, can it impose any limitation on the exercise of papal power? In attempting to answer that question, we shall focus on three principal areas: the sense of the faithful (*sensus fidelium*); the reception of papal teaching; and the nonreception of papal teaching.

The Sense of the Faithful

The Church of Christ is a community of laity, clergy, religious, and bishops who are united in faith and the sacraments and have the common task of acting as sign and instrument of Christ in the world.

---

* *Clericis laicos*, February 25, 1296. *Magnum bullarium romanum*, (1741), IX, 110.

† *Lumen gentium*, article 33.

The Church, in the words of St. Thomas, "is constituted, made, founded, and consecrated through faith and through the sacraments of faith."[1] The laity, according to Vatican II, share both "a common dignity from their rebirth in Christ," and "a true equality with regard to the dignity and to the activity of all the faithful for the building up of the Body of Christ" (*Lumen gentium*, art. 32). The Church is not formed on the basis of prior merit or sanctity; it depends ultimately on the call we receive to participate in the life of the Risen Savior. All members of the Church share in the one Lord, one Spirit, one Word, one faith, one baptism, one call to holiness, and one common mission. This emphasis on the fundamental sacramental equality and dignity of all the faithful opposes any sectarianism among the People of God. How does the *sensus fidelium* fit into this understanding of the Church and does it limit the Pope?

The Meaning of the *Sensus Fidelium*

In the history of theology we find many terms that refer to the presence of faith within believers: *sensus fidei, sensus fidelium, communis sensus fidei, sensus Ecclesiae, sensus Christi,* and *consensus fidelium.* These terms are interrelated and are often used interchangeably.

The *sensus fidei* (the sense or understanding of the faith) refers to a subjective quality—a supernatural gift, graced sensitivity, or instinct—given to all believers, enabling them to perceive the truth of the faith. The intuition or understanding of the faith allows believers to perceive God's revelation and the Church's teaching as consonant with divine truth. It is not an amorphous or nebulous feeling but a firm adherence to the essential truths of revelation and a self-awareness of Christian identity.

More precisely, the *sensus fidei* belongs to the category of prethematic, preconceptual, connatural knowledge and should have no superstitious or magical overtones. The perception of faith may be more intuitive than reasoned, but it is, nonetheless, real and transformative.[2] The *sensus fidei*, a function of the entire Church, creates a climate, a communal instinct that enables Christians to grasp the truth that saves.

---

1. IV Sent., dist. 17, q. 3, a. 1; dist. 18. q. 1, a. 1.
2. See John Glaser, "Authority, Connatural Knowledge, and the Spontaneous Judgment of the Faithful," *Theological Studies* 29 (1968):742-751.

The *sensus fidelium* (the sense or mind of the faithful) has a more objective quality, referring rather to what is believed than to the believer. It is the corporate presence of the *sensus fidei* in the community of believers, the objective mind of the Church—what the faithful believe. It is similar to the expressions *communis sensus fidei, sensus Ecclesiae,* and *sensus Christi.* The *consensus fidelium* (agreement of the faithful) is the unanimous agreement of the faithful in regard to a specific revealed truth.[3]

Through the special gift of the Holy Spirit, the Church as a whole is infallible, incapable of error, and indefectible in the faith. Many Fathers of the Church taught that the unanimous agreement (*consensus fidelium*) of Christians on matters of faith and morals is without error.[4] In appealing to the faith of the people—their identity with Christ manifested through genuine Christian living—the Fathers affirmed the infallibility of the believing Church. Thus in the fifth century, Vincent of Lerins wrote: "If at any time, a part is in rebellion against the whole or if there is a dissension of one or a few involved in error against the consent of all or the vast majority of Catholics, then they should prefer the integrity of the whole to the corruption of the part."[5] St. Thomas Aquinas agreed. He stated that a heretic is one who cuts himself from the common faith[6] and that it is impossible for the judgment of the universal Church to err in matters of faith.[7] Catholic theologians after the Protestant Reformation, including Robert Bellarmine, held the same position.

John Henry Newman presented a perceptive study of the *sensus*

---

3. The descriptions given above closely follow Yves Congar: "On the one hand, there is the *sensus fidei,* which is a quality inherent in a subject, on whom the grace of faith, charity, the gifts of the Spirit confer a faculty of perceiving the truth of the faith and of discerning anything opposed to it. The *sensus fidelium,* on the other hand, is what can be grasped from the outside, objectively, about what the faithful, and especially layfolk, believe and profess" ("Toward a Catholic Synthesis," in Jürgen Moltmann and Hans Küng, eds., *Who Has the Say in the Church? Concilium* no. 148 [New York: Seabury, 1981]:74).

4. See Yves Congar, *Lay People in the Church* (Westminster, Md.: Newman, 1957), pp. 441–443, and Robert B. Eno, "Consensus and Doctrine: Three Ancient Views," *Eglise et théologie* 9 (1978):473–483.

5. *Commonitoria,* chapter 27. *Patrologia latina* 50:674.

6. IV Sent. dist. 13, q. 2, a. 1, c.

7. Quodl. IX, 8, 1.

fidelium in *On Consulting the Faithful in Matters of Doctrine.*[8] He examined at length the meaning and historical development of the consent of the faithful—the agreement of believers on points of doctrine—defining its subjective basis as "a sort of instinct, or *phronema*, deep in the bosom of the mystical body of Christ."[9] This idea is related to the *phronesis* of Aristotle—the instinctive capacity of the virtuous and morally sensitive person to discern moral matters accurately and spontaneously. For Newman the Christian community is able to discern doctrinal truth. The *phronema* is that instinctive judgment by which the faithful are able to interpret tradition and discover the true content of revelation. The consent of the faithful, then, objectively speaking, is "the voice of the Infallible Church,"[10] because the faithful are witnesses to the tradition of revealed doctrine. Newman spoke often of the "*pastorum et fidelium conspiratio.*" "*Conspiratio*," literally a "breathing together," referred to the harmony and cooperation of both the bishops and the faithful as witnesses to the faith.

Newman gave five examples from history to illustrate the critical role played by the faithful in preserving and developing Catholic doctrine: the Arian controversy over the divinity of Christ in the fourth century, the affirmation of Mary as Mother of God (*theotokos*) in the fifth century, the debate over the real presence of Christ in the eucharist in the ninth century, the opposition to the theory proposed by Pope John XXII (1316-34) on the beatific vision,[11] and the definition in 1854 of the Immaculate Conception.

In speaking of the Arian controversy, Newman said that the Church had to have recourse to the faithful to determine the true meaning of the apostolic tradition, since "the body of the Bishops failed in their confession of faith."[12] In a revised version of *On Consulting*, he explained that he was using the term "body" in the sense of "the

---

8. Edited with an introduction by John Coulson (New York: Sheed and Ward, 1961). Hereafter cited as Coulson. Also see Samuel D. Feminano, *Infallibility of the Laity* (New York: Herder and Herder, 1967), and John T. Ford, "Newman on '*Sensus Fidelium*' and Mariology," *Marian Studies* 28 (1977):120-145.

9. Coulson, p. 73.

10. Ibid., p. 63.

11. See Decima Douie, "John XXII and the Beatific Vision," *Dominican Studies* 3 (1950):154-174.

12. Coulson, p. 77.

great preponderance" of bishops and not in the technical sense of *corpus*—the entire body of bishops.[13]

The role of the *sensus fidelium* in preserving the faith has been important, but it should not be overestimated or viewed in an uncritical or romantic way. The history of the Church gives us many examples of when Christians—both lay and clerical—have failed to maintain the faith. One could point to the spread of Islam in the seventh century; the Protestant Reformation in Germany, England, and Scandinavia; the various superstitions that have distorted true Christian piety; and the sinful actions of Christians throughout history. At times, the sense of the faith has been feeble and ineffective.

Newman's organic view of the Church as a union of all believers, clerical and lay, contributed to a reinterpretation of the formerly rigid distinction between the *Ecclesia docens* (the hierarchy) and the *Ecclesia discens* (the laity). This distinction assigned an active teaching role to the hierarchy and a passive learning role to the laity. In reality there is a complementarity between the two, since they both share a common faith. Members of the hierarchy also are learners. As Cyprian noted: "It behooves a bishop not only to teach but to learn, for the best teacher is one who daily grows and advances by learning better."[14] The Church is one body with a variety of charisms or gifts of the Spirit whose function is to contribute to the building up of the community.

Vatican II often referred to the meaning and value of the *sensus fidelium*.[15] In the early discussions on the *Constitution on the Church* at Vatican II some Fathers presented a very juridical understanding of the Church's indefectibility in the faith, assigning a largely passive role to the laity. Cardinal Ruffini, for example, defended the view that the *sensus fidelium* is "an echo" of the magisterium.[16] Yet Cardinals Paul Emile Léger and Franziskus König

---

13. Ibid., pp. 116–117.

14. *De oratione dominica* 23, in G. Hartel, ed., *Corpus scriptorum ecclesiasticorum latinorum*, I:285.

15. For an analysis of the conciliar debates see Antonio Acerbi, *Due ecclesiologie: Ecclesiologia giuridica ed ecclesiologia di communione nella "Lumen gentium"* (Bologna: Dehoniane, 1975), pp. 133 ff., 304 ff., 351 ff., passim, and Gérard Philips, *L'Eglise et son mystère au IIe Concile du Vatican* (Paris: Desclée, 1967), I:167–179.

16. *Acta et documenta concilio oecumenico Vaticano II apparando*, Series II (Vatican City: Typis Polyglottis Vaticanis, 1968), vol. II, part 4, 640.

insisted that the infallibility of the magisterium is rooted in the infallibility of the Church, and they attributed an active role to the *sensus fidelium.*[17]

The Council taught that the laity participate in the mission of the Church and continue the messianic work of the Lord. They share in the threefold mission of Christ as priest, king, and prophet. The *sensus fidei,* an exercise of prophetic ministry of the People of God, manifests the indefectibility of the Church; the whole Church possesses an infallible character. This concept is clearly present in the following text from *Lumen gentium*, article 12:

> The holy People of God shares also in Christ's prophetic office. It spreads abroad a living witness to him, especially by means of a life of faith and charity and by offering to God a sacrifice of praise, the tribute of lips which give honor to his name. The body of the faithful as a whole [*universitas fidelium*], anointed as they are by the Holy One, cannot err in matters of belief [*in credendo*]. Thanks to the supernatural sense of the faith [*sensu fidei*] which characterizes the People as a whole, it manifests this unerring quality when, "from the bishops down to the last member of the laity," it shows universal agreement [*universalem consensum*] in matters of faith and morals.[18]

The most important element of the *sensus fidelium* is its catholicity, which is not a spatial or temporal universality but a consistent relationship to apostolic tradition. Vincent of Lerins taught that one distinguishes truth from error by appeal to sacred Scripture, which must be interpreted according to the following norm: "We must hold that which has been believed everywhere, always, and by all."[19] Ancient tradition is of immense value for determining the content of the faith, but the Vincentian canon has to be seen in a broader context. Whatever is universal, ancient, and accepted by all Catholics is

---

17. Ibid., 640–644. Bishop Pedro Cantero Cuadrado of Huelva, Spain, gave a balanced description of the *sensus fidelium* at the second session of the Council. *Acta synodalia sacrosancti concilii Vaticani II* (Vatican City: Typis Polyglottis Vaticanis, 1972), vol. II, part 3, 283–286.

18. See *Relatio* on article 12 of *Lumen gentium*, in *Acta synodalia sacrosancti concilii oecumenici Vaticani II* (Vatican City: Typis Polyglottis Vaticanis, 1973), vol. III, part 1, 198–200.

19. "Id teneamus quod ubique, quod semper, quod ab omnibus creditum est." *Commonitoria*, cap. 3. *Patrologia latina* 50:639.

true, but there are also truths that are clearly Catholic which have not been explicitly believed always, everywhere, and by all.

Yves Congar, for example, has pointed out that the Vincentian canon has a legitimate value, but it is limited because "it substitutes the reality of the living Church for a historical view."[20] What has been defined remains valid and is a sign of the action of the Holy Spirit, but one cannot assign any particular point in history as the end of the growth of the Church in truth. The dynamic and creative quality that is present in the development of Church doctrine by the official teaching Church and the faithful should not be overlooked. Thus article 8 of *Dei Verbum* of Vatican II spoke of the continued growth in the understanding of tradition by believers through contemplation and study. Apostolic tradition remains a constant rule of faith; it is not an archaic remnant of the past but a vital energy within the present People of God.

The *sensus fidelium* is dependent on revelation. The faith of believers is determined and shaped by revelation and not the reverse: "The *sensus fidei* is not constitutive of revelation," declared the Dutch bishops.[21] It is not a normative source of the faith, but rather its sign. Moreover, the *sensus fidelium* is not the same as the free interpretation of Scripture. The belief of the faithful must always be related to the objective data of faith as it is expressed in Scripture and tradition and authentically interpreted by the Church. But the self-communication of God given in revelation is not an abstract and sterile reality. It is always linked to the concrete historical life of the Christian community as it is authenticated by the Church's teaching authority. The real issue is how the faith is lived. Catholic identity resides in the unity of its faith and is mediated by the Church, the universal sacrament of salvation.

The Pope and the *Sensus Fidelium*

The *sensus fidelium* is, obviously, an essential element in the life of the Church. It is also important in relationship to the papacy, since the Pope, himself one of the *fideles,* must act in harmony with the

---

20. *Diversity and Communion* (Mystic, Conn.: Twenty-Third Publications, 1985), p. 124.

21. Dutch Synod (1980), *Origins,* February 14, 1980, vol. 9, no. 35:560.

genuine expression of faith in the Church. The *sensus fidelium*, then, introduces a possible limit in the exercise of papal authority. What role does the *sensus fidelium*—the mind of the Church—play in the development and preservation of doctrine? Does it limit in some way papal power? The following observations will attempt to answer these questions.

First, not every position held by the faithful is necessarily equivalent to tradition nor is a valid manifestation of the *sensus fidelium*. The latter is a gift given to the Church by the Spirit and can be a genuine criterion of truth, but it is not self-justifying. The genuine *sensus fidelium* is only one theological source (a *locus theologicus*), and it does not take the place of other sources, such as Scripture, the magisterium, or theology. Not every and any group that is opposed to a Church doctrine and demands that it be changed expresses the faith of the Church. At times, as Avery Dulles says, authentic teaching may be upheld not by the great majority of Church members but only by a faithful minority: "We must not look so much at the statistics, as at the quality of the witnesses and the motivation for their assent."[22]

The *sensus fidelium* is above all a spiritual reality and not a sociological device, a counting of heads, or an opinion poll.[23] What is to be said of polls that reveal positions not in accord with the teaching of the Church?[24] Poll-taking is a controversial technique—even in the political arena—and may well create opinion rather than merely report it. Several elements can affect the reliability of a poll: the phrasing of the questions and the age, sex, education, and culture of the respondents.

The use of polls in doctrinal matters is especially problematic, depending largely on whether the respondents are practicing or

---

22. "Sensus Fidelium," *America*, November 1, 1986, p. 242.

23. The point made by John Paul II in the apostolic exhortation *Familiaris consortio* (1981), *On the Family* (Washington: USCC, 1982), p. 4.

24. A New York Times/CBS opinion poll by telephone of 927 adult American Catholics taken in November, 1985, just before the Synod of Bishops, indicated that a majority of those contacted held views that contradicted the official teaching of the Church. The results showed that 68 percent favored the use of artificial means of contraception; 52 percent favored the ordination of women as priests; 63 percent favored letting priests marry; and 73 percent favored remarriage for divorced people. *New York Times*, November 25, 1985, p. A7.

nonpracticing Church members.[25] It may be, as Archbishop William Levada has observed, that opinion polls, rather than reflecting the true faith of the Church, indicate "the enormous invasion of secular values—I might say values directly opposed to the Gospel and inimical to discipleship in Christ."[26]

Opinion polls are not infallible indications of ecclesial agreement or disagreement.[27] At the same time polls may be one indication among others of whether or not the faithful follow Church doctrine and discipline. *Humanae vitae* is a classic example. Polls should be judiciously evaluated and correlated with other indices. They are not in themselves genuine expression of the sense of faith.[28] Consultation—a broader and more reliable category than the opinion poll —is, as we shall see later, an important element in Church teaching.

Second, the *sensus fidelium* is not self-sufficient; it is necessarily related to the hierarchical magisterium for its full functioning. The Pope and the bishops make the ultimate judgment concerning the genuineness of the *sensus fidelium*. The final and authentic interpretation of the Word of God has been given exclusively to the Church's teaching authority, but it "is not above the Word of God but serves it" (*Dei verbum*, art. 10). All bishops, including the Bishop of Rome, must recognize the *sensus fidei*, determine its truth, and encourage the faithful to discern what the faith truly means.[29] The bishops, as *fideles*, share in the collective discernment of the faith

25. The September 1986 Gallup telephone survey of 264 Roman Catholics is illustrative of this point. They were asked: "Some people say that the official position of the Catholic Church on sexual morals should not be changed. Others say that this position should be changed to reflect modern trends in the modern world. Which point of view more closely reflects your own opinion?" The majority (57 percent) favored change, but there was a significant difference between practicing and nonpracticing Catholics. Nearly 70 percent of nonpracticing Catholics favored change, compared with only 46 percent of practicing Catholics. Asked about the action of the Vatican against Charles E. Curran, practicing Catholics supported the decision by a 5-to-3 ratio, but nonpracticing Catholics opposed it 6 to 1. *Washington Post* (Health section), November 18, 1986, p. 8.

26. *Origins*, August 14, 1986, vol. 16, no. 10:200.

27. William M. Thompson writes: "It would be a perversion of the tradition to image the *sensus fidelium* as a kind of 'majority vote,' a 'head count' of the faithful, according to which truth is found in the majority will or mind" ("*Sensus Fidelium* and Infallibility," *American Ecclesiastical Review* 167 [1973]:482).

28. See John Paul II, *Familiaris consortio*, p. 4.

29. Idem.

when they speak in the name of the Church. In judging the authenticity of the *sensus fidelium*, the Pope and the bishops act within the community of the faith that they serve. Their teaching, reflecting the vital faith of the community, has an impelling power and conviction that mere juridical pronouncements lack.

Third, the magisterium and the *sensus fidelium* are complementary and not opposing realities. They are interdependent: both are joined by the Word of God and both are instruments of the same Holy Spirit. The teaching Church does not depend solely on the opinions of the faithful nor do the faithful only passively accept the teaching of the magisterium.[30] Interaction between the magisterium and the faithful is crucial. A balanced ecclesiology recognizes that each part of the Church has its own proper charisms, which should not be neglected.

Cardinal Newman insisted that both the faithful and the bishops contribute to the formation of doctrine, but that "there is something in the '*pastorum et fidelium conspiratio*' which is not in the pastors alone."[31] The Pope and the bishops are not separate from the Church; the articulation of Church dogmas reflects the belief of the living Christian experience.[32] "The magisterium," writes Jean M. R. Tillard, "should draw from the very life of the People of God the reality to be discerned, judged, and promulgated or 'defined.'"[33]

At certain times the faithful, on the basis of their own experience, may contribute to the understanding of the faith in a way different from that of the magisterium. The magisterium, limited by cultural, social, or political biases, may be unable to appreciate problems fully. Their pronouncements about them may be inadequate.[34]

Fourth, broad consultation should be part of the process by which the Church teaches, even when it teaches infallibly. Vatican I taught that the Pope possesses that infallibility "with which the divine Redeemer willed His Church to be endowed."[35] What is taught infallibly

---

30. See Congar, *Lay People in the Church*, p. 276.
31. Coulson, p. 104.
32. Bishop Gasser at Vatican I: "We cannot separate the Pope from the agreement (*consensus*) of the Church, because this agreement is never lacking" (Mansi 52:1214 A).
33. "*Sensus Fidelium*," *One in Christ* 11 (1975):28.
34. On this issue see Glaser, "Authority, Connatural Knowledge," 745–746.
35. DS 3074.

is what the whole Church believes. At Vatican I several of the Council Fathers spoke out in favor of consultation before the Pope may make an *ex cathedra* definition. Cardinal Dechamps, for example, agreed with Bellarmine that the Pope does not rashly define dogmas but should consult with wise men, councils, and bishops.[36] Cardinal Guidi referred to a limit on the Pope when he stated that the Pope depends on the Church in that he must ascertain "whether the truth to be defined is truly contained in the deposit of revelation."[37] Bishop Gasser was also in favor of consultation, but he qualified it. He noted that although there is no "strict and absolute necessity" for the Pope to consult with the bishops, there may be a "relative necessity" for consultation that rests with the decision of the Pope.[38] The Pope, then, is not juridically bound to consult, but he should.

Wide consultation was conducted before the definitions of the Immaculate Conception (1854) and the Assumption (1950). Both Pius IX and Pius XII asked the bishops throughout the world to give their opinion concerning the appropriateness of the definitions and to report to him the devotion the clergy and faithful have regarding these doctrines. The results of these questionnaires were positive. Thus the Marian definitions were not imposed on the Church but rather developed from below.

Vatican II repeated the doctrine of Vatican I on infallibility but expanded the idea of consultation. It declared that the Pope and the bishops, in preserving and expounding revelation, should "strive painstakingly and by appropriate means to inquire properly into that revelation and to give apt expression to its contents" (*Lumen gentium*, art. 25.) In practice, this means that the Pope should engage in collaboration and consultation with the bishops—and

---

36. Mansi 52:68 A.

37. Mansi 52:746 A.

38. Mansi 52:1215 C D. Gasser also stated that the Pope, in virtue of his office and the gravity of the matter, is bound to investigate revealed truth through appropriate means (*media apta*) such as the seeking of advice from bishops, cardinals, theologians, and others (Mansi 52:1213 D). He said, however, that this obligation belongs to the moral order, thus binding in conscience, rather than to the dogmatic (Mansi 52:1214 C). Yves Congar has suggested that these ethical elements should be introduced into the very ontology of pastoral duty ("Apostolicité du ministère et apostolicité de doctrine," in Remigius Bäumer and Heimo Dolch, eds., *Volk Gottes: Festgabe für Josef Höffer* [Freiburg: Herder, 1967], p. 110).

through them the faithful—before issuing a statement affecting the entire Church. The Council did not say that failure to consult would invalidate a papal decision. Theoretically, the Pope could refuse to consult with anyone, bishops included. He is always free, as both of the Vatican Councils attest, to excercise his supreme and full authority. Although such authoritarian behavior might displease the bishops and weaken the Pope's own credibility, there is no canonical prohibition against it. A Pope who refuses to take any counsel may be acting imprudently and perhaps may even sin seriously against the moral law, but he would be breaking no canonical prescription.[39]

The present Code of Canon Law contains at least two instances that require the Pope to consult. Canon 431, 3 refers to the competency of the supreme authority of the Church to establish, suppress, or change ecclesiastical provinces, "after hearing the bishops involved." The Pope asks the bishops for advice, but the final decision is his. Canon 449, 1 states that "after hearing the bishops involved," the supreme authority of the Church alone can erect, suppress, or change the conferences of bishops.

If consultation is desirable before the Pope makes an infallible pronouncement, then it would seem prudently necessary that it be present in the ordinary, noninfallible teaching of the Pope and the bishops. Rahner insists that "the believing Church can and must be consulted by the magisterium."[40] The ideal of dialogue and consultation is enshrined in Vatican II: "Let the laity realize that their pastors [bishops] will not always be so expert as to have a concrete solution to every problem—even every grave problem—that arises; such is not the role of the pastors" (*Gaudium et spes*, art. 43).

The bishops of the United States have employed broad consultation in their teaching. This procedure was clearly evident in the

---

39. The observations of Joseph Ratzinger are pertinent: " . . . among the claims which his very office makes upon the Pope we must undoubtedly reckon a moral obligation to hear the voice of the Church universal. . . . Juridically speaking, there is no appeal from the Pope even when he acts without the college [of bishops], and the college cannot act without him at all. Morally speaking, the Pope may have an obligation to listen to the bishops, and the bishops may have an obligation to take the initiative themselves." In Herbert Vorgrimler, ed., *Commentary on the Documents of Vatican II* (New York: Herder and Herder, 1967), I:304.

40. Karl Rahner and Herbert Vorgrimler, *Theological Dictionary* (New York: Herder and Herder, 1965), p. 269.

preparation of the pastorals on moral life, peace, and the economy and also for the National Catechetical Directory. There were hearings, publication of preliminary drafts, and invitations to submit suggestions. After the first draft of the pastoral on the economy, for example, some ten thousand pages of comments were submitted by Catholics and non-Catholics. Wide consultation also took place in the studies of seminaries and religious orders and in preparation for the synod of 1987.

The Pope and the bishops do not have a monopoly on the faith. If faith and tradition are possessed by the entire Church and if the universal Church cannot err in matters of faith, then the Pope in teaching —even in a noninfallible manner—should have some way to discern what is the faith of the Church. Consultation appears to be a most suitable way for this to take place, granting of course that the ultimate decision rests with the Pope. This consultative process is especially necessary when the Church teaches in areas that directly concern the lives of the laity, such as questions of social and sexual morality.

Present structures are inadequate to ensure full dialogue between the universal Church and the local Churches, to channel input from the faithful to the bishops and the Pope, and to guarantee proper consultation. Several episcopal conferences in their reports for the 1985 Synod of Bishops made similar observations. The bishops of England and Wales were the most forthright. They spoke of the frustration over the present consultative process at all levels of the Church—local, national, and international. In particular, they referred to the poor communication by Rome of the arguments justifying specific Church decisions. Their own words are direct.

> The exercise of the teaching office in the Church is an area of difficulty calling for clarification. It operates in the context of community where dialogue is appropriate. Its relationship to the *sensus fidelium* and subsequent reception of teaching is not well understood. In its relationship with the work of theology, common interests need to be recognized and mutual respect built up. The controversies regarding *Humanae vitae* are examples of these difficulties.[41]

In conclusion, let us return to our initial question: Does the *sensus fidelium* in some way limit papal authority? This question cannot be

---

41. *Origins,* September 5, 1985, vol. 15, no. 12:184.

answered in a juridical way, since the *sensus fidelium* is a spiritual and not a legal concept. As knowledge by connaturality, it should not be confused with the magisterium, absorbed by it, or made a substitute for it. The same Holy Spirit guides both the faithful and the hierarchy; the understanding of the faith is shared by the entire Church. Papal authority, however, is not unlimited and absolute. It is not an end in itself but always at the service of the believing community. In proclaiming the Word of God and in governing the Church, the Pope operates within the context of a community that is linked by common beliefs and animated by a common source of truth in the Spirit.

The Pope is not simply an administrator outside the Church nor an executor of every desire expressed by the body of the faithful. He must function with respect and reverence to the lived faith of the members of the Church. He too is a believer. In clarifying, preserving, and judging the authenticity of the faith of the Church, he cannot depart from it. His own teaching must expound what has been revealed and what belongs to the patrimony of the Church. The Pope, then, is limited by the *sensus fidelium* in that he cannot neglect the faith of his fellow believers and should recognize it as one among many channels by which God's self-communication is transmitted.

The Reception of Papal Teaching

The phenomenon of reception is as old as the Church itself. The New Testament communities received the teaching of the Apostles, and throughout its history the Church has been engaged in the process of reception: the formation of the canon of Scripture and the acceptance of doctrinal truths, conciliar decisions, papal and episcopal judgments, laws, and liturgical feasts and practices. Today some theologians even speak of re-reception; because of new concerns, new questions, and advanced historical research, the Church must re-receive the truths of the past and apply them to the present. There is a growing interest in the reinterpretation of some of the Councils, for example, Chalcedon, Trent, and Vatican I. Reception, then, remains a continuing task for every generation of Christians.

The Bearers of Reception

The term "reception" is frequently used in jurisprudential studies as the process by which a law is received.[42] Applied to the ecclesiastical sphere, reception is the acceptance by local Churches of doctrinal statements or conciliar decisions issued by Church authorities. Yves Congar defines reception as "the process by which an ecclesial body truly takes as its own a determination which it did not originate, in acknowledging, in the measure promulgated, a rule suitable to its own life."[43] Other theologians have given similar descriptions of reception.[44] Reception has also been applied to ecumenism: the acceptance of common theological positions agreed upon by separated Churches.[45]

Reception is a multilayered reality. It is not a purely juridical concept, a technical device, nor a sociological norm. Nor is it the exclusive task of the magisterium. When the Church teaches a doctrine or mandates a discipline, the process of reception is not ended. Reception of papal and episcopal teaching involves the entire People of God; the hierarchy and the faithful are together the bearers of reception. Full reception involves the official promulgation of a doctrine by the Church, its communication, its reflection in the liturgy, its presence in the spiritual and moral life of the faithful, and its articulation by theologians. Christian truth is not an abstraction but

---

42. Franz Wieacker describes the way the Germans received Roman law in the fifteenth century in *Privatrechtsgeschichte der Neuzit unter besonderer Beruchsichtigung der deutschen Entwicklung,* 2nd ed. (Göttingen: Vandenhoeck & Ruprecht, 1977).

43. "La 'réception' comme realité ecclésiologique," *Revue des sciences philosophiques et théologiques* 56 (1972):370. A shortened version of this article is found in "Reception as an Ecclesiological Reality," in Giuseppe Alberigo and Anton Weiler, eds., *Election and Consensus in the Church. Concilium* no. 77 (New York: Herder and Herder, 1972):43-68. This quotation is on page 45.

44. See Alois Grillmeier, "Konzil und Rezeption: Methodische Bermerkungen zu einem Thema der ökumenischen Diskussion der Gegenwart," *Theologie und Philosophie* 45 (1970):321-352, and "The Reception of Chalcedon in the Roman Catholic Church," *Ecumenical Review* 22 (1970):383-423; also Edward J. Kilmartin, "Reception in History: An Ecclesiological Phenomenon and Its Significance," *Journal of Ecumenical Studies* 21 (1984):34-54.

45. This idea is discussed by Thomas P. Rausch, "Reception Past and Present," *Theological Studies* 47 (1986):497-508, and by Cardinal Johannes Willebrands, "The Impact of Dialogue," *Origins,* April 18, 1985, vol. 14, no. 44:720-724.

exists only in the living faith of people. Church officials play a critical role in the process of reception by their formal teaching and also by their continued preaching and explaining of that teaching. But it is the faithful themselves who appropriate the teaching of the Church.

Reception, even in the full sense, is not an action that confers validity upon a conciliar declaration or doctrinal decrees. "They obtain their legitimation and their obligatory value," as Congar notes, "from the authorities who have supported them."[46] These same authorities act as ministers to the community to which they belong. Although reception does not confer validity, it does declare and give witness that a doctrine is beneficial for the entire Church. The level of the efficacy of a Church doctrine is linked to the level of its reception.

The doctrine of infallibility provides a good illustration of the theological meaning of reception and also reveals a further aspect of the limits of the papacy. Vatican I defined the dogma of infallibility or "charism of truth" and gave certain necessary conditions for *ex cathedra* and hence infallible teaching. These conditions, as we saw earlier in Chapter Three, amount to explicit limitations in the exercise of the infallible papal magisterium. The Pope, when he teaches *ex cathedra*, must follow those conditions; he does not have absolute, unrestricted power to teach infallibly on any subject and in any way he desires. If these conditions are followed, then the definitions are irreformable "of their very nature, and not from the consent of the Church."[47] Infallibility says as much about the Church as it does about the Pope, since he shares that infallibility with which the Lord willed his Church to be endowed.

Infallible definitions reflect the faith of the Church and will be accepted by believing Christians. Because of the action of the Holy Spirit, as Vatican II explains, "the assent of the Church can never be wanting" to definitions (*Lumen gentium*, art. 25). The faithful will accept the authenticity of a definition and recognize it as the faith of the Church. Jacques Bénigne Bossuet (d. 1704) declared: "Since he [the Bishop of Rome] is in effect at the head of the ecclesial commun-

---

46. "La réception," pp. 396–397, and "Reception as an Ecclesiological Reality," p. 64.

47. DS 3074.

ion and since his definition intends nothing other than what he knows to be the feeling of all the Churches, the subsequent consent only attests that everything has been done in due order and in accordance with the truth."[48]

But what of the intriguing theoretical case in which assent to a definition may not be present among a significant group of committed Catholics who have serious doubts about its authenticity? This lack of assent, according to Avery Dulles, "could be interpreted as a sign that the Pope had perhaps exceeded his competence and that some necessary condition for an infallible act had not been fulfilled."[49] Joseph Ratzinger has a similar position: "Where there is neither consensus on the part of the universal Church nor clear testimony in the sources, no binding decision is possible. If such a decision were formally made, it would lack the necessary conditions and the question of the decision's legitimacy would have to be examined."[50]

Reception, then, is a sure sign that an infallible judgment is a true and binding expression of the faith, but it does not confer ex post facto infallibility on a definition. The Pope, as Ratzinger says, does not "merely ratify such processes of reception, but also has the authority to make definitive decisions and interpretations against the background of the faith of the Church."[51]

The Process of Reception

The process of reception culminates in the recognition of a common faith; it emerges from the living tradition of the Church. Dogmas, canons, or moral norms are true not because they are taught by the hierarchy; they are true because they conform to apostolic faith.

---

48. *Dissertatio praevia* of 1696 in the *Defensio Clerici Gallicani*, no. 78, *Oeuvres de Bossuet* (Versailles: J. A. Lebel, 1817), 31:161.

49. "Moderate Infallibilism" in Paul C. Empie, T. Austin Murphy, and Joseph A. Burgess, eds., *Teaching Authority and Infallibility in the Church: Lutherans and Catholics in Dialogue VI* (Minneapolis: Augsburg, 1978), p. 89. Also see p. 92.

50. *Das neue Volk Gottes* (Düsseldorf: Patmos, 1969), p. 144.

51. Interview with German Catholic News Agency (KBA), *The Tablet* (London), March 1, 1982, p. 434. *Mysterium ecclesiae* made the following statement: "However much the Sacred Magisterium avails itself of the contemplation, life, and study of the faithful, its office is not reduced merely to ratifying the assent already made by the latter" (*Acta apostolicae sedis* 65 [1973]:399).

The hierarchy's mission is to communicate this faith and to be its responsible guardians. Ecumenical councils and doctrinal decisions have authority ultimately because of their truth content and not because of their juridical standing.

Acceptance of dogmatic statements is more than the repeating of a linguistic formula; it touches the very heart of the Christian life. St. Thomas noted that "the act of believing does not end with a proposition but with reality."[52] The main reason for formulating a proposition is that we may know the reality. The believer internalizes the reality of faith that the words proclaim and express.

Reception is grounded in the vision of the Church as a communion, animated by the Holy Spirit, and unerring in matters of faith. A rigid monarchical or pyramidal view of the Church, in which the hierarchy dominates and the faithful have only a passive role, cannot adequately deal with the process of reception. If truth is central to reception and if the Holy Spirit is present in all believers, then the faithful play an important role in the discernment and reception of the faith. Reception involves the entire Church. "The People of God," says Cardinal Willebrands, "under the guidance of the Holy Spirit, recognizes and accepts new insights, new witnesses of truth and their forms of expression because they are deemed to be in the line of the apostolic tradition and in harmony with the *sensus fidelium* of the Church as a whole."[53]

Reception takes time; it is not automatic. It does not end when an ecumenical council is concluded and the participants return home. Its decisions have to be made part of the life of the Church throughout the world. Doctrinal and disciplinary decisions of a council—and also in the less formal ways of Church teaching—rarely present a permanent solution to a problem and rarely receive immediate and universal assent. The Creed of Nicaea (325), for example, was not fully received until nearly sixty years after its appearance. Constantinople I (381) was accepted by Rome as the second of the four great Councils only in 519, by Pope Hormisdas (514-523). It was nearly seventy years before Chalcedon (451) was received by the same Hormisdas. The first Pope expressly to receive Nicaea II (787) was Leo IX

---

52. "Actus credentis non terminatur ad enuntiabile sed ad rem." *Summa theologiae*, II-II, q. 1, art. 2, ad 2.

53. "The Impact of Dialogue," 722.

(1049-54) in 1053. The reforms of the Council of Trent (1545-63) took decades before they were received in all places. Who is to say when Vatican II will be fully receieved into the life of the universal Church?[54]

The process of reception for councils involves, according to Alois Grillmeier, three interacting and coexisting levels: the kerygmatic, spiritual, and theological.[55] The kerygmatic refers to the official promulgation of the conciliar teaching and its dissemination. This is done by ecclesiastical authorities—the Pope and the bishops. At the spiritual level the truth enunciated by the council nourishes the life of the faithful and is reflected in the spirituality and liturgy of the Church. The principle of *lex orandi lex credendi* is operative here. At the theological level theologians delve into the deeper meaning of the council and by their discussions contribute to its clarification and development.

These three elements of reception are not restricted to ecumenical councils; to some extent they are also present in the acceptance by the Church of other realities such as liturgical practices, canonical norms, and nonconciliar doctrines. Full reception, both intellectually and spiritually, exists when the Church incorporates the truth into its lived experience. In some sense reception is never finished because each age, in light of its own particular situation, must reaffirm the meaning of doctrines previously taught and apply them. Furthermore, every reception also leads to a new understanding of the faith and creates new challenges.

In one sense, reception can be viewed as a limitation of papal authority. No Pope, however exalted his office may be and however extraordinary his talents, can mandate by sheer juridical force the reception of his teachings or legislation. Reception is only gradually realized and can take a long time. The Pope may encourage reception and create an atmosphere in which it can develop, but he may not live long enough to see the fruit of his labors. Furthermore, he can expect opposition, criticism, and at times disloyalty, even though objectively his actions may be for the good of the Church. In the last analysis, reception occurs because of the continual guidance of the Holy Spirit within the Church.

---

54. See Giuseppe Alberigo and Jean-Pierre Jossua, eds., *La réception de Vatican II* (Paris: Cerf, 1985).

55. In "The Reception of Chalcedon."

The Nonreception of Papal Teaching

History is filled with examples of the nonreception of papal teaching. After nearly every ecumenical council there have been some—at times a large number—of individuals who rejected the conciliar teachings: Vatican I had its Old Catholics and Vatican II the followers of Archbishop Lefebvre. At times local Churches have refused to accept validly appointed officials. The classic example is the Corinthian community at the end of the first century. Some of its members deposed presbyters on their own authority and were rebuked by Clement of Rome. He declared that their action was gravely wrong and a violation of a divine ordinance, since the presbyters had been appointed indirectly by the Apostles and had ministered blamelessly.

Church laws have not always received universal acceptance. *Veterum sapientia*, the apostolic constitution issued by John XXIII in 1962, which mandated the use of Latin in seminaries and other institutes of higher learning, was almost universally ignored. Canonists for centuries debated the question of whether the acceptance by the community was necessary for constituting a Church law.[56] The present Code of Canon Law does not refer explicitly to the idea of reception or acceptance; it mentions custom but reduces the role that an earlier tradition attached to it.

Custom is the best interpreter of the Church's positive law (can. 27), since the community plays a role in shaping the Church's legal system. But no custom contrary to divine law can obtain the force of law (can. 24); only a custom introduced by the community and approved by the legislator has the force of law (can. 23). A custom that is contrary to the existing canon law or apart from it (*praeter ius*) obtains the force of law only after thirty continuous years; only a centenary or immemorial custom can prevail over a canon that explicitly forbids future customs (can. 26). The nonacceptance of a law may not necessarily be an act of disobedience or recalcitrance. It may be a sign that the law is unreasonable, unworkable, or that it fails to take into account the particular sociocultural conditions of

---

56. See Geoffrey King, "The Acceptance of Law by the Community: A Study in the Writings of Canonists and Theologians, 1500-1750," *The Jurist* 37 (1977):233-265.

the people. Initial nonreception may sometimes be the first step in eventual reception.

Our concern in this section is mainly with the nonreception of papal teaching and whether it affects or limits the authority of the Pope. Is it possible to speak of legitimate dissent from noninfallible teachings? This issue obviously is relevant in view of the actions of Rome taken against such theologians as Küng, Schillebeeckx, and Curran, discussed in Chapter One. We shall treat here the kinds of Church teaching and assent, the possibility of dissent, and the response of Church authority to dissent.

The Kinds of Church Teaching and Assent

Church teaching is either infallible (definitive) or noninfallible (nondefinitive).[57] Let us examine the sphere of Church teaching as it extends to three classes of objects.

1. *Primary Objects*. The Pope, either in an *ex cathedra* pronouncement or with the accord of an ecumenical council, may formally and infallibly teach that a particular truth is revealed by God. Some examples are the dogmas of the divinity of Christ, the institution of the sacraments by Christ, papal primacy, the Immaculate Conception, and the Assumption.

The Church may also infallibly propose a truth as revealed when the bishops in their ordinary teaching are in union with the Pope and declare that truth to be definitive and binding. This type of infallibility is called the teaching of the ordinary and universal magisterium. Thus, although individual bishops cannot teach infallibly, through their collegial union with the Pope and other bishops they can do so even without forming an ecumenical council. Vatican II explained this kind of episcopal teaching:

> This is so, even when they [bishops] are dispersed around the world, provided that while maintaining the bond of unity among themselves and with Peter's successor, and while teaching authoritatively on a matter of faith or morals, they concur in a single viewpoint as the one which must be held definitively (*Lumen gentium* , art. 25).

---

57. For a balanced and detailed study of the entire range of issues concerning the teaching authority of the Church see Francis A. Sullivan, *Magisterium: Teaching Authority in the Catholic Church* (New York: Paulist, 1983).

Examples of this kind of infallible teaching are the bodily resurrection of Jesus, the virginity of Mary, and the prohibition against the deliberate taking of innocent human life.[58] These truths have not been formally defined, but they are part of the Catholic tradition.

The irrevocable and unconditional assent of divine and Catholic faith is required for the primary objects of infallibility when taught by either the Pope or an ecumenical council or by the ordinary and universal magisterium. The doctrines so taught then enjoy a guarantee of absolute certainty, since the ultimate reason for believing is God as revealing. Vatican I decreed: "All those things are to be believed by divine and Catholic faith which are contained in the Word of God, written or handed down, and which the Church, either by a solemn judgment or by her ordinary and universal magisterium, proposes for belief as having been divinely revealed."[59] To dissent from infallibly proposed teachings knowingly, obstinately, and publicly is heresy and separates the dissenter from the Church.

2. *Secondary Objects.* Infallible teaching may probably extend also to doctrines necessary to maintain or defend the content of revelation. These doctrines are not revealed but are so connected with revelation as to be necessary for its understanding and preservation. These truths include: the condemnation of propositions contrary to revelation; certain speculative truths, such as the preambles of faith; theological conclusions derived from revelation; "dogmatic facts" both historical (Trent is a genuine ecumenical council) and doctrinal (the teachings of Jansenius are not compatible with revealed truth); the canonization of saints; and the final approbation of religious orders.

---

58. Karl Rahner's observation is instructive: "It is therefore quite untrue that only those moral norms for which there is a solemn definition . . . are binding in faith on the Christian as revealed by God. . . . When the whole Church in her everyday teaching does in fact teach a moral rule everywhere in the world as a commandment of God, she is preserved from error by the assistance of the Holy Spirit" (*Nature and Grace* [New York: Sheed and Ward, 1964], p. 52). Some theologians argue that the Church's prohibition of contraception is infallible on the basis of the ordinary and universal magisterium: John C. Ford and Germain Grisez, "Contraception and the Infallibility of the Ordinary Magisterium," *Theological Studies* 39 (1978):258-312. For a different view see Joseph A. Komonchak, "*Humanae vitae* and Its Reception: Ecclesiological Reflections," ibid., 221-257.

59. DS 3011; TCC 38.

There is a question whether there are secondary objects of infallibility at all. Some theologians prefer to restrict the object of infallibility only to revealed truths, pointing out that Vatican I did not teach explicitly that infallibility extends to the secondary objects. Others, however, justify such an extension because of Vatican I's use of the expression "to be held" (*tenenda*) in the definition of infallibility; they argue that since the Council did not say "to be believed" (*credenda*), it would appear that the object of infallibility is broader than revealed truths. This view is supported by the discussions at Vatican I. The Deputation on the Faith said that such an opinion was theologically certain.[60]

Vatican II was in agreement. It referred to the secondary objects in *Lumen gentium*, article 25, declaring that infallibility extends "as far as the deposit of divine revelation, which must be religiously guarded and faithfully expounded." Even more explicit was the 1973 declaration of the Congregation for the Doctrine of the Faith, *Mysterium ecclesiae*: "The infallibility of the Church's magisterium extends not only to the deposit of faith but also to those matters without which the deposit cannot be rightly preserved or expounded."[61]

The assent required for secondary objects is disputed. In general, such truths require absolute assent, internal and external, but not the assent of divine and Catholic faith. Theologians are divided on the specific kind of assent. The more common view is that the assent required is that of ecclesiastical faith—an assent based on the authority of the Church.[62] Others, however, propose the assent of

---

60. Mansi 52:258 D. At Vatican I, Bishop Gasser said that the secondary objects of infallibility are not simply connected with revelation but are *necessary* if the deposit of faith is to be guarded and explained (Mansi 52:1226 B). Theologians debate whether specific moral norms can be infallibly taught. The majority of moral theologians hold that they cannot. In Sullivan, *Magisterium*, p. 227, n. 46, a list of authors favoring that position include F. Böckle, C. E. Curran, J. Fuchs, R. McCormick, B. Schüller, and others. Some moralists, however, contend that moral norms can be infallibly proposed. See Germain Grisez, *The Way of the Lord Jesus*, vol. I: *Christian Moral Principles* (Chicago: Franciscan Herald, 1983), chapters 35 and 36, and "Infallibility and Specific Moral Norms: A Review Discussion," *The Thomist* 49 (1985):248–287.

61. *Acta apostolicae sedis* 65 (1973):401.

62. See Gerard Van Noort, *Dogmatic Theology*, vol. III: *The Sources of Revelation and Divine Faith*. Trans. and rev. J. J. Castelot and W. R. Murphy (Westminster, Md.: Newman, 1961), pp. 188, 265–270.

Catholic faith.[63] Either way, to dissent from infallible teaching on the secondary objects would be to deny the faith, either Catholic or ecclesiastical.

3. *Tertiary Objects.* The ordinary magisterium of the Pope and the bishops can also teach about a wide range of objects, doctrinal and disciplinary. This teaching is authoritative but noninfallible. The vehicles of such papal teaching are encyclicals, apostolic exhortations, declarations, and other communications directly from the Pope or indirectly from Roman congregations. The ordinary teaching of the bishops is found in pastoral letters, preaching, and the other ways that bishops exercise their magisterial role. As part of the ordinary pastoral care of the faithful, the magisterium proposes its teachings as true but not definitive in light of the promise that the Spirit guides this kind of teaching.

The assent required for the tertiary objects is true internal and external assent. Members of the Church are expected to give an obediential assent, which Vatican II refers to as "religious submission of mind and will"—"*religiosum voluntatis et intellectus obsequium*" (*Lumen gentium*, art. 25).[64] Catholics are to receive these nondefinitive teachings as safe and well-founded opinions, prudently believing they are free from error. Even though such teachings are not absolutely guaranteed as true and unchangeable, they are to be followed by the faithful. To dissent from this category of teaching would be an act of disobedience, unless the justifying reasons are personally compelling and the dissent properly circumscribed, as we shall see in the following section. This assent is described in canon 752:

> A religious submission of intellect and will, even if not the assent of faith, is to be paid to the teaching which the Supreme Pontiff or the College of Bishops enunciate on faith or morals when they exercise the authentic magisterium, even if they do not intend to proclaim it

---

63. See Ioachim Salaverri in M. Nicolau and I. Salaverri, *Sacrae theologiae summa*, vol. I: *Theologia Fundamentalis* (Madrid: Biblioteca de autores christianos, 1952), 788-789.

64. The term "*obsequium*" is best translated as "submission." Bishop B. C. Butler, however, suggested that "due respect" is a more accurate translation ("Infallible: *Authenticum: Assensus: Obsequium*. Christian Teaching Authority and the Christian's Response," *Doctrine and Life* 31 [1981]:77-89). Francis A. Sullivan has argued convincingly against Bishop Butler's view in *Magisterium*, pp. 158-160.

with a definitive act; therefore the Chirstian faithful are to take care
to avoid whatever is not in harmony with that teaching.

The Possibility of Dissent

Are there any instances when one can legitimately dissent from some
of the ordinary, noninfallible teachings of the Church? Clearly, the
Church, by labeling certain propositions as noninfallible, recognizes
that the teaching could be erroneous. Why, then, the current controversy over dissent? To see this issue in perspective and to narrow
the discussion, it is helpful to present briefly several traditional pre-
suppositions, accepted even by most Catholics who argue for the
possibility of dissent.

First, the hierarchical magisterium—the Pope and the bishops—
has the duty and responsibility to teach matters of faith and morals.
Authoritative teaching is an integral part of the ministry of the
hierarchy and should be generally accepted.

Second, the teaching of the Church enjoys the presumption of
truth; it is not simply one opinion among many, but the authentic
voice of the Church guided by the Spirit. Only serious and convincing reasons can challenge that presumption

Third, everyone has the obligation to follow one's conscience in
making personal moral and doctrinal decisions. An essential element
in the proper formation of conscience, however, includes the truths
that are taught by the Church, even those that are not infallible.

Fourth, a refusal to accept the ordinary noninfallible teaching of
the Church should be an exception. Catholics are expected to follow
Church teaching, all the more so because the Holy Spirit assists the
hierarchy when it proclaims truths of faith and morals.

Fifth, every Church teaching, even the most formal infallible definition, can be further understood and developed. The entire Church
—hierarchy, theologians, and laity—share in the task of grasping
more fully and accurately the truth of what the Church teaches.

Sixth, the term "noninfallible" does not mean that a teaching is
merely probable; it may be as certain as any natural truth. Noninfallible means only that it is not protected by a religious guarantee of
absolute inerrancy. A noninfallible teaching, however, is in theory
reformable; and it may, at least conceivably, be incorrect. Several
past teachings of the ordinary magisterium of the Church have eventually changed, for example, those dealing with interest taking or

usury, juridical torture, slavery, religious liberty, and the ecclesial quality of the Roman Catholic Church and other Christian Churches. These teachings, however, have to be understood in their origin and development, taking into consideration their cultural context, their concrete justification, and their abstract formulation.

The present debate over the nonreception of some noninfallible teachings of the ordinary magisterium centers primarily on the distinction between private and public dissent with special concern for the modalities of the exercise of the latter. Each type requires special analysis.

Private dissent refers to the personal decision of an individual not to follow a specific teaching of the Church. Dissent, however, is not objectively self-justifying; the reasons for the dissent are determinative. Is the judgment to disagree based on valid reasons or is it the result of misunderstanding the meaning of the teaching, hostility to Church authority, or intellectual pride? Has the person studied the matter, sought counsel, and tried sincerely and prayerfully to arrive at assent? Very convincing reasons for private dissent are needed, especially if the teaching concerns important matters and if it has been taught deliberately, repeatedly, and with great emphasis at the highest levels of Church authority. The decision to dissent is a serious one, because it implies that the Church's teaching is either wrong in itself or in its application to one's particular case.

A clear theological tradition, however, allows the possibility of internal dissent by one who has tried honestly, conscientiously, and with docility to make a sincere assent to the ordinary teaching of the Church, but is unable for good reasons to do so. Such a person may find the arguments and the conclusion proposed by the Church to be so unconvincing and arguments to the contrary so weighty that in conscience he or she cannot agree with the Church's teaching. Dissent ever remains the exception, but as the German bishops noted, it is "in principle admissible"; the Christian "must ask himself in sober self-criticism before God and his conscience, whether he has the necessary depth and breadth of theological expertise to allow his private theory and practice to depart from the present doctrine of the ecclesiastical authorities."[65]

---

65. Pastoral Letter of German Bishops (1967). Quoted in Karl Rahner, *Theological Investigations* (New York: Seabury, 1976), XIV:87.

Public dissent, however, takes another big step; it refers to open nonconformity or disagreement with a Church teaching, which is communicated publicly in a spoken or written manner. Reasons that justify private dissent do not automatically justify public dissent. A new component—communication of disagreement—brings dissent into the open. Its impact is a function of the person and his or her role in the Church: individual lay persons, religious educators, catechists, theologians, priests, and even bishops.

Of special concern here is the theologian. Theologians have an ecclesial ministry of service to the truth of the Gospel. Their mission is to explore the origins, meaning, and development of faith, to probe the relationship between Christian truths, and to show how revelation responds to the challenges of contemporary society. In a critical and systematic way, they seek to be mediators between faith and culture. May theologians, then, in exercising their professional duties dissent publicly from noninfallible teachings of the Church? Again it is a question of the modalities of public dissent in view of the circumstances.

Professional theologians must be able to evaluate official Church teaching, to analyze the arguments adduced by the Church in support of its positions, and to suggest modifications. This critical analysis—which is an essential part of the theological enterprise—emerges in theological journals and conferences. There, provisional and hypothetical conclusions that differ from Church teaching may be properly submitted to other theologians and to Church officials for critique. This kind of public dissent may be more correctly called nonassent or witholding of assent.

Contemporary proponents of public dissent often refer to Vatican II and the Code of Canon Law to justify their position. Often cited are canon 212 (*Lumen gentium*, art. 37) and canon 218 (*Gaudium et spes*, art. 62). Canon 212, 3, states that the Christian faithful have the right and "even at times a duty" to make known their opinions to the bishops and to other Christian faithful on matters which pertain to the good of the Church. Canon 218 says that those engaged in the sacred sciences enjoy a lawful freedom in seeking the truth and in prudently expressing their views.

These canons, however, do not directly speak of dissent. Indeed, canon 212, 1, refers to the obligation of the faithful to follow the teaching of their bishops, and canon 218 says that the experts in the sacred sciences must, in manifesting their views, show "due submission" (*obsequium*) to the magisterium of the Church. A theologian may be convinced that he or she ought to make known certain dissenting views, but the authorities may, in particular instances, prohibit such expression on the grounds that such dissent does not promote the good of the Church.

Some Catholic theologians, however, often publicly assert with full confidence that their views are correct and the clear teaching of the Church wrong. Note the radical difference between withholding assent and actively promoting dissent. Theologians who present their own ideas as pastoral norms are publicly putting their own judgment above that of the Church and attempting to function as an alternate magisterium. Bishops alone are the official teachers in the Church by divine right; they alone are what Thomas Aquinas called the "pastoral magisterium" ("*magisterium cathedrae pastoralis*").

Theologians run a risk when they disseminate their dissenting views to nonspecialists throughout the media or in public talks. An audience not schooled in the subtleties of theological discourse may perceive that which is presented as debatable or probable as if it were a certain and acceptable norm of action in their own lives. Many nontheologians feel they have the right to hold any theological opinion, especially in moral matters, as long as they can cite some dissenting theologian. Lost or ignored are the nuanced distinctions made by theologians between infallible and noninfallible, probable and certain, and private and public. Church authorities are rightly concerned with public dissent so perceived, since it may threaten the unity of the believing community.

Like other believers, Catholic theologians sometimes find themselves personally unable to give internal assent to some noninfallible teachings and may propose arguments critical of a particular teaching. They may discuss their difficulties with other theologians and members of the hierarchy; nevertheless, even this so-called scholarly dissent has its limits. Factors relevant to the limiting of public dissent look to the degree of opposition to current magisterial teaching, the seriousness of the matter, the forum of the dissent, and the subsequent polarization of the faithful.

The Church often tolerates such public discussion and dissent for a while, but at some point, exercising its right to teach authoritatively, it may for good reason impose a cloture, forbidding the theologian (whatever his or her private views) from teaching that opinion publicly. In such a case, the Church requires that the theologian, as a member of the ecclesial community, defer to higher authority for the sake of the public order and the common good of the Church. James H. Provost has espoused this same view:

> A theologian should not express opinions that differ from the position of the magisterium in such a way as to lead to disrespect for the magisterium. If after observing appropriate procedures, a determination is made that the position of the theologian is not to be taught, due respect for the magisterium includes witholding the expression of the opinion as required.[66]

The Response by Church Authority

In 1950, Pius XII (1939–58) issued the encyclical *Humani generis*. That document, which affirmed that theologians must follow the teaching of the ordinary magisterium, contained this passage: "But if the supreme pontiffs in their official acts purposely pass judgment on a matter debated until then, it is obvious to all, according to the mind and will of the same pontiffs, that the matter cannot be considered any longer a question open to free discussion among theologians."[67]

Vatican II, assuming that assent would be given to Church teaching, did not discuss the issue of dissent. The Theological Commission of the Council, however, responded to a case, "at least theoretically possible," raised by three bishops about a learned person who for well-founded reasons cannot give an internal assent to a noninfallible doctrine. The Commisssion replied that "approved theological treatises should be consulted."[68] It should be carefully noted that the question dealt with internal assent and not the public assent we described above.

---

66. In J. A. Coriden, T. J. Green, and D. E. Heintschel, eds., *The Code of Canon Law: A Text and Commentary* (New York: Paulist, 1985), p. 152.

67. *Acta apostolicae sedis* 41 (1950):568. This point was made in an earlier draft of *Lumen gentium* but was not included in the final text. *The Decree on Priestly Formation (Optatam totius)*, article 16, note 31, has a reference to this section of *Humani generis*.

68. *Acta synodalia sacrosancti concilii oecumenici Vaticani II* (Vatican City: Typis Polyglottis Vaticanis, 1976), vol. III, part 8, 88, n. 159.

In the United States during the height of the controversy over *Humanae vitae* (1968), the American bishops in their pastoral, "Human Life in Our Day," referred to the norms of licit theological dissent. They stated: "The expression of theological dissent from the magisterium is in order only if the reasons are serious and well-founded, if the manner of the dissent does not question or impugn the teaching authority of the Church, and is such as not to give scandal."[69]

Archbishop Daniel Pilarczyk has understood these criteria as the "outer limits" that determine how much dissent the Church will tolerate. The Church itself must judge if these norms have been followed. But when theologians dissent from noninfallible teachings, Pilarczyk said, "they do so at their own risk, subject to a final determination by Church authority."[70]

That final determination by the Church is a difficult exercise in discernment. It has to balance the rights of the theologian and the rights of the Church. Two extremes should be avoided.

First, the Church in its teaching ministry should avoid "creeping infallibilism," whereby everything that is taught appears to come under the mantle of infallibility. Not all magisterial teaching is at the same level, and the Church should make that clear. Furthermore, Roman intervention should be used sparingly, lest the Church create a climate of fear that would stifle theological creativity. Theologians need sufficient freedom of inquiry if they are to explore the revealed message and relate it to the challenges of the present. A theology that simply repeated what the magisterium asserted would soon stagnate.

The history of Catholic theology demonstrates that harsh judgments by the Church have not always been justified. The examples are numerous: the bishop of Paris formally condemned some teachings of Thomas Aquinas; a papal bull condemned many propositions from the writings of Meister Eckhart; Joan of Arc was burned at the stake; Teresa of Avila underwent much persecution from Church authorities. In more recent times John Henry Newman, Yves Congar, Pierre Teilhard de Chardin, Henri de Lubac, and John Courtney Murray humbly and submissively suffered from Roman displeasure.

The lesson from history is not that Rome should abdicate its role

---

69. No. 51. *The Pope Speaks* 13 (1968):386.
70. *Origins,* July 31, 1986, vol. 16, no. 9:177.

as teacher of the faith and its function as the authentic interpreter; history also lists the great number of theologians whose theories have been legitimately condemned. Strict action by Rome has helped preserve the unity of the Church in the face of error and opposition. The ultimate norm is truth itself. The Church and its authority, under the guidance of the Holy Spirit, seeks to preserve, foster, and communicate accurately the truth of the Christian tradition.

Second, theologians must avoid underestimating the authority of the magisterium. The Church must decide what is and what is not consonant with Scripture and tradition. If the opinions of theologians and the teaching of the magisterium are of equal value regarding the truth of noninfallible teaching, then the latter would soon be reduced to the choice of either defining infallibly or remaining virtually silent. The Church must sometimes present teaching that is noninfallible and possibly provisional if the faith is to be integrated as a decisive force within the concrete Christian community. The German bishops in their 1967 letter made this point:

> In order to maintain the true and ultimate substance of faith she [the Church] must, even at the risk of error in points of detail, give expression to doctrinal directives which have a certain degree of binding force, and yet, since they are not *de fide* definitions, involve a certain element of the provisional even to the point of being capable of including error.[71]

The Church cannot countenance within itself a "free market of ideas" without any control or limit. Even ordinary teaching of the Church is not just "another opinion" that can be cavalierly dismissed. Occasionally, the official Church may have to proscribe some theological opinions. Rome may tolerate dissent for a time, but it cannot endorse it.

In conflict situations, Rome has several options. The most common one is to wait and see if the offending theological opinion is more accurately formulated in later writings in response to peer judgment. The Vatican may issue a document pointing out the Church's teaching on a specific question or evaluating the work of a particular theologian. In more serious and protracted cases, Rome has other choices: to require the theologian to clarify the point at issue in future

---

71. Pastoral Letter of German Bishops, p. 86.

publications (Schillebeeckx), to silence the theologian for a period of time or prohibit publication or teaching (Boff and Pohier), to withdraw the right to be called a Catholic theologian (Küng), or declare that the theologian is not eligible nor suitable to teach Catholic theology (Curran). A theologian who obstinately denies an infallible teaching may be excommunicated.

To put these concerns into more definite categories, I shall describe four models for dealing with dissent in noninfallible matters. Of course, additional variations are possible, but these four are the basic alternatives. The first two deal with dissent from the perspective of liberty; the last two from the perspective of authority.

1. *The free-market model* brings all opinions into the public arena. The Pope's position is just one of the many positions presented for serious consideration. The basis of this model is the generally laudable one of freedom of individual conscience. It comprises thoughts, actions, and communications in the private and public sector. The decision, if there really is one, is not final but ongoing; it is a kind of public consensus, a majority vote of laity, theologians, and hierarchy, Catholic and non-Catholic, secular and religious. This model is the *consensus fidelium* writ large in an egalitarian world community, but as such effectively undermines the unique authority of the Church: theologians do not speak for the whole Church; only the Pope and the bishops do.

2. *The peer-review model* stays within the same genus but narrows the circle of decision makers. Professional theologians, whether exclusively Catholic or inclusively Christian, debate various opinions, giving special deference to the Pope as a theologian, the *primus inter pares*, but still merely a theologian. All together, they look to Scripture, tradition, and the *sensus fidelium*; they attend to the noninfallible statements issuing from the Vatican but do not feel automatically obliged by them. Here again the authority of the Church is diminished.

3. *The open-season model* contrasts squarely with the free-market model. It is an authoritarian method of dealing on an ad hoc basis with opinions that diverge from Vatican policy even on noninfallible matters. The Church does not argue; it sanctions. As a result, it fails to profit much from the creativity of theologians; nor does it manifest publicly that openness to the Spirit that is a sign of authenticity.

4. *The court-of-last-resort model* replaces authoritarianism with due process. The Church does not abdicate its magisterial role, but exercises it through dialogue and a shared concern for unity. The formal procedures should show sensitivity to the *sensus fidelium* as the Spirit works through the minds of the members of the Church, but the Church retains as its own the final right and responsibility of authoritative teaching and decision-making.

According to this model, the magisterium does more than structure a formal debate with reasonable rules; it is also able, under the guidance of the Spirit, to establish even in noninfallible matters norms of assent and action that demand "religious assent." After the representations of divergence and discussions of objections, it brings the matter to a timely and authoritative cloture, so that the hearts and minds of the faithful may be in peace.

Sanctions are not the norm but may function, when necessary, as the public promulgation of a magisterial decision. Even in noninfallible matters, the magisterium is the court of last resort; its primary mandate is not to punish but to bring guidance to all of the faithful. It does not, however, abolish freedom of conscience, but rather operates in private and in public to help in the formation of a truly Christian conscience. In doing so it fulfills its mission with fear and trembling but with a confidence, which all the faithful can share, in the ever-abiding and efficacious presence of the Spirit of truth. The divinely given structure of the Church and the promised guidance of the Spirit make this last model the only one that promotes the proper tension between freedom and authority, between individual conscience and the Church of Christ.

In the last decade, Rome has not acted precipitately in correcting theologians. It acts not in response to trivial matters but only when there is clear dissent from doctrines, even noninfallible ones, which the Church has consistently and repeatedly taught. Abortion, contraception, euthanasia, and homosexuality are not marginal issues. After repeated warnings and opportunity for clarification, a lengthy process begins, entailing extensive dialogue and communication between the theologian and Church authorities; twelve years in the case of Hans Küng and seven years in the case of Charles E. Curran. The penalties imposed have admittedly been severe, even though they did not involve excommunication or dismissal from the priesthood.

Unfortunately, the issue of dissent was not adequately addressed in *Lumen gentium,* article 25, canon 752, or by the International Theological Commission.[72] The present situation in the Church and the continuing debate over theological dissent should prompt Rome to issue a thorough clarification of the meaning and limits of dissent. Such guidelines, however, should be the product not just of one Roman congregation but the result of extended dialogue between bishops and theologians.

An essential element in any procedure that seeks to resolve a doctrinal dispute between a theologian and the magisterium is respect for the basic sacramental and human rights of the theologian.[73] Thus, the first attempts at resolution would begin at the local level and, if unsuccessful, be brought to the attention of Rome.

The Sacred Congregation for the Doctrine of the Faith (SCDF), in 1971, made public its procedure for doctrinal investigations called the *"Ratio agendi."*[74] This procedure, used in the investigations of Küng, Schillebeeckx, Curran, and others, could be improved in the interest of fairness to better serve the Church. I would suggest the following changes in the *Ratio agendi*: the theologian should be informed of the charges and, if relevant, the names of the accusers; time limits should be reasonable; the theologian should have access to the full record; the procedures for the colloquium (the meeting of the theologian with representatives of the SCDF) should be published; the theologian should be able to have counsel present at the colloquium; appeal procedures should be more clearly indicated; and, finally, members (hierarchical and staff) of the SCDF should not comment publicly on the positions of the theologian before the investigation is completed.

---

72. *Theses on the Relationship between the Ecclesiastical Magisterium and Theology* (Washington: USCC, 1977), pp. 8–9.

73. I treated this issue in "Theological Evaluation of Current Procedures," in Leo J. O'Donovan, ed., *Cooperation between Theologians and the Ecclesiastical Magisterium: A Report of the Joint Committee of the Canon Law Society of America and the Catholic Theological Society of America.* (Washington: CLSA and CTSA, 1982), pp. 117-143. This same committee also published procedures dealing with disputes between bishops and theologians. It is found in *Proceedings of the Catholic Theological Society of America* 39 (1984):209-234.

74. *Acta apostolicae sedis* 63 (1971):234-236. English translation in *Origins,* March 16, 1972, vol. 1, no. 39:648.

Conclusion

In this chapter we have examined at length the *sensus fidelium* and reception and their relationship to the limits of the papacy. The *sensus fidelium*, together with Scripture and tradition, limit the Pope in that he has the responsibility to communicate accurately the lived faith of the Christian community and not depart from it. Exercising his authority within the Church, the Pope must be sensitive to the Spirit working in Christians and protect the common faith he shares with them.

Reception of Church teaching is a complex process involving the entire Church. Nonreception does not invalidate a papal decision any more than reception confers legitimacy. Refusal to accept the teaching of the Church does not limit papal authority in itself, but it may impede or weaken its exercise. Continuous and widespread disagreement with Church teaching, however, may prompt the magisterium to reassess its positions or to communicate them more effectively. Dialogue between the hierarchy, the laity, and theologians can only contribute to the common task of all believers seeking to grasp the mystery of Christ "who is the light of the world, from whom we go forth, through whom we live, and toward whom our journey leads us" (*Lumen gentium*, art. 3).

The Pope and Other Christians

*The Roman Pontiff is the successor
of Peter, the true Vicar of Christ,
the head of the whole Church, the
father and teacher of all Christians.*

—*Council of Florence**

*The Pope, as we well know, is undoubtedly
the greatest obstacle in the path of ecumenism.*

—*Paul VI*†

I n its two-thousand-year history, the office of the papacy has been
both a symbol of unity and an occasion of division. For those
Christians who are not Catholic the papacy remains a major problem.
Antipapal literature has often contended that Catholics understand
the Pope as a Hobbesian "mortal god" or as a benevolent but totali-
tarian despot. The two following passages, one from the East and one
from the West, dramatically illustrate these views. The first is a statement of the Greek bishops made at Nicaea in 1204 who, in their opposition to the Latin Church, rejected the claims of the Roman
primacy.

They [the Latins] say and believe that the Pope is not the successor of
Peter but rather Peter himself in person. They make him almost into
a god and place him over Peter by proclaiming him to be the lord of
the whole of Christendom. They say that the Roman Church itself is
the one, catholic, and apostolic Church which, within itself alone,
comprehends all others. The Pope becomes, as Pontifex, the sole

---

*Decree for the Greeks (DS 1370). Repeated at Vatican I (DS 3059).
†Address to the Secretariat for Promoting Christian Unity, Rome, April 29, 1967.
Documentation catholique, May 21, 1967, p. 870.

connecting link between all, since he alone is Peter and the whole flock of Christ must be subject to him.[1]

The second statement is from the *Apology of the Augsburg Confession* of 1531. This Lutheran document is even more detailed in its opposition to the papacy.

> It [the Church] is the supreme outward monarchy of the whole world in which the Roman pontiff must have unlimited power beyond question or censure. He may establish articles of faith, abolish the Scriptures by his leave, institute devotions and sacrifices, enact whatever law he pleases, excuse and exempt men from any laws, divine, canonical, or civil, as he wishes. From him the emperor and all kings have received their power and right to rule, and this at Christ's command. . . . Therefore the pope must be lord of the whole world, of all the kingdoms of the world, and of all public and private affairs.[2]

These two statements, made three centuries apart, reflect the then intense animosity between the Roman Church and other Christian bodies. The Orthodox East and the Protestant West did not accept the doctrine of the papacy and were not reluctant to say so. Polemics, rhetoric, and exaggeration were common currency in these theological debates; their principal argument, although overstated, focused on what they perceived to be the unlimited, absolute, and monarchical power of the Pope. To some extent, this objection, admittedly in more nuanced terms, has persisted to this day. Most non-Catholics, the ecumenical movement notwithstanding, do not subscribe to Vatican I's definition of the Pope's primacy of jurisdiction. They might acknowledge that the Pope cannot abolish Scripture, violate divine or natural law, nor reject Christian tradition, that he is a Christian and even a spiritual leader among Christians, but they do not accept the Pope's authority as "supreme, full, ordinary, and immediate."

A united Church comprising all Christians may not be imminent,

---

1. "Criminationes adversus Ecclesiam Latinam," in J. B. Cotellier, ed., *Ecclesiae graecae monumenta* (Paris, 1868), III:501.

2. Theodore G. Tappert, ed., *The Book of Concord* (Philadelphia: Fortress, 1959), p. 172.

but more and more Christians agree with the words of the *Decree on Ecumenism* of Vatican II that a divided Church "contradicts the will of Christ, scandalizes the world, and damages that most holy cause, the preaching of the Gospel to every creature" (art. 1). They are beginning to recognize that a universal ministry of unity is necessary for a united Church. This openness to some form of primacy within the Church demands a better understanding of the nature and the limits of the primatial office. In this chapter we shall discuss the relationship between the Pope and other Christians and the possibility of a voluntary limitation of papal authority.

The Scope of the Petrine Ministry

Non-Catholic Christians were encouraged that Vatican II set the doctrine of the papacy within the context of the Church and proposed a collegial understanding of authority. The Council's commitment to ecumenism inspired Christians to work for reunion. This movement has been advanced by the dialogues or bilateral consultations between the Roman Catholic Church and other Christian denominations. Many of these dialogues have discussed the question of ecclesial authority and papal primacy, but none more fully than the Lutheran–Roman Catholic Dialogue in the United States and the Anglican–Roman Catholic International Commission.[3] They have examined in detail how the Pope could function as a "father and teacher of all Christians."

The Need for a Universal Primate

The initial and continuing question that Orthodox and Protestant Christians face is whether a primatial office is, in fact, necessary for the Church. All Christians may desire unity, but many do not want any formal relationship with Rome; furthermore, some non-Catholics wonder about a possible need for the papacy in the protecting and fostering of their own ecclesial communities. Of course, the Orthodox

---

3. See J. Michael Miller, *What Are They Saying about Papal Primacy?* (New York: Paulist, 1983).

Church has survived over nine hundred years without the papacy and the Protestant Churches nearly five hundred years; the rejection of the papacy has become part of their self-definition. And they ask themselves whether the papacy would contribute anything significant to their own ecclesial character or prove a restrictive and unnecessary burden.

One answer has been given by the Lutheran–Roman Catholic Dialogue. It declared that among Lutherans today there is an increasing awareness "of the necessity of a specific Ministry to serve the church's unity and universal mission."[4] Such a ministry might help relate the local Churches to the universal Church and would provide the world with a credible, visible witness of Christian unity. The tasks of this universal ministry or "Petrine function" are many: to preserve the unity of the Church, to facilitate cooperation, communication, and mutual assistance, and to encourage collaboration in the Church's mission. Moreover, the Bishop of Rome has been "the single most notable representative of this ministry toward the Church universal."[5]

The Reformers, as the Dialogue pointed out, did not reject the "Petrine function" as such but only its abuses as manifested in the historical papacy at the time of the Reformation; they sought not an abolition of the primacy but rather its reform. Although Lutherans do not accept the Catholic interpretation of the divine institution of the papacy, its jurisdiction, and its infallibility, they consider the recognition of papal primacy possible to the degree that a renewed papacy could truly serve the Gospel by protecting Christian freedom and by fostering the unity of the Church. "God may show again in the future that the papacy is his gracious gift to his people."[6]

An even more positive approach is found in the international dialogue between Anglicans and Roman Catholics. It held that the unity of Christians needs a visible expression which would promote fidelity to the apostolic teaching and act as a safeguard of catholicity for each local Church. A primatial authority is necessary for the unity of the whole Church. The participants developed an understanding of authority in the Church around the idea of *koinonia*: sharing in

---

4. Paul C. Empie and T. Austin Murphy, eds., *Papal Primacy and the Universal Church: Lutherans and Catholics in Dialogue V* (Minneapolis, Minn.: Augsburg, 1974), p. 10.

5. Ibid., p. 12.

6. Ibid., p. 21.

the life of God in Christ Jesus through the Spirit. They concluded that "a universal primacy will be needed in a reunited Church and should appropriately be the primacy of the bishop of Rome."[7]

The Anglicans pointed out that Anglicanism never rejected the principle of a universal primacy but objected only to the way it was exercised and to some of the claims of the Roman primacy. The divine institution of the primacy of Rome and even the divine-right language of Vatican I are not major stumbling blocks for Anglicans. They accept the primacy as an expression of God's purpose for his Church, as long as it does not imply that Churches out of communion with Rome are not fully Churches. Both communions understand jurisdiction as "given for the effective fulfillment of office and this fact determines its exercise and limits."[8]

The Anglicans, concerned over the possible uncontrolled use of primatial authority, insisted that authority must be understood in a pastoral rather than in a juridical sense. The moral limits of universal jurisdiction derive from the nature of the Church itself and from the nature of the function of the primate.

> Although the scope of universal jurisdiction cannot be precisely defined canonically, there are moral limits to its exercise: they derive from the nature of the Church and of the universal primate's pastoral office. By virtue of his jurisdiction, given for the building up of the Church, the universal primate has the right in special cases to intervene in the affairs of a diocese and to receive appeals from the decision of a diocesan bishop.[9]

The two dialogues mentioned above have obviously not reached complete agreement on the doctrine of papal primacy nor on its practical consequences. Serious obstacles remain; the suspicions and prejudices of the past have not yet been overcome. At the same time "it is becoming increasingly clear," writes the Protestant ecumenist Max Thurian of Taizé, "that Christian unity can only be achieved and maintained thanks to a universal ministry of unity."[10] Chris-

---

7. Anglican-Roman Catholic International Commission, *The Final Report* (Cincinnati: Forward Movement; Washington: USCC, 1982), p. 85.

8. Ibid., p. 88.

9. Ibid., p. 90.

10. "The Ministry of Unity of the Bishop of Rome to the Whole Church," *One in Christ* 22 (1986):132.

tians of the mainline Churches are beginning to recognize the value of a universal Petrine ministry and many are committed to its realization. The dialogues have created a climate of genuine Christian reconciliation and collaboration marked by shared faith and fellowship.

The Authority of the Pope over Other Christians

If the Pope is the "father and teacher of all Christians," does he have any authority over those who are not members of the Catholic Church? Let us examine this interesting question of limits first in terms of legal authority, by comparing the 1917 and 1983 Codes of Canon Law.

The 1917 Code accepted as a given that the Church of Jesus Christ and the Roman Catholic Church are coterminous. On the basis of this conviction, canon 87 stated that by baptism one is constituted a person in the Church of Christ with all the rights and duties of a Christian, unless, in regard to rights, there exists an obstacle that impedes the bond of communion or a censure imposed by the Church.[11] Baptism of water confers a juridical personality; by it one enters into the Church. Communion with the Catholic Church, however, is lost by apostasy, heresy, and schism, which also entail a loss of ecclesial rights. Neither membership in a non-Catholic denomination nor censure excuses one from the duties incumbent on all Christians.

The subject of ecclesiastical laws is treated in canon 12 of the 1917 Code. It declared that persons who are baptized, have attained the use of reason, and have completed the seventh year of age are bound by all merely ecclesiastical laws. Infants, the unbaptized, and the mentally incompetent are not bound. But heretics, schismatics, apostates, and excommunicated persons are bound to observe ecclesiastical laws.

What of non-Catholic Christians? Most commentators noted that in general they too are bound by ecclesiastical laws, unless expressly exempted. The 1917 Code itself made two exemptions: non-Catholics in their own marriages are exempt from the impediment of

---

11. Compare this view with the declaration of the Council of Trent: "If anyone says that the baptized are free from all the precepts of Holy Church, whether written or handed down, so that they are not bound to observe them unless they wish to submit to them on their own accord, let him be anathema" (DS 1621).

disparity of cult (can. 1070) and from the law regarding the form of marriage (can. 1090). Commentators added that Christians who in good faith belong to other denominations are practically speaking excused from certain laws (e.g., laws of fast and abstinence). This was not an exception in the strict sense but rather an excuse because of invincible ignorance and thus the lack of moral imputability.

The 1983 Code of Canon Law approached this question differently by recognizing the ecclesial reality of Churches not in union with Rome. It clearly reflected the theology of Vatican II and the famous passage in article 8 of *Lumen gentium*, when it stated that the Church of Christ subsists in the Catholic Church (can. 204, 2). Before the Council, it was commonly accepted that the Church of Christ is the Roman Catholic Church. Pius XII taught explicitly in *Mystici corporis*[12] and in *Humani generis*[13] that the Mystical Body of Christ, the Church of Christ, and the Roman Catholic Church were one and the same reality. The Council's use of the term "subsists" indicated that the Church of Christ is broader than any one denomination, even though it is present in a special or full manner in the Catholic Church. To say that the Church of Christ subsists in the Catholic Church means, as Francis A. Sullivan correctly observed, "that it is in the Catholic Church that it is to be found existing with all its essential properties: oneness, holiness, catholicity, and apostolicity."[14] The Church of Christ thus includes other Christian Churches in the East and the West, although they are not in full communion with the Church of Rome.

The 1983 Code, in a clear departure from the 1917 Code, restricted the subject of ecclesiastical laws to Catholics. In so doing, the Pope —who promulgated the law voluntarily—limited his own authority. Canon 11 states that merely ecclesiastical laws bind only those who were baptized in the Catholic Church or received into it, who have the use of reason, and who have completed seven years of age. Non-Catholic Christians are, therefore, not bound by the ecclesiastical laws of the Catholic Church.

---

12. *Acta apostolicae sedis* 35 (1943):221 ff.

13. Ibid., 42 (1950):571.

14. "'*Subsistit in*': The Significance of Vatican II's Decision to Say of the Church of Christ not that It 'Is' but that It 'Subsists In' the Roman Catholic Church," *One in Christ* 22 (1986):119.

It follows, then, that anyone who is baptized a Catholic or received into full communion with the Catholic Church is always bound by Church law even if that person loses the faith and severs all bonds with the Catholic Church. The only exceptions relate to marriage: a person who has left the Catholic Church by a formal act is exempted from the impediment of disparity of cult (can. 1086) and is not bound by the canonical form of marriage (can. 1117). The two latter exemptions are identical to those of the 1917 Code in regard to non-Catholic Christians.

A related question concerns the duties and rights of the Christian faithful that are mentioned throughout the Code but particularly in canons 208–231. Some examples of *duties* incumbent on all the Christian faithful are the following: to maintain communion with the Church, to observe ecclesiastical laws, to be faithful to the doctrine of the faith, to live a holy life and promote the growth of the Church, to spread the Gospel, to obey Church authorities in doctrinal and disciplinary matters, to express opinions to Church authorities on matters that concern the good of the Church, to help provide for the needs of the Church (talent, time, and financial support), and to promote social justice.

Some examples of *rights* are: to spread the Gospel; to make known one's needs, especially spiritual, to Church authorities; to receive help from the spiritual goods of the Church, especially the sacraments and the Word of God; to found and govern associations devoted to religious purposes and to hold meetings; to promote or sustain apostolic action; to receive a Christian education; to have freedom of inquiry and expression as long as it is in obedience to Church teaching; to choose one's state of life without coercion; and to protect one's privacy and good reputation.

Do these rights and duties apply to non-Catholic Christians? Canon 96 states that by baptism one is incorporated into the Church of Christ and has certain duties and rights which, in accordance to each one's status, are proper to Christians, to the extent that they are in ecclesiastical communion and unless a legitimately issued sanction intervenes. This canon admits of at least two interpretations.[15]

---

15. See observations by James H. Provost in James A. Coriden, Thomas J. Green, and Donald E. Heintschel, eds., *The Code of Canon Law: A Text and Commentary* (New York: Paulist, 1985), pp. 124 ff.

The first interpretation is that baptized persons have the duties and rights in the Church of Christ according to their status and degree of communion in it, so that only those in full communion—that is Catholics—have rights and duties fully and simply. Canon 205 explains that full communion with the Catholic Church (in which the Church of Christ subsists) involves the bonds of profession of faith, sacraments, and ecclesiastical governance.

A second view is that all baptized persons, since they are incorporated into Christ and his Church by baptism, have, at least potentially, all the rights and duties of Christians according to their status, but their exercise is limited to the extent that they can be enforced or vindicated in the Catholic Church. Even though all Christians may potentially have the rights and duties that flow from baptism, they may not be able to actuate them; pragmatically the Catholic Church cannot enforce the duties nor can non-Catholic Christians realistically be permitted to exercise the rights.

Although the Pope may not choose to take full canonical authority over Christians separated from Rome, he may well exercise moral authority. In fact the greatest asset of the papacy may well be this parenetic role, which enables the Pope to act as the "father and teacher of all Christians." By tirelessly preaching the Word of God, the Pope can reach out to all humanity, Christian and non-Christian, and move the hearts and minds of people through exhortation and example. Recent Popes have seen their ministry of evangelization in this broad perspective.

One sign of this new approach is that the major encyclical letters of the Popes, since *Pacem in terris* of John XXIII, are now addressed to a wider audience and not simply to the hierarchy or even to the Catholic faithful. Thus the first encyclical of John Paul II, *Redemptor hominis*, had the following salutation: "To his venerable brothers in the episcopate, the priests, the religious families, the sons and daughters of the Church, and to all men and women of good will." The papal ministry can offer love, hope, truth, and compassion to people who are longing for a renewed sense of spiritual values. By demonstrating his solidarity with all humanity, the Pope, through his unique role as head of a large, international, and influential religious organization, is able to communicate effectively the saving message of the Gospel.

The Possibility of Further
Voluntary Limitation

In the minds of many Protestant and Orthodox Christians the papacy is often identified with arbitrary authoritarianism. They point to instances in the past where Popes have acted unilaterally without regard for the rights of others. Distrusting a supreme office that is highly centralized and monarchically operative, they doubt that such an organization can help the cause of Christian unity. Undoubtedly, the papacy has been guilty of abuses; these distortions have diminished its credibility. But the papacy is a historical reality; it has changed in the past and it is capable of further change. One would hope that the papacy will become more collegial in the future.

Papal prerogatives are admittedly broad, but there is a difference between what a Pope may do and what he will do, between the possession and the exercise of authority. The Pope should use only that amount of authority needed to fulfill his mandate as supreme shepherd. "The differentiation between supreme authority and its use enables the pope to limit the exercise of his jurisdiction voluntarily," writes Heinrich Fries.[16] Likewise, the Lutheran-Roman Catholic dialogue is hopeful that "voluntary limitation by the Pope of the exercise of his jurisdiction will accompany the growing vitality of the organs of collegial government."[17] Voluntary limitation can be a symbol of significant value as long as it does not unduly restrict the freedom of the Pope nor prevent him from carrying out his mission.

The rest of this chapter will cover some of the possible ways a Pope may voluntarily limit his authority. These instances are drawn largely from the ongoing bilateral consultations between the Roman Catholic Church and other Christian communions and from the theological literature on ecumenism. They are proposed tentatively as suggestions and not as ultimate resolutions. Some are controversial, with ramifications that may make their implementation difficult.

Three cautions are in order. First, voluntary limitation of authority usually means that power is transferred to other bodies. Similar

---

16. In Heinrich Fries and Karl Rahner, *Unity of the Churches: An Actual Possibility* (Philadelphia: Fortress; New York: Paulist, 1983), p. 72.

17. *Papal Primacy and the Universal Church*, p. 21.

abuses may be present in the way these other groups exercise their power. Second, voluntary limitation represents a move toward decentralization. Note, however, that a decentralized model of governance has a certain inherent weakness. As the history of the Churches in the West separated from Rome amply demonstrates, the absence of a center of unity easily leads to fragmentation and individualism. Extreme decentralization may be a greater impediment than extreme centralization. Third, canonical guidelines that limit papal power would, of course, depend on the consent of the Pope himself. They would not necessarily bind him in every instance nor could they bind his successors. But they would provide an ideal to be followed in most instances. "Voluntary limitation," as Kilian McDonnell writes, "would be a public commitment and an evangelical imperative of great force and weight which would assure against the exercise by future popes of those powers voluntarily limited."[18] With these reservations in mind, we will consider three areas in which voluntary limitation of papal authority may be applicable: legitimate diversity, collegial action, and teaching authority.

Legitimate Diversity

The unity of Christians is ultimately the gift of the Spirit who animates and guides the life of believers. Institutional structures are ineffective without the action of the Spirit. Communion is the fruit of the Spirit who bestows a wide variety of gifts on the Christian community for the purpose of building up the Body of Christ which is the Church. Unity in Christ does not exist despite diversity nor in opposition to it, but exists in and with diversity. Not all diversity is legitimate, only that which does not violate the Gospel imperatives and the relationship with other Churches.

The "legitimacy" of diversity is determined by its consonance with the unity of faith and communion. The unifying Spirit bestows diverse gifts in order to create a unity of love and truth. These gifts, given to people in specific geographical and cultural situations, help create different ways of interpreting the Christian message; they

---

18. Ibid., "Papal Primacy: Development, Centralization, and Changing Styles," p. 192.

contribute to the formation of diverse customs, laws, theologies, and liturgical practices.

The history of the Christian Church reveals the continued presence of diversity. Communities in the New Testament and in the subapostolic periods exhibited significant ecclesiological differences in their view of Church order, authority, moral norms, and theological truths.[19] These communities were far from identical in their vision of the Church, and yet, because of their insistence on sound doctrine, they were not divided; they did not break *koinonia* but continued in communion with one another.

In the contemporary Roman Catholic Church the coexistence of some eighteen canonical rites is also evidence of considerable diversity. There are already great differences, for example, in the traditions, theologies, structures, languages, and liturgies of the Latin, Coptic, Byzantine, and Armenian rites. Moreover, the oriental Churches have their own legal system as canon 1 of the 1983 Code of Canon Law implies: "The canons of this Code affect only the Latin Church." The rites are not simply tolerated; their autonomy is affirmed and appreciated. Thus, Vatican II in the *Decree on Eastern Catholic Churches* stated: "The Catholic Church holds in high esteem the institutions of the Eastern Churches, their liturgical rites, ecclesiastical traditions, and Christian way of life" (art. 1).

If the universal Church is understood as the dynamic communion of local Churches, then the function of the universal primate is to be a sign of this communion. Primacy should recognize the freedom of the local Churches, respect their diversity, and promote unity without demanding uniformity. "The ministry of the Bishop of Rome is to serve the unity of the universal Church and legitimate diversity in the Church," declared the international Lutheran-Roman Catholic dialogue.[20] Unity is not divorced from catholicity; the primatial responsibility for the unity of the local Churches also requires respect for their legitimate customs and traditions. Individual Churches

---

19. See Raymond E. Brown, *The Churches the Apostles Left Behind* (New York: Paulist, 1984).

20. "The Ministry of the Church" (1981) in Harding Meyer and Lukas Vischer, eds., *Growth in Agreement: Reports and Agreed Statements of Ecumenical Conversations on a World Level* (New York: Paulist; Geneva: World Council of Churches, 1984), p. 269.

contribute to the vitality of the universal Church and help foster the fullness of Christian life and witness. The multiplicity of diverse ecclesial expressions should never encourage divisiveness but must always operate according to the rule of faith.

The non-Roman Churches that recognize the value of an efficacious sign of world-wide unity and support the possibility of a universal ministry desire that their legitimate diversity be respected in the "one Church to be." The Anglicans, for example, want assurance that their acceptance of the primacy of the Bishop of Rome would not mean the suppression of their own traditions nor the imposition of a wholly different tradition.[21] They fear that jurisdictional primacy could undermine or usurp the rights of the local bishops and that a centralized authority might not fully understand local conditions and cultural diversity. If this were the case, then freedom of conscience, thought, and action would be threatened.[22] Likewise the Lutherans ask if the Roman Church is willing to protect the legitimate traditions and spiritual heritage of Lutheran Churches, to recognize them as sister-Churches, and to grant them some measure of self-governance within the same communion.[23]

The Bishop of Rome, on the necessary assumption that he would exercise a primatial role in a reunited Church, could accept these requests. He could voluntarily agree not to demand complete uniformity from those Churches desirous of reunion with Rome, but to accept their traditions insofar as they did not contradict the faith or destroy the communion of the Churches. This relationship would be analogous to the present position of the Eastern Catholic Churches who preserve their own traditions but still acknowledge the primacy of the Bishop of Rome.

The Pope, as the protector of unity, would remain the ultimate arbiter of conflicts. Unless the primatial office were to be only a vague and ineffective symbol of unity, the Pope would need the right to make the final decision on the legitimacy of certain traditions and theological articulations of the faith. As the universal primate in collegial association with bishops in other Churches, the Pope's task would be to safeguard the faith and the unity of the entire Church.

---

21. See *The Final Report*, p. 91.
22. Ibid., p. 89.
23. See *Papal Primacy and the Universal Church*, p. 23.

He would not make decisions regarding the legitimacy of specific teachings or practices in an authoritarian manner but only after proper consultation, discernment, and clarification. The procedures for arriving at a judgment should respect the rights of all the parties.

The issue of legitimate diversity has taken on new meaning in view of the recent Roman interventions described in Chapter One. Some Protestants, but by no means all, consider these events harmful to the ecumenical movement. Some have asked if union with the Roman Church is possible if that Church cannot accept diversity in its own membership. The faculty of the General Theological Seminary of New York, for example, felt that the Vatican's treatment of Charles E. Curran raised a "fresh and grave obstacle for Christian intellectual freedom and ecumenical credibility." It wondered what kind of relationship Anglicans could have with a Church that seems determined to suppress public discussion, debate, and dialogue. The faculty also requested that the Anglican-Roman Catholic International Commission II place on its agenda "the question whether responsible Christian intellectual freedom is presently denied by official policies of the Roman Catholic Church."[24]

It would be unfortunate if these issues permanently blocked the progress of ecumenism. In the short term, however, that seems to be a realistic prediction. In the long term, however, the controversy may have good effects, forcing those Christian Churches interested in reunion to discuss these issues candidly with the Catholic Church in order to arrive at a consensus. It presents an opportunity for them to examine carefully the entire question of legitimate diversity, the role of intellectual freedom, theological pluralism, the limits of dissent, and the authority of the Pope in all of these matters. Such a dialogue, in any case, would be necessary before Christian Churches formed a corporate union that recognized the primatial role of the Pope. It would be enormously beneficial at the present time to confront these questions honestly, lest the Churches labor under unrealistic expectations about the nature of a united Church.

---

24. These quotations come from "An Open Letter to the Members of ARCIC II," approved by the Dean and Faculty of the General Theological Seminary of New York. The letter, dated May 23, 1986, has not, to my knowledge, been published.

Collegial Action

The doctrine of episcopal collegiality taught by Vatican II was enthusiastically received by non-Catholic Churches. A typical comment
is that of the international Lutheran-Roman Catholic dialogue which
stated that collegiality "placed the primacy in a new interpretative
framework and thereby avoided a widespread one-sided and isolated
way of understanding it."[25] Collegiality is seen as balancing the
papalism of the past, thus making the office of the papacy more
acceptable.

In support of the doctrine of collegiality from an ecumenical perspective two arguments may be given—one sociological and the other
theological. First, the complexities of the world-wide Church require that the Pope collaborate with the College of Bishops in his
universal ministry. No Pope can govern the Church alone. If the
united Church ever became a reality, the task of the primate would
be even more complex; collegiality would contribute to efficiency,
accountability, and solicitude.

Second, the theological basis for collegiality is the continuity between the apostolic college and the episcopal college; bishops by
their sacramental ordination form a hierarchical communion with
other bishops under the leadership of the Pope. The entire College
of Bishops has responsibility for the whole Church. Collegiality, as a
corrective to excessive centralization, means that the Pope exercises
his ministry in collegial association with his fellow bishops and not in
isolation from them. It enables the primate to perform his pastoral
diakonia within the Church and to avoid the impression of
autocratic power.

The concrete shape of the Petrine ministry has varied greatly
throughout the centuries. Each Pope exercises his authority in a different way and creates a particular image characteristic of his pontificate. Papal style is an important factor in ecumenical circles. Is
the Pope, as perceived by other Christians, aloof, dictatorial, and
uncaring or, on the other hand, is he trusting, humble, and concerned? The Methodists made this point in 1971, when they said
that "half-a-dozen John XXIII's or Paul VI's in the next century

---

25. "The Gospel and the Church," (1972), in *Growth in Agreement*, p. 184.

would do more than anything to dispose of a thousand years of conflict and misunderstanding."[26] Only an authority given in love and received in love can be truly effective.

Some ecumenists have suggested that one way to change the image of the papacy would be for the Pope to be more visible in his ministry as the Bishop of Rome. In overseeing his own local Church, the Pope would more clearly appear as a pastor, servant, and guide.[27] "On the basis of his incorporation in and service to a particular Church we may understand his universal ministry," observed Max Thurian.[28] John Paul II has tried to emphasize his local episcopal ministry by frequent visits to Roman parishes and institutions. His remarks concerning the various papal titles are revealing:

> It is said—and this is true—that the Pope is Vicar of Christ. It is true and I accept it with all humility. . . . The attribution, the phrase in question, is undoubtedly a strong one that arouses trepidation. I must tell you that I prefer not to abuse this phrase, and to use it only rarely. I prefer indeed to say "Successor of Peter"; but I prefer even more to say "Bishop of Rome."[29]

The Anglicans, however, are still troubled by the Catholic claim that the Pope has universal and immediate jurisdiction, since the limits of such authority are not clearly expressed. As a result, they "fear that the way is thus open to its illegitimate or uncontrolled use."[30] In response to such concerns, some theologians have suggested possible changes in the structure and exercise of the primacy, in order for the Pope to exercise more pastorally his universal ministry of unity. In effect, these suggestions amount to voluntary limitations of papal authority. They deal with the papal term of office, the adaptation of a patriarchate system, and the legal determinations of collegial activity.

The first proposal suggests that the Pope would not have to be

---

26. Denver Report (1971), in *Growth in Agreement*, p. 333.

27. See Groupe des Dombes, *Le ministère de communion dans l'Eglise universelle* (Paris: Centurion, 1986), pp. 96–98.

28. "The Ministry of Unity of the Bishop of Rome," p. 132.

29. Address at the Seminary of Rome, *Osservatore Romano*, March 5–6, 1984, p. 6.

30. *The Final Report*, p. 65.

elected for life, but that he would have either a specific term of office or retire at a fixed age.[31] The advantages of this suggestion would include the following: the regular introduction of officeholders with new ideas and more vigorous energies; a sign of fraternity with other bishops who must retire at seventy-five years of age; the diminution of complacency, vested interests, or ineffective leadership that might accompany lifelong tenure; and the avoidance of those difficult times when a venerable or sickly Pope would be unable to provide strong direction. The disadvantages would be a possible weakening of the papacy as an enduring, visible sign of unity; disruption in the universal Church because of frequent changes; the increase in political maneuvering before a Pope ended his term; and the inability of a Pope to implement any long-term planning. Any proposal for a fixed papal term would have to be carefully weighed before the Church would change a system that has survived for nearly two millennia. The ultimate criterion will always be the greater good of the Church.

A second suggestion deals with the adaptation of the ancient system of patriarchates. The ecumenical group of French priests, ministers, and theologians called *Le groupe des Dombes*—so named after the abbey in Ain where they meet—proposed this change.[32] They argued that since the separation of the Eastern Churches from the West, the Bishop of Rome has exercised a twofold responsibility: minister of the whole Church and Patriarch of the West. This development has led to excessive centralization by creating a gap between local and universal jurisdictions. In order to resolve this difficulty, they suggested a structure by which the large conferences of Catholic bishops would function as did the ancient regional patriarchates. With greater canonical authority given to them, the episcopal conferences would be in charge of the organization of the local Church, the nomination of bishops, and liturgical and catechetical matters. Their decisions—with the exception of those that immediately affect

---

31. See Patrick Granfield, *The Papacy in Transition* (Garden City, N.Y.: Doubleday, 1980), pp. 147-150; Joseph Blank and Gotthold Hasenhüttl in Georg Denzler, ed., *Papsttum heute und Morgen* (Regensburg: F. Pustet, 1975), pp. 38, 71; Richard P. McBrien, *The Remaking of the Church* (New York: Harper & Row, 1973); and Joseph A. Burgess, "Lutherans and the Papacy: A Review of Some Basic Issues," in Peter J. McCord, ed., *A Pope for All Christians? An Inquiry into the Role of Peter in the Modern Church* (New York: Paulist, 1976), p. 42.

32. *Le ministère de communion*, pp. 93-95.

the common good of the universal Church—would not need confirmation by Rome.

This internal decentralization of the Catholic Church might, in turn, provide a model that could be followed by other Christian groups: Orthodox, Protestant, and Anglican Christians in the reunited Church might each become perhaps the patriarchates of Constantinople, Geneva, and Canterbury. They would have authority in their own territories, be allowed to preserve their cherished traditions, and remain in union with the universal primate.

This suggestion, similar in substance to many raised in the current ecumenical dialogues, is challenging. It would enable various Christian groups to form a united Church and still keep their own heritage. Several questions, however, still need to be answered. What would be the leadership structure in each patriarchate? How would they relate to one another? What would be their relationship to the Church of Rome? These questions are not insurmountable, but they require study and dialogue.

The third suggestion raises the possibility of formulating legal norms that would govern the collegial activity of the Pope. The underlying reason for this is that there are moral norms governing the exercise of collegiality, and these can be made into canonical laws; no intrinsic incompatibility exists between the primacy and the norms determining its exercise. Wilhelm De Vries, the eminent Jesuit orientalist, supports this idea:

> The Pope is not the source of all rights in the Church. The jurisdiction of the bishops is not derived from him, but directly from Christ. This jurisdiction is not a participation in the papal power, but stands independently. The relations between the Pope as head of the college of bishops and the remainder of the college should be positively and legally determined.[33]

The Pope could, therefore, "legitimately bind himself to follow the decision of a qualified majority" of the bishops, but "he would naturally in all cases preserve the right to make the reservation: insofar as

---

33. "Limits of Papal Primacy," in P. S. Achútegui, ed., *Cardinal Bea Studies II: Dublin Papers on Ecumenism* (Manila: Ateneo University, 1972), pp. 194–195.

this is compatible with his conscience."[34] This compatibility would also seem to involve objective criteria founded in revelation.

The De Vries suggestion is similar to the synodal principle of decision making followed in the Orthodox Churches. If adopted, it would apply canonical specifications to several papal actions. The Pope, for example, would be required to consult with the bishops before making a decision affecting the entire Church, to call a synod if the majority of the bishops request it, and to approve the selection of episcopal candidates made by the bishops. Such legislation, voluntarily agreed to by the Pope, would undoubtedly limit his plenitude of power and oblige him to act coresponsibly with the bishops in all important events.

Karl Rahner made a similar proposal, suggesting that the process by which definitive or *ex cathedra* teaching is made be explained and even codified in Church law.[35] If the one Church of the future is to become a reality then the Pope should agree that he would use his *ex cathedra* teaching authority in a way that conforms juridically or substantially to a general council of the Church. Rahner explained that the Pope should use all the available human means in arriving at a definitive judgment. He referred approvingly to the survey of bishops conducted before the definitions of the Immaculate Conception (1854) and the Assumption (1950). A law could state the necessity of wide consultation before a teaching is issued. It would be only a human law, but it "would assure the transparency of any future survey of all the bishops in the future Church."[36]

An immediate objection to this suggestion might be that it would seem to make the Pope simply the executor of the will of the bishops. Rahner was quick to answer this criticism by insisting that his proposal does not mean that future decisions are possible only after the bishops have agreed. The Pope would still be free to make definitive decisions on the basis of his authority as Pope. Any binding episcopal decision would always be dependent on the acceptance by the Pope who is the head of the College of Bishops. Furthermore, any ecclesiastical law requiring certain steps for the Pope to take

---

34. Ibid., p. 190.
35. *The Unity of the Churches*, pp. 83–92.
36. Ibid., 88.

before he teaches infallibly would have to be antecedently agreed upon by the Pope and, as supreme legislator, he could decide, in any given case, not to follow the procedures.

On the positive side, legal guidelines that determine relations between the Pope and the College of Bishops might assist a consenting Pope in his governance of the Church and help reduce the potential for the abuse of papal power. They would also assure other Christians that papal decisions are not made in an arbitrary or unilateral manner. Canonical norms, if accepted by the Pope, would help dispel fear among other Christians that the Pope is isolated from the Church and from his fellow bishops.

On the negative side, the legal determination of collegial action might be harmful to the papal office. The decision-making process would become extremely burdensome if the Pope had to consult with the bishops on every major judgment. Any such canonical guidelines would have to indicate clearly that they are freely accepted by the Pope, that he remains free to act otherwise on his own discretion, and that they do not bind his successors. Furthermore, legal norms could polarize the bishops themselves and create an unhealthy tension between the Pope and the bishops. A powerful and authoritarian College of Bishops might attempt to control the Pope by undue political pressure. In the final analysis collegiality cannot be satisfactorily realized by legal prescriptions. Although there have been tensions between the Pope and the College of Bishops in the past and there will be in the future, they will not be ultimately resolved by law but by the perduring guidance of the Holy Spirit. The words of the late Bishop B. C. Butler are apropos: "In the end the Church lives by conscientious charity rather than by law."[37]

Teaching Authority

The teaching authority or magisterium of the Pope is another possible object of voluntary limitation. One of the principal duties of the universal primate within the *koinonia* is to preach the Gospel. As an authentic teacher, endowed with the authority of Christ, the Pope communicates the doctrine of the faith and, guided by the

---

37. *The Theology of Vatican II*, rev. ed. (Westminster, Md.: Christian Classics, 1981), p. 94.

Holy Spirit, witnesses to the truth that saves. The Pope, teaching only what has been handed down, serves the Word of God and is not above it. Papal infallibility, however, is a major obstacle to Christian unity.

Infallible judgments are rarely made by Popes—the last one being the definition in 1950 of the Assumption of Mary. For Karl Rahner, the frequent use of definitive, *ex cathedra* teachings by the Pope in the future would lessen the credibility of papal teaching and create fear among non-Catholics. Rahner, however, believed that because of the existing pluralism in culture, philosophy, terminology, and theology, "in the forseeable future there will be no further really new definitions."[38] He distinguishes between "new" dogmas and other dogmas. A "new dogma" would be a surprise to Catholic believers and would be an addition to the existing body of Catholic truth. Thus the definition of Mary as "Queen of the World" would be "more new" than the definition that the resurrection of Jesus is not simply an event within the subjective understanding of the believer. The Pope, according to Rahner, is not likely to define "new" dogmas, but rather will preserve and clarify the substance of the faith already present in the Creeds.

Rahner may be correct about the likelihood of future definitions, but the fact that Catholics believe that the Pope *can* teach infallibly—whether it be "new" or old truths—remains a problem for non-Catholics. With this in mind, then, are there any ways that the papacy itself can make the magisterium more understandable and ultimately more acceptable to non-Catholics? I shall mention just two suggestions for voluntary limitation by the Pope, which are taken from contemporary ecumenical theology: the nonimposition of dogmas on Churches seeking unity with Rome and ecumenical cooperation in teaching.

The first suggestion is that the Catholic Church would not require other Christian Churches to accept all its dogmas if they wish to unite with Rome. The most controversial dogmas are the two Marian definitions and the teaching of Vatican I on the papal primacy of jurisdiction and infallibility. Thus, the Anglicans ask in reference to the Marian definitions if "in any future union between

---

38. *Theological Investigations* (New York: Seabury, 1976), XIV:71.

our two Churches, they would be required to subscribe to such dogmatic statements."[39]

In the past, Protestant theologians have addressed this question in various ways. For example, Lutheran theologian George Calixtus (d. 1656) proposed the *consensio quinquesecularis*: agreement by Protestants and Catholics on the essential truths of Christianity that are found in the first five centuries. In that period the first four ecumenical councils were held, and most Christians accepted their Trinitarian and Christological doctrines.[40] A contemporary Protestant theologian, Max Thurian, has suggested that the first seven ecumenical councils could act as the basis for Christian unity.[41] Others have argued that the Catholic Church should not require assent to those dogmas that were defined after the separation of the Churches, since the participation of all Christians was lacking. As a result, dogmas that have been defined by the Catholic Church since the sixteenth century should not be binding on Protestants. Orthodox theologians have used similar arguments especially in regard to the definitions concerning papal authority.

Catholic theologians have assumed that Orthodox and Protestant Christians must assent to the dogmas of the papacy and Mary if they desire full union with Rome. Joseph Ratzinger, however, suggested another solution. His concern was with the Orthodox and their clear rejection of Vatican I's definition of the jurisdictional primacy of the Pope. He looked at the first millennium, during which the Eastern and Western Churches lived together in communion. Despite tensions, fundamental unity was preserved. What, then, must Rome require of the Orthodox on the doctrine of the primacy as the minimum condition for reunion?

> Rome must not require more of a doctrine of the primacy from the East than was formulated and experienced in the first millennium. On July 25, 1976, when the Patriarch Athenagoras addressed the visiting Pope as the successor of Peter, the first in honor among us, and the presider over charity, this great Church leader was expressing the essential content of the declarations on the primacy of the first mil-

---

39. *The Final Report*, p. 96.
40. Discussed in Yves Congar, *Diversity and Communion* (Mystic, Conn.: Twenty-Third Publications, 1985), pp. 113 and 122.
41. *Visible Unity and Tradition* (Baltimore: Helicon, 1962).

lennium. And Rome cannot ask for more. Reunion could occur if the East abandons its attacks on the Western development of the second millennium as being heretical and accepts the Catholic Church as legitimate and orthodox in the form which it experienced in its own development. Conversely, reunion could occur if the West recognized the Eastern Church as orthodox and legitimate in the form in which it has maintained itself.[42]

Karl Rahner took an even broader view.[43] He contended that full communion of the Churches is possible as long as they accept the teaching of Scripture and the Creeds and do not reject the binding dogmas of other Churches as being totally irreconcilable with the substance of Christianity. This would mean that non-Catholic Churches in a reunited Church would not have to affirm the truth of the dogmas of the Catholic Church, but they could not condemn them as definitively opposed to the faith of the Gospel.

In response to the Rahner proposal, Avery Dulles has raised several questions.[44] He wondered whether the mere noncondemnation of doctrines provides sufficient grounds for full unity and whether it would confuse Catholic believers about the value of recent dogmas. If Protestants and Orthodox could enter into full communion with Rome without assenting to these dogmas, would Catholics then be justified in doubting or denying these same dogmas? Unlike Rahner and Fries, who proposed immediate communion of the Churches, Dulles contended that doctrinal agreement leading to full communion can be achieved only after much time and effort. One important stage in this process would be that Christian Churches can gradually come into closer, albeit incomplete, communion if they refrain from condemning the binding doctrines of other Churches as contrary to the Gospel.[45]

---

42. *Theologische Prinzipienlehre: Bausteine zur Fundamentaltheologie* (Munich: E. Wewel, 1982), p. 209.

43. *The Unity of the Churches,* pp. 25–41.

44. "Paths to Doctrinal Agreement: Ten Theses," *Theological Studies* 47 (1986):32–47, esp. 37–39.

45. Avery Dulles has also proposed that the Marian dogmas should not be taught under anathemas: "I am suggesting that the Catholic Church, while continuing to propose these doctrines as true, should abolish the canonical penalties presently connected with the questioning or denial of these doctrines" (*Origins,* December 26, 1974, vol. 4, no. 27: 419–420).

The second way the Pope could agree to limit his teaching authority would be to have non-Catholic Christians share in the teaching task of the Catholic Church. This suggestion was made by the Catholic members of the Lutheran-Catholic Dialogue VI. They recommended that "Catholic leaders invite Lutheran Church authorities to participate in the formulation of Catholic doctrine in a consultative capacity."[46] A precedent was set by the presence of non-Catholic observers at Vatican II. In practice this could mean that the Pope would invite representatives from the major Christian denominations to take part in the work of some of the Roman congregations. They would act as more than observers, take part in all the meetings, and have a voice but not a vote in the deliberations.

At first glance this suggestion might appear strange, especially since very few lay Catholics, male or female, have any official connection with the Roman Curia. Some might consider the presence of non-Catholics in the congregations as weakening the unique Catholic identity and restricting the way the official Church teaches. Yet there would be advantages to magisterial cooperation among Christians. It would establish an active liaison between Rome and other Churches, encourage ecumenism at the highest levels of the various Churches, and give firsthand experience to Christian leaders of the workings of the central administration of the Catholic Church. Such ecumenical collaboration would provide a strong and persuasive witness to the world and could be a significant step in the advancement of eventual Christian unity.

Conclusion

In examining the ecumenical perspective of the limits of the papacy, we have explored some areas in which the Pope might voluntarily limit his authority. Although significant convergence on the nature of papal authority has been made in the ecumenical dialogues, the papacy remains a major barrier. The road to reunion will be long

---

46. Paul C. Empie, T. Austin Murphy, and Joseph A. Burgess, eds., *Teaching Authority and Infallibility in the Church: Lutherans and Catholics in Dialogue VI* (Minneapolis: Augsburg, 1978), p. 59.

and difficult. Despite real, unresolved differences among Christians, there is also a genuine communion that binds them together. John Paul II, in an address to religious leaders in New Zealand, expressed our common hope: "We are convinced that the goal is not simply partnership; it is nothing less than the fullness of communion in a visible, organic unity."[47]

47. *New York Times*, November 24, 1986, p. A10.

Epilogue

B y focusing on the limits of the papacy, we have been able to take a fresh view of the tension between authority and autonomy, which inevitably and properly exists in every community of human beings.

This study of the dialectics of unity in the Church recognizes the Pope's constitutional primacy—with this difference: the constitution and the primacy come from God and not from the people.

Papal authority is thus essentially limited both by divine natural law and by divine positive law; reason and faith circumscribe the power of the Pope. Moreover, papal authority may be voluntarily limited through heeding the demands of prudence as it faces the totality of changing circumstances in the living Church, which is also a world Church. In sanctifying, teaching, and ruling, the Pope may for the sake of the community of believers nuance or even freely forego the exercise of certain rights in a kind of Spirit-prompted response to the exigencies of a Church in dialogue.

The present crisis in the Church over the use of papal power, however, must be understood in its historical context. The Church is entering a new phase of the ongoing dialectical process. This process ideally should have only two phases: creativity and consolidation; in practice, there are two more, anarchy and formalism. In other words, creativity can be derailed into a fragmented pluralism, just as consolidation can be transformed into a defensive uniformity.

The recent history of the Church chronicles the deterioration of the old formalism, which was superseded at Vatican II. The years immediately after the Council produced a creative ferment that many felt was being carried away by its enthusiasm for unrestricted change. John Paul II gradually initiated what has been called a restoration, but not as if he wanted a return to the static formalism of the past. His goal—however its exercise may be interpreted—is better understood as an attempt at consolidation.

This disturbing transition sets the stage for the working out of the dialectical process. Unfortunately, the interaction sometimes tends toward the confrontational, a classic stand-off between power and freedom. To the extent that the dialectical partners are adversarial, they slow down the harmonization process.

In these times of ecclesial anxiety, we do well to recall that the Holy Spirit who guides the Church is a Spirit of wisdom and love. For us, responding to differences with mutual love is the key to the full functioning of the dialectical process. What is important is that all members of the Church be open to Christ, who through his Spirit, "bestows on it the various hierachical and charismatic gifts, and adorns it with his fruits and leads it to all truth and to perfect union in communion and ministry" (*Lumen gentium*, art. 4).

Addendum

Recent developments in the Hunthausen case that occurred while this book was in proofs have necessitated the following additions to the text.

Following the fourth full paragraph on page 30
From February to May, the commission conducted lengthy interviews with Hunthausen, Wuerl, and other bishops, priests, and lay leaders. It presented its report in Rome, on May 19–20, to John Paul II and the Congregation for Bishops. The commission recognized that the divided governing arrangement in Seattle was ineffective and had to be changed. It made the following recommendations: the restoration of full faculties to Archbishop Hunthausen, the transfer of Bishop Wuerl to another diocese, and the appointment of a coadjutor bishop. On May 27, 1987, Archbishop Pio Laghi announced that the Vatican had accepted the commission's recommendations and that Bishop Thomas J. Murphy, bishop of Great Falls–Billings, Montana, had been appointed as the coadjutor archbishop of Seattle with right of succession. The commission will remain in existence for one year to assist the archdiocese to accomplish the directives of the Holy See.*

Following the second full paragraph on page 120
The procedure employed by the commission differed considerably from the earlier investigation. First, it was more informal, since the commission's task was not to conduct an apostolic visitation, but to provide an assessment of the current situation in Seattle. Second, it was more open. The commission based its conclusions only on docu-

---

*The report of the commission and other documents are found in *Origins*, June 4, 1987, vol. 17, no. 3:37, 39–43.

ments seen by Archbishop Hunthausen and on discussions with persons designated by him or those consulted with his agreement. Each person interviewed was free to share with the archbishop everything that was discussed.

The commission pointed out that although Hunthausen had made sincere steps to carry out the directives of the Holy See, there was still confusion in the minds of some in the archdiocese about certain teachings of the magisterium and certain practices mandated by Rome. Noting an inadequacy in communication, the commission insisted that the overall attitudinal orientation needed to be changed.

The appointment of the commission and, more importantly, the acceptance of its recommendations by Rome, was a clear affirmation of the theory and practice of collegiality. The final resolution, granting full episcopal powers to Hunthausen and appointing a coadjutor, balanced the concerns of both the archbishop and the Holy See. It enabled the Church in Seattle to move forward after a long and difficult period of uncertainty.

Addressing the relationship between a diocesan bishop and the Bishop of Rome, the report of the commission quoted *Lumen gentium*, art. 27, that the bishop is not the vicar of the Pope, but one who exercises power in his own right. It added, however, that every bishop must be in communion with and in obedience to the head of the College of Bishops, the successor of Peter, the Pope. Any intervention by the Bishop of Rome in a local Church is determined by the good of the Church. The final resolution of the conflict in Seattle, by means of an episcopal commission approved by Rome, affirmed belatedly the principle of subsidiarity: problems, when possible, should be settled on the local level. It may well have established a precedent for resolving future tensions between a local Church and Rome.

Index